REFLECTIVE AUTHENTICITY

Has the Linguistic Turn sounded the death knell for the project of modernity? How can we appraise theoretical, practical and aesthetic claims in a universalist way without violating the premises of pluralism? *Reflective Authenticity* offers a challenging answer – an answer equally critical of the belief that the end of "grand narratives" implies the end of all kinds of universalism and of the intimation that conceiving of reason along communicative lines will by itself solve all the problems incurred by the project of modernity. Alessandro Ferrara suggests that the notion of reflective authenticity offers the key to a new kind of *exemplary* universalism which, differently from the *generalizing* universalism typical of modern thought, does not fall under the critique of foundationalism articulated by postmodernist thinkers.

While those uneasy with the "groundlessness" handed over to us by the Linguistic Turn will find that a "groundless ground" can be found in the rationality without principles of oriented reflective judgment, those with postmodernist sympathies will find in this book an argument about what may come next, after the critique of foundationalism. *Reflective Authenticity* will be essential reading for all those interested in continental philosophy, social and political theory, and psychoanalysis.

Alessandro Ferrara is Senior Lecturer in the Faculty of Sociology of the University of Rome "La Sapienza." He is the author of *Modernity and Authenticity: A Study of the Social and Ethical Thought of Jean-Jacques Rousseau* (1993) and of *Justice and Judgment. The Rise and the Prospect of the Judgment Model in Contemporary Political Philosophy* (1998).

REFLECTIVE AUTHENTICITY

Rethinking the project of modernity

Alessandro Ferrara

London and New York

First published 1998
by Routledge
11 New Fetter Lane, London EC4P 4EE

Simultaneously published in the USA and Canada
by Routledge
29 West 35th Street, New York, NY 10001

© 1998 Alessandro Ferrara

Typeset in Goudy by Routledge
Printed and bound in Great Britain by Clays Ltd, St. Ives PLC

British Library Cataloguing in Publication Data
A catalogue record for this book is available from the British Library

Library of Congress Cataloguing in Publication Data
A catalogue record for this book has been requested

ISBN 0–415–13061–1 (hbk)
ISBN 0–415–13062–X (pbk)

FOR EMANUELE

CONTENTS

CONTENTS

PREFACE

As the twentieth century draws to its close, it seems clearer than ever that the rift opened in our understanding of validity by the philosophical developments of the beginning of the century that go under the conventional name of the Linguistic Turn cannot be remedied through a simple refurbishing of the philosophical means that have proven to be part of the problem. Any view of validity, theoretical or normative, which aspires to be consistent with the Linguistic Turn will have to dispense with the pretense to justify itself through appeals to any kind of description, however minimal or formal, of an uninterpreted, "real" reality – be it the reality of the human subject, of a direction in human history, of perception or of the presuppositions of argumentation. What is called for is an entirely new way of explicating what it means for our statements to be true and for our norms to be right, as well as a new understanding of the reason why one of the competing explications is better than the others.

Since the beginning of the 1980s I've been working at the idea that the normative notion of *authenticity*, initially elaborated within one of the traditions of Western ethics in modern times, possesses a crucial significance in this connection. In *Modernity and Authenticity* (1993), drafted in the mid-1980s and first published in Italy in 1989, I tried to elucidate some aspects of this significance in relation to the evolution of modern ethical thought. I located in Rousseau's implicit "ethic of authenticity" the starting point of a line of thinking centered on the idea that the singular requisites of the authenticity of an individual identity – what is uniquely indispensable for an individual to be himself or herself – provide a better anchoring for moral normativity than general principles or the rational nature of the moral subject.

In the present book I build on this basic idea and explore several facets of the thesis that a general (and not just ethical) notion of validity consistent with the Linguistic Turn is best understood as somehow connected with the authenticity of a relevant individual, collective or symbolic identity. In the meantime, the intellectual context has undergone interesting modifications. The notion of authenticity is no longer used mainly in an existentialist sense or as a shorthand term for capturing the cipher of a moral climate characterized by a onesided emphasis on self-realization, intimacy, privatism and skepticism concerning all values that transcend the self – as was the case in the wave of cultural criticism inaugurated in the late 1970s and early 1980s by authors like Christopher Lasch, Richard Sennett, Robert Bellah, Daniel Bell, David Riesman, Philip Rieff and many others, a kind of cultural criticism whose internal difficulties I tried to bring out in *Modernity and Authenticity*. For example, the genealogy of the ethic of authenticity has recently been reconstructed by Charles Taylor along lines quite similar to those followed in my text, and some version of the concept of authenticity has finally found a place, under the rubric of "the ethical," in the systematic work of a thinker like Jürgen Habermas. None of these more receptive accounts of the contemporary relevance of the notion of authenticity, however, captures one aspect of it which, in my opinion, possesses crucial importance, namely the relation of authenticity to a new understanding of validity based on reflective judgment and potentially capable of effecting a true reconciliation of universalism with the "fact of pluralism" – not just the pluralism of comprehensive conceptions of the good that John Rawls has in mind but, in a broader sense, the pluralism of cultures, of traditions, of political cultures, of scientific paradigms and of language games that finds its point of origin in the Linguistic Turn.

The nexus of authenticity and validity is thus at the center of this work. I try to account for it in three ways. First, I try to highlight the philosophical context within which it has arisen and acquired its meaning. Second, I explore some illustrious views of validity based on judgment rather than on principles – Aristotle's notion of *phronesis* and Kant's concept of *reflective judgment*. My intent is not philological, however. Rather, my revisitation aims at tracing some elements of those conceptions that can still be part of a postmetaphysical notion of judgment.

For judgment on the authenticity of identities to work and engender results that, in turn, possess some kind of validity over and beyond their context of origin we must presuppose, however, that some equivalent of what Kant identified as a *sensus communis* allows people who are differently situated to make sense of and communicate their assessment of the state of the concerned identities. This postmetaphysical equivalent of Kant's *sensus communis* is found in a vocabulary, drawn from a reconstruction of the idea of fulfillment implicit in psychoanalytic theory, which supposedly is differentiated enough for allowing the articulation of different understandings of the authenticity of identities of various sorts, starting from individual identities and moving on to collective and symbolic ones.

Third, the authenticity view of validity implicitly raises a claim to validity that needs to be discussed and accounted for in terms fully consistent with the postmetaphysical assumptions that the Linguistic Turn has bequeathed us. Such an account requires a rethinking of the project of modernity and a radical reflexivization of the authenticity view of validity – in Chapter 8 "reflective authenticity" will be shown to turn *reflexive* in that it self-validates as the view of validity that is most authentic for us to entertain.

For a long time I have believed that one of the terrains on which the authenticity view of validity can show its fruitfulness is the debate on justice and its justification in a pluralistic world. No specific chapter is devoted to the issue, however, for the simple reason that my interest for this theme has in turn given rise to another book in its own right – *Justice and Judgment The Rise and Prospect of the Judgment Model in Contemporary Political Philosophy* (1998b) – in which I use the framework outlined here in order to make sense of the transformations undergone by the liberal theories of justice over the past few decades and to develop a judgment view of justice that builds on the authenticity approach to validity. In a way the two books are meant to work in tandem: while in *Reflective Authenticity* I outline my broader thesis about authenticity as the new ground for conceiving of validity in (exemplary) universalistic terms, in *Justice and Judgment* I try to offer an account of the implications of this conception of validity in the realm of political philosophy.

Some of the chapters of this book have appeared in the form of articles in a number of journals. In most cases the materials have been extensively reworked, but a grateful acknowledgment is owed to the editors and publishers of the journals mentioned below. Chapter 1 and the first section of Chapter 8 appeared as "Authenticity and the Project of Modernity" in the *European Journal of Philosophy*, 1994 (Volume 2, number 3, pages 241–73). Significant parts of Chapters 2 and 3 appeared as "On Phronesis" in *Praxis International*, 1987–8 (Volume 7, numbers 3–4, pages 246–67). Chapter 4 was published pretty much in its present shape as "Authenticity as a Normative Category," in *Philosophy and Social Criticism*, 1997 (Volume 23, number 3, pages 77–92). Chapters 5 and 6 are an expansion of my article "Postmodern Eudaimonia," in *Praxis International*, 1992 (Volume 11, number 4, pages 387–411). Some among these materials, as well as the essays from which Chapter 7 is derived, were also included in my volume *L'eudaimonia postmoderna*, published in Italy in 1993 – and I am grateful to Liguori Editore for permitting me to use them.

Over the long years of gestation of this work I have incurred many more intellectual debts than I can possibly acknowledge. Among the institutions, I wish to thank the Alexander von Humboldt Foundation for having financed, in the Fall of 1987, a four-month period of research at the Department of Philosophy of the J.W. Goethe Universität of Frankfurt during which I worked at the draft later developed into Chapters 2 and 3; the Italian C.N.R. and the Commissione per gli Scambi Culturali fra l'Italia e gli Stati Uniti for having financed, in the Fall of 1989, a four-month period spent as a Research Associate at the Department of Sociology of the University of California at Berkeley, during which I outlined a draft later incorporated in Chapters 5 and 6; and the Society for Phenomenology and Existential Philosophy for having invited me to give a paper, which was later to become Chapter 4, at the 1995 Conference held at De Paul University in Chicago.

I have benefited from comments on parts of the manuscript that were addressed to me on the occasion of various debates, presentations and personal conversations by Seyla Benhabib, Richard Bernstein, Franco Cassano, Jean Cohen, Maeve Cooke, Lucio Cortella, Franco Crespi, Maurizio Passerin D'Entreves, Teun van Dijk, Gianpaolo Ferranti, Jürgen Habermas, Michael

Halberstam, Dick Howard, Paolo Jedlowski, Ernesto Laclau, María Pía Lara, Charles Larmore, Sebastiano Maffettone, Rudolf Makkreel, Thomas McCarthy, Christoph Menke, Walter Privitera, David Rasmussen, Loredana Sciolla, Carlos Thiebaut, Gabriella Turnaturi and Bernard Williams.

Also, I am very grateful to the participants of the Critical Theory Seminar that meet every year in Gallarate, Italy, for having discussed the Italian volume *L'eudaimonia postmoderna*, of which the present one constitutes a development, and in particular to Ferruccio Andolfi, Marina Calloni, Lucio Cortella, Paolo Costa, Virginio Marzocchi and Stefano Petrucciani.

Finally, special thanks are due to Pieter Duvenage, Axel Honneth and Joel Whitebook for having read and commented on extensive parts of the manuscript, and to Massimo Rosati for having accompanied with many challenging remarks the slow growth of the manuscript.

Alessandro Ferrara
Roma, July 1997

1

AUTHENTICITY AND VALIDITY

Metaphors based on Babel abound in the literature on contemporary culture: Babel as the poisoned fruit of modern value pluralism, of the inconsiderate project "of finding a short cut to heaven," of the enamorment of the modern self with itself. There is something unconvincing about them. For there begins to emerge, within the condition that the image of Babel is designed to capture, new ways of coming to terms with the task of forming common orientations, projects, interpretations – new ways which all involve a rethinking of universalism, justice and the project of modernity. This book is about making sense of these transformations and at the same time trying to initiate a rethinking of the notion of validity that might eventually bring it in line with our intuitions about the irreducible pluralism of lifeforms and conceptions of value. The nexus of validity to authenticity and the sphere of aesthetic value will play a decisive role in this respect.

One of the assumptions underlying this book is that the cultural change which over the past few decades has swept the advanced industrial societies affects not only the peripheral stratum of values, beliefs and lifestyles, but also that deep core of any culture constituted by the *foundations of validity*. Norms, values and beliefs, as well as scientific theories or political institutions, are in a state of almost constant change. Yet the *kinds of reasons* in the name of which these symbolic entities demand our consensus or bind our conduct change much less frequently. To Heraclitus' saying "You cannot step twice into the same river" we can object, following Wittgenstein, that while the continuous flowing of the waters may prevent us from doing so, the bedrock on which the waters of a river flow – a culture's basic assumptions concerning what counts as valid – changes much more rarely. To be precise, up to now Western culture has gone through only *one* cultural transformation so deep as to affect not just cultures, values and norms but also that bedrock of the symbolic network through which we relate to reality and reproduce our lifeforms – a bedrock constituted by what I will call the foundations of validity. Such transition is the transition to the Modern Age.

Today we in the West might be in the midst of another transition of similar magnitude. The notion of *eudaimonia* or well-being, reformulated as a *normative*

1

ideal of *authenticity*, constitutes the center of this cultural change and at the same time one of the avenues through which the fragmentation of value that has made the Babel metaphors popular may begin to give way to a new cultural constellation. But in order to understand what the rise of such an ideal of authenticity means and what its implications are we must retrace our steps and reconstruct the path through which we have come to our present predicament. This path originates in the particular way in which Western modernity has connected rationality, subjectivity and validity, and subsequently undergoes turning points which again are specifically Western. As we shall see at the end, however, the congruence of our notion of validity with this path bears a significance that projects itself beyond the immediate circle of who we are. Paradoxically, the best way to ensure a significance of our conception of validity beyond that circle is to keep our view firmly within it.

The caravan at the ford

Supposedly, subjectivity is the seal of modernity – so founding fathers like Descartes, Kant and Hegel, as well as countless textbooks in their wake, have taught us. Where the truth of propositions and the normative cogency of norms are no longer thought to derive from their corresponding to an order inherent in the world, but merely from their conformity with laws of reason inherent in the mind of a human *subject*, there we enter the modern territory. The "principle of subjective freedom" formulated by Hegel sums up this insight in a canonical way.

According to the classical, premodern world-view, the validity of norms, theoretical statements about nature, and institutional arrangements rested on their capacity for reflecting the objective order of the world. When the order of Cosmos provided the foundations of validity, also Reason was conceived as *objective*, i.e. as Logos. Its objectivity trickled down to the various branches of knowledge. Physics was supposed to be the "mirror of nature" in a strong ontological sense. Ethics was supposed to draw prescriptions for the good life from insights into human nature and these prescriptions did not yet have a different status from that of true propositions. Political philosophy tried to derive from the same insights indications as to the institutional order most likely to promote virtue among the citizens.

The detachment of Western culture from this conception of validity – indeed, a tortuous and far-from-linear process which developed slowly and with occasional backlashes through the Middle Ages – came to a completion when, at the onset of modernity, the basis on which the validity of knowledge and practical conduct is supposed to rest was equated with their being "rational," i.e. with their satisfying the requirements of the rationality of an ideal human subject. These requisites of reason, often condensed in the form of a method or of a set of categories or rules of inference, were no longer conceived as attributes of Being as such but as having a *subjective* quality. For the first time the rationality of Reason was thought of as an entirely human quality. The bearer of this rationality, however, was conceived in early modern times either as an abstract and ideal Subject, supposedly "inherent" in each concrete individual (Descartes, Kant), or as a macro-subject to which we all belong *qua* individuals (Spirit in Hegel, the human species in Marx).

This narrative of modern rationality is so trite that it would be of no import to relate it once more, were it not for an ambiguity implicit in it, the unraveling of which can help us to understand our own relation to modernity. The ambiguity lies in the notion of subjectivity. The subjective quality of the modern form of rationality was subjective only in a peculiar sense. In fact, the subjectified reason of early modern times continued to be in a certain sense objective. As classical Logos, it continued to constitute a "larger than life" or transsubjective standard of validity. The criteria for evaluating the truth of propositions and the rightness of actions continued to be somehow *external* to the individual. Rationality was no longer objective in the sense of reflecting the order of Cosmos, but was still objective in the sense of being as independent of common opinion and personal judgment as classical philosophical discourse.[1] Up until now, the heritage of the early modern notion of rationality is still so vital, that to be rational for many is still synonymous with being impartial, where being "impartial" in turn means being "unsubjective." From the very beginning, this notion of rationality showed cracks and proved to be quite unstable. Rousseau's work, for instance, offers a testimony of the early uncertainty as to the modern view of foundations, at least in the realm of morality.

Furthermore, while early modernity took it for granted that the kind of subjectivity capable of providing foundations for validity was that inherent in an *autonomous* subject, today the very notion of an *autonomous subject* has become disputable. Both of its components, primarily the notion of the subject but also, though to a lesser extent, that of autonomy – understood as the ideal of *self-legislation guided by general principles* – have become problematical. It remains unclear, however, with what the notion of autonomous subjectivity should be replaced.

From this perspective our situation resembles the period between the Renaissance and the Enlightenment, when the classical ontological view of validity had been discredited but no consciousness of a new paradigm yet existed. We are like a caravan standing uncertain in the middle of a ford. The secure shores of the early modern understanding of validity in terms of autonomous and rational subjectivity are definitively behind us, but we haven't yet come ashore to the other side, where a *new* way of grounding the validity of statements and norms awaits us. Worst of all, a great confusion reigns among our guides.

Some want to take us back to the shore of Reason writ "Large." They propose versions irrelevantly different of the same notions of a macro-subject, of an abstract rational subject and of an impartial "method" or "form of rationality" which led us to where we are. Among these we find the last defenders of

3

"critical rationalism" in the philosophy of science who ironically find themselves in the company of most of those who call themselves "analytical Marxists." In political and social theory the diehard defenders of the modern constellation occupy regional strongholds of some consequence in certain cases: game-theory, the theory of rational choice, methodological individualism, some theories of social movements and of cultural reproduction, systems theory, Artificial Intelligence and computer science.

Others among our guides protest that we should retreat much further back than to the shore behind us. According to them we should have never left the great plains of Logos in the first place, and we are paying now for that earlier mistake. If validity does not rest on *objective* foundations, as it did for Plato and Aristotle, then the only coherent conclusion is that it expresses the will to believe and to make believe, ultimately a will to power. The greatest of all illusions, continue these critics, is the Enlightenment project of envisaging validity as more "subjective" than in the classical view, and yet in another sense as equally "objective," in the sense of undisputable and impartial. Once typical of conservative Roman Catholic theology, this position has been revamped in the 1980s from a radical perspective by MacIntyre and other authors of neo-Aristotelian inspiration. The task of the day for these authors is to recover as much as possible of the classical understanding of objective validity and to reconcile it with certain transformations that appear irreversible: for example, a certain notion of freedom. Charles Taylor provides another example of this attempt to bring together the freedom of the modern self and the classical sense of a meaning that transcends the self.[2]

Then a very vociferous group of guides denounces as a prejudice the preference, taken for granted by all others, for the mainland. As a solution they advocate settling on boats that float downstream and giving up once for all the pernicious myth of the existence of standards of validity. This is what the best among French intellectuals (Derrida, Foucault, Lyotard), together with Rorty, invite us to do.

Finally, other guides – and these are the ones I personally prefer – do their best to spot out some clearings on the other shore through which it might be easier to accede to the new land. Some of them, for instance Rawls and Habermas, have much to say on how to rescue a notion of validity and rationality without invoking the early modern notion of an abstract or superindividual rational subject. Important as their attempt to rescue the positive aspects of modern autonomous subjectivity and to reformulate them in terms of *intersubjectivity* might be, they seem unable to convince the caravan to move toward the indicated point, probably because they still keep too close to the early modern ideal of a dehistoricized and depersonalized knowledge. The position defended in this book is that the goal of finding an entry point into a new land is best served by replacing the modern notion of a rational and autonomous subject not so much with the notion of *intersubjectivity* as with that of *authentic* subjectivity and by working out the methodological conse-

4

quences of such move. In Chapter 8 I will briefly return to these alternatives and to the different stances that they presuppose with respect to the "project of modernity."

In a nutshell, the *authenticity-thesis* claims that the notion of authentic subjectivity is to contemporary modernity as the notion of autonomous subjectivity is to early modernity. While the Enlightenment is the age of autonomy *par excellence*, ours is the age of authenticity. This could be taken as a statement that belongs in the sociology of culture or at best in the history of moral ideas. But there is more to it. The normative ideal of authenticity brings with it a methodological appendix which implicitly calls into question the early modern universalism and replaces it with a new universalism based on the model of reflective judgment. I cannot claim to do justice to the full scope of this thesis in the context of this book. I will be satisfied if I succeed in making it plausible by way of highlighting some of its main points and implications. In the next sections of this chapter I will elucidate the distinction between autonomy and authenticity, the intersubjective nature of the concept of authenticity and some of the methodological implications of the *authenticity-thesis*.

Autonomy and authenticity

The *authenticity-thesis* presupposes a distinction between autonomy and authenticity. They are not just versions of the same concept. While authenticity includes the notion of autonomy, and should not be construed – at least in the version that I try to defend – as implying a radical break with it, there is no way of generating the notion of authenticity from within the perspective of autonomy alone. Some "additional content" is needed, which represents the specific contribution of contemporary modernity – wherever one conventionally sets its temporal watershed – to the "discourse of Western rationality." The meaning of that "additional content" is the object of the contest between the various notions of authenticity that will be examined in Chapter 6.

"Autonomy" and "authenticity" can best be contrasted with reference to a theory of social action and to moral theory. From the standpoint of a theory of social action, autonomy and authenticity are properties of human conduct. "Autonomy" refers to the actor's accountability in his or her choosing a course of action, regardless of the grounds and type of rationality that inspire his or her choice. Weber's typology of action may be useful here. Only *purposive-rational* and *value-rational* action fully qualify as "autonomous" conduct – *traditional* and *affective* action, instead, fall short of it.[3] "Authentic" conduct cannot be accommodated within this typology. It can neither be reduced to "self-determined" conduct nor be derived from it. Why? What does the notion of authentic conduct require that self-determination cannot supply? Authentic conduct has the quality of being somehow connected with, and expressive of, the core of the actor's personality. It brings into play the actor's uniquely personal, as opposed to culturally or socially shared, identity. If I am insensitive to my deepest needs,

5

if I betray them, or if I inscribe my action into a life-plan which in turn fails to fit with who I am, then I may act in a purposive-rational or value-rational way inauthentically.

Autonomy and authenticity appear, then, to be related in an asymmetrical way. On one hand, authenticity *presupposes* autonomy. Neither traditional nor affective action, as Weber understands them, can be authentic. These types of action exhibit a deficit of individuation and self-determination which prevents us from making sense of "authentic traditional action" or "authentic affective action." Of course, we could revise our theory in such a way that these expressions would then make sense, but that would lead us beyond Weber's categorization, only to find the same problem cast in a different vocabulary.

On the other hand, the conceptual gap between autonomous and authentic conduct cannot be bridged with materials derived analytically from autonomy. Weber offers an implicit illustration of this point. He never uses the term "authentic conduct," but his notion of political action inspired by an ethic of responsibility – the "Here I stand. I can do no other" stance that Weber's responsible politician borrows from Luther – shares all the characteristics of authentic conduct. It combines considerations of expediency and value with a deep emotional resonance which stems from the link that this kind of action manifests with the *identity* of the actor. The exemplary interplay of affective, moral and pragmatic moments accounts for Weber's description of such conduct as "immensely moving"[4] – a qualification that usually does not apply to purposive-rational or even to value-rational action. In sum, while on one hand the conduct of the politician inspired by an ethic of responsibility *presupposes* the categories of purposive and value rationality, on the other hand there is no way of *deriving* the "immensely moving" quality of the responsible politician's conduct from the concepts of purposive or value rational action.

It is interesting to note that the conditions of success or validity for autonomous and authentic action vary dramatically. While the validity or success conditions for purposive- and value-rational action are captured by the principle of maximization of utility or of value realization – and thus fall entirely within the scope of what Kant has called *determinant judgment* – in the evaluation of the conduct of the responsible politician no rules, no principles, not even concepts, let alone demonstrations, can be produced under which the correctness of a given course of action can be exhaustively subsumed – and thus the validity of action seems to be conceivable only in terms of exemplary uniqueness, in a way similar to what Kant called *reflective judgment*.[5]

From the standpoint of *moral theory*, autonomy and authenticity can be contrasted as two comprehensive ideals which shape concrete ethical and moral theories to a different extent. By virtue of their common modern origin, ethical and moral views oriented towards autonomy (e.g. the Kantian ethics) share with conceptions centered on authenticity (e.g. Kierkegaard's conception of the ethical life) an understanding of the normative force of moral norms as stemming from the actor's capacity to observe consistently a *self-imposed* principle.

Beyond this point, however, the two conceptions part company. Views centered on autonomy tend to understand moral worth as total reconciliation of action and reason. For example, in Kant's view of the *Wille*, the moral will is good insofar as it is oriented entirely and solely to the moral law. For the ethic of authenticity, instead, the willingness to abide by formal principles is not the exclusive constituent of moral worth. Rather, all ethics of authenticity start from the assumption that in order to be a worthy moral being, we must not deny or try to suppress, but rather acknowledge the urges which deflect us from our principles, while at the same time continuing to orient our conduct to the moral point of view. The difference between the two approaches, best exemplified by the internal tensions of Rousseau's ethical thought, concerns the value to be attributed to our deviations from the ethical principle. For the ethics of autonomy, *all* these deviations subtract something from the worthiness of the person – the less deviations the better, no matter how impoverished in other dimensions our life will look as a result. For the ethic of authenticity, instead, the discrepancy between the ideal and the real self is not simply an undesirable imperfection. As Rousseau suggests through the case of Julie (the main character of *La nouvelle Heloise*) any attempt at mastering the motivations that deflect us from the moral principle without fully grasping the pattern underlying them is bound to result in the undermining of the individual's identity.[6] Autonomy, again, though it constitutes a necessary ingredient of moral worth, cannot exhaust the meaning of it. For Rousseau other qualities are needed, which can be grouped under the heading of *authenticity*. These qualities include having a capacity to distinguish those aspects of a person's inner world which are crucial from those which are expendable, having knowledge of oneself, empathy, a capacity to accept emotionally the undesired aspects of one's real self, and the courage to follow one's moral intuitions even when it is difficult to translate them into the language of abstract reflection.

These analytic distinctions, however, may be misleading. They tend to obscure an important fact – often missed by neo-conservative critics such as Daniel Bell, Christopher Lasch, Richard Sennett, Allan Bloom, Philip Selznick, Philip Rieff and Peter Berger who, however, do perceive the notion of authenticity as the normative core of the culture of advanced industrial societies.[7] The normative ideals of autonomy and authenticity sink their roots in the same cultural context.[8] They represent two distinct lines of development taken by our moral culture at the onset of modernity. Both originated in the Reformation's response to the clash between a secularizing polity and the market on one hand, and the medieval Catholic ethos of brotherliness on the other hand. Arguably, to the Protestant response to those tensions,[9] not only the releasing of a potential for societal modernization can be imputed, but also the rise of *new* cultural tensions which in turn are the sources of two rival ethical traditions or moral cultures. The institutionalization of Protestantism, in fact, determined an erosion of motivation for social solidarity in a context where rapid social change, the beginnings of the Industrial Revolution and processes of urbanization and secularization made the strong solidarity of the premodern community an ever scarcer resource, and also contributed to the diffusion of attitudes of self-censorship and repression in a context in which, again, rapid cultural change and the increasing abstractness of the new ethics of principle demanded more refined interpretive abilities of the moral actor.[10]

This social and cultural predicament, determined by the fact that Protestantism was the first ethic of principle to play a public role in the West, accounts for the peculiar dual path that characterizes the development of modern ethics. After the Reformation, one stream of moral theory took the first kind of tension as primary and placed at the center of moral reflection the question "What is the relation between right conduct and self-interest?", but overlooked the relation of morality to self-realization and authenticity. This line of moral reflection, which cuts across the traditional categories of deontological and consequentialist ethics, adopted the "autonomy of the subject" as its catchword. We also have another line of ethical reflection, however, which addressed primarily the second tension and focused on the relation between acting ethically and "being oneself." This second strand of modern ethical thought, inaugurated by Rousseau and enriched by the contributions of, among others, Herder, Schiller, Kierkegaard, Nietzsche and Heidegger, is the seed-bed where the contemporary normative notion of authenticity was shaped.

Throwing these names together under the heading of a "tradition of authenticity" might at first sound bizarre. While Kierkegaard's inquiry into the existential viability of the moral point of view presupposes the meaningfulness of the moral law, the main point of Nietzsche's *Genealogy of Morals* is to call that very idea into question. Heidegger, on the other hand, understands his own inquiry as topographically located before the bifurcation of theoretical and practical philosophy and dismisses ethics as an unimportant philosophical subject. Yet, these authors do share something in common that sets them against the tradition of autonomy. They share (1) a notion of the human being according to which the *capacity for being oneself*, as opposed to the ability to modify the world instrumentally, or the propensity toward sociation, or the capacity to follow self-chosen principles, is the fundamental feature of the person and builds the core of human dignity; (2) the view that Western modernization has left unfulfilled the promise of individuation that it contained; (3) the intent to justify their overall philosophical stance with reference to the idea of "being oneself," "choosing oneself," "asserting oneself" or "becoming who one is"; (4) a denunciation of the generalizing universalism of early modernity.

During the last decade, considerations such as the ones presented above have acquired an ever wider intellectual acceptance, which they did not enjoy in 1982 when I first began to formulate them. The intellectual trajectory of Habermas's thought is instructive in this connection. In the typology of social action underlying the *Theory of Communicative Action*, just as in the one formulated by Weber in *Economy and Society*, there is hardly a trace of anything that might resemble "authentic action." Nevertheless, like an invisible planet the notion of authenticity has influenced the formation of other concepts. In fact, while it is possible to act strategically (and, of course, instrumentally) in an inauthentic way, the idea of someone acting communicatively in an inauthentic way is somewhat problematic. The concept of "systematically distorted communication" is designed to cover this ground. The actor who engages in systematically distorted communication believes himself or herself to be acting communicatively toward others, but in fact he or she is acting manipulatively without being aware of it.[11] Within the theoretical framework of the *Theory of Communicative Action*, autonomous and authentic conduct are fused in communicative action. Later, between 1982 and 1984, when working on his first systematic formulation of the "discourse ethics" and on the *Philosophical Discourse of Modernity*, Habermas began to distinguish the two concepts of autonomous and authentic conduct at the level of moral theory. He still maintained, however, that the distinction between autonomy and authenticity is spurious and must be understood, rather, as the distinction between two varieties of autonomy: autonomy as the quality of a *rigid* moral consciousness and autonomy as the property of a *mature* moral actor capable of applying the moral point of view with flexibility and good judgment. The transition from the early modern "age of autonomy" to the so-called "age of authenticity" was then conceived as the transition from a rigid to a flexible postconventional moral consciousness. The Kantian notion of autonomy, interpreted along intersubjective lines – namely, as the willingness to submit candidate norms to the test of dialogical generalization – and purified of Kant's rigorism, was assumed not to miss any of the qualities of moral agency that the notion of authenticity was supposed to capture.[12] Recently Habermas's overall framework has undergone further modifications. Habermas has felt compelled to introduce a whole new sub-domain of practical reasoning – *das Ethische* – where the object of discussion is the appropriateness of practical projects to concrete identities, individual or collective.[13] Over the years, the lower status of ethical questions – a lower status signaled, among other things, by the fact that the term "discourse" would not apply to them – has been constantly upgraded, until the recent use, in *Faktizität und Geltung*, of the term "ethical discourse." The most important shift, however, lies in the fact that in *Faktizität und Geltung* we no longer find a merely analytic distinction between moral and ethical questions, but also the attempt to trace genealogically the realm of *das Ethische* back to a tradition of self-realization which is now presented as a *competitor* of the tradition of autonomy. The two traditions of autonomy (*Selbstbestimmung*) and authenticity (*Selbstverwirklichung*) are now said by Habermas "not to harmonize with each other without difficulty."[14] In Habermas's case, as well as in Weber's, however, an important ambiguity remains. While developing an increasing receptiveness for the dimension of authenticity, both seem reluctant to draw the methodological implications of a normative notion of authenticity. In fact, a case could be made that Habermas's discursive account of practical validity derives some of its difficulties from the attempt to run together two incompatible ways of

9

understanding validity embedded respectively in the models of universalism presupposed by the "tradition of autonomy" and by the "tradition of authenticity."[15]

The universalism of authenticity

The *authenticity-thesis*, as presented thus far, lends itself to a reductive interpretation. First, one might be led to think that the rise of a tradition of authenticity and its recent comeback against the rival tradition of autonomy results only in phenomena of personal and private consciousness, or in certain social movements or, put more generally, in the rise of a "cultural climate." Second, one might get the impression that even if the consequences of the rise of authenticity reached deeper than the moods of popular culture, their significance would be somehow confined to the history of ethics.[16]

What this interpretation leaves out of focus is the fact that the rise of a *normative* notion of authenticity is associated with the demise of the fascination with form, method, procedure and generalizing universalism typical of the culture of autonomy, and brings with it a new ideal of universal validity, ultimately linked with the model of exemplary uniqueness or enlightening singularity thus far associated with "aesthetics."

The *authenticity-thesis* contains a *methodological* claim which amounts to the following proposition:

> *The form of universalism most appropriate to a postmetaphysical standpoint is that proceeding from the exemplary self-congruency of a symbolic whole – two significant models of which are, at the level of life-world practices, the congruency of a life-history and, at the level of expert-practices, the congruency of the well-formed work of art.*

Let me briefly clarify the meaning of some of the terms occurring in this methodological claim. First, by "universalism" I mean the capacity, on the part of a statement or norm, to project some kind of cogency over and above the context within which it was first formulated, i.e. to be *actually* relevant for actors who operate in *other* contexts, and not to just be *reputed to possess such a relevance* by the members of the context of origin. For early modern thought universalism was made possible by the existence of principles, theoretical or moral, under which any given issue could be *subsumed* and whose validity spanned local contexts. Instead, if we take seriously the Wittgensteinian idea of a plurality of language games, and if we want to maintain a conceptual distinction between the relevance of a norm for contexts other than the one from which it originates and our mere *supposition* that the norm possesses such relevance, then one route that remains open is to have that normative relevance rest on the universalism of exemplary self-congruency. To borrow once more from Weber, we contemporary moderns accept only exemplary prophecy.

In "Two Kinds of Universalism" Michael Walzer has traced the origin of this non-generalizing universalism to one of two prophetic traditions that in the Bible contend over the meaning of God's relation to the various nations.[17] According to one tradition – the one which constitutes the point of origin for the generalizing model of universalism – God judges each nation according to the degree to which its laws and mores reflect one and the same divine Law. According to the other, however, God covenants with and blesses each nation separately, holding each nation "to its own standard."[18] As long as the first kind of universalism, in its secularized version up to Hempel's "covering law" model, maintained its plausibility, the second seemed a softer kind of "aesthetic" universalism or no universalism at all. But since the Linguistic Turn, as exemplified in the work of the later Wittgenstein, has made all Archimedean points look suspicious, the normative aspects of the second version of universalism have come to the fore. What Walzer fails to adequately highlight is the fact that also within the second kind of universalism there is judgment and normativity, even though each nation is judged according to different and local standards. There is a sense in which the reality of existing arrangements can be criticized and a sense in which the exceptional success of a collectivity in devising an institutional order suited to its members can inspire other collectivities, though not – as early modern universalism would have it – by virtue of its embodying the one and only set of principles that should inspire all collectivities.[19]

Second, the expression "postmetaphysical standpoint" stands for the assumption that there is simply no way of grasping reality from outside an interpretive framework, and that there exists *an irreducible multiplicity* of interpretive frameworks. Consequently conflicts between competing frameworks, conceptual schemes, paradigms, moral cultures, traditions, symbolic universes and the like cannot be overcome through recourse to decisive evidence or crucial experiments designed to let reality speak.

Third, "self-congruency" is not to be understood as mere coherence or, even more reductively, as consistency. Coherence is but one dimension of that exemplary degree of self-congruency which we designate by authenticity. Other dimensions are needed if we want to reconstruct our intuitions concerning the fulfillment of an identity. By looking at the convergence of various strands of psychoanalytic theory, taken as the most differentiated and fine-grained vocabulary that we have for articulating our sense of what it means for an identity to flourish, a case will be made in Chapter 5 for understanding the notion of *authentic subjectivity* in terms of the dimensions of *coherence, vitality, depth* and *maturity*. These dimensions of *authentic subjectivity* – whose applicability to the cases of collective identities and the symbolic identities of texts and works of art will be discussed in Chapters 6 and 7 – are the keystone elements of a vocabulary within which we make sense of what it means for identities to excel and to attain exemplary-universal relevance – to become embodiments of what Simmel has called an "individuelle Gesetz" and Sartre has called a "universel singulier."[20] In a sense, they cut across the traditional dichotomy of "descriptive" and "prescriptive": their status is similar to that of a vocabulary with which we sum up who we are when we are in the process of redefining who we want to be. That "reconstruction" is neither purely descriptive nor prescriptive.[21] The same is true of the categories which we use in the process of articulating it.

Moving to notions not explicitly mentioned in the methodological claim associated with the normative notion of authenticity, but included in the background assumptions underlying it, *phronesis* can be understood as the judgment that guides us in selecting the combination of values on the various dimensions that best suits who we, individually or collectively, are. Its nature and functioning, as well as its relation to Aristotle's ethics, will be discussed in the next chapter. The phrase "best suits" leads us to the idea of "best fit," which also plays a crucial role in the authenticity-based conception of validity. "Best fit" is not to be understood in descriptive terms, as fitting the current state of an individual identity at a given moment. If that were the case, in fact, the authenticity view of validity would collapse into an uninspiring traditionalism hinging on the imperative to assert or actually reiterate whatever exists. Rather, the notion of "best fit" must be understood along exemplary-normative lines, namely as the property of bringing the concerned identity (ranging from that of an individual to that of humankind, as in the case of judgment in matters of justice) closer to the unique combination of the dimensions of self-realization which realizes the highest aggregate value while being also the least dispersed. A claim of this sort should be supported by an argument concerning the greater adequacy of this notion of self-realization, relative to rival notions (e.g. a consistency view of self-realization, a Dionysian or "multiple self" view, or even the same view without the "least dispersed" clause), to our postmetaphysical intuitions. Again, this argument cannot be developed in this context. Let me mention, instead, two implications that follow from a conception of validity based on a postmetaphysical reconstruction of the notion of *phronesis*.

First, a new idea of *degrees of fit* will replace the early modern dichotomies of rational/irrational, valid/invalid, just/unjust, true/false, legitimate/illegitimate and so on. This is one way to vindicate the intuition that there are indefinitely many ways in which identities can attain their flourishing, as there are indefinitely many ways in which works of art can elicit an exemplary aesthetic experience, while at the same time for each given identity or work of art there is one optimal way, within the field of the conceivable alternatives, of attaining realization.

Second, if we adopt a notion of validity based on authenticity and *phronesis* or judgment, many of the problems usually connected with the impact of the Linguistic Turn on the paradigm of the philosophy of the subject disappear and give way to an entirely new configuration, distinctive of the contemporary predicament. For instance, the problem of incommensurability evaporates. If, to recall Walzer's formulation, each nation is judged by God according to its own standards, then we no longer have the problem of translating the "local" ways of

12

understanding a universal principle into some kind of neutral language in order to evaluate the extent to which they approximate the general standard. In its place, we have a constellation of new problems within which the problem of "authentic evil" (i.e. of identities whose realization can be attained only through evil) stands out as most in need of solution.

Authenticity and intersubjectivity

One point that remains to be addressed is how the *authenticity-thesis* stands *vis-à-vis* that *intersubjective perspective* with which it shares a propensity to call the caravan to proceed across the ford and, more specifically, *vis-à-vis* the claims put forward by the *communicative paradigm* developed by Habermas. The proponents of the different versions of the intersubjective framework share the same basic criticism of the early modern notion of autonomous subjectivity. Autonomous subjectivity is irremediably flawed by an instrumentalist reductionism and by a *subjekt-philosophisch* bias. These two flaws, however, are conceived by the defenders of intersubjectivity as connected more with the notion of the subject than with that of autonomy. It would be possible, in other words, to rescue the notion of autonomy independently of the assumptions typical of the "philosophy of the subject." All the authors who share this paradigm – for example, Habermas and Taylor, Wellmer and Honneth – entertain the hope that by replacing the old notion of subjectivity (solipsistic, monological, instrumentally biased) with a new notion of subjectivity (interactive, linguistically constituted, communicative), all that is problematic in the concept of "autonomous subjectivity" will dissolve.

The *authenticity-thesis* and the *perspective of intersubjectivity* are complementary. The *authenticity-thesis* shares the assumption that the kind of subjectivity capable of "grounding" validity is an intersubjectively constituted sort of subjectivity but, unlike the intersubjective paradigm, does not assume that such capacity to ground validity derives from the subject's property of being intersubjectively constituted. In the rest of this section I would like to elucidate these two statements. First, in what sense does the notion of "authentic subjectivity" presuppose an intersubjective dimension? Second, why is the crucial characteristic of subjectivity, insofar as its capacity for grounding validity is concerned, identified with the subject's potential for authenticity rather with its intersubjective constitution?

As far as the first question is concerned, let me briefly consider three ways in which the *authenticity-thesis* can be said to entail a genuinely intersubjective perspective. First, the category of identity, central to the *authenticity-thesis*, is best understood along intersubjective lines. Second, the category of *self-realization*, which also plays an important role, presupposes the notion of *recognition*, which in turn holds centerstage within certain versions of the intersubjective paradigm. Third, the model of universalism presupposed by the *authenticity-thesis* rests on the notion of reflective judgment, and reflective judgment, as Kant has shown, is inherently intersubjective.

The idea of an "authentic identity" which we moderns of the late twentieth century see as connected with our own understanding of validity is entirely internal to the intersubjective horizon inaugurated by the Linguistic Turn. It cannot be equated with the notion of identity *qua* "self-consciousness" of a subject reflecting on its praxis. It presupposes, among other things, that to possess an identity as a subject, *any* identity whatsoever, means to be able to see oneself through the eyes of another – a presupposition, however, which does not exhaust the meaning of the expression "authentic identity." As George Herbert Mead has put it:

> The individual experiences himself as such, not directly, but only indi-
> rectly, from the particular standpoints of other individual members of
> the same social group, or from the generalized standpoint of the social
> group as a whole to which he belongs. For he enters his own experi-
> ence as a self or individual, not directly or immediately, not by
> becoming a subject to himself, but only in so far as he first becomes an
> object to himself just as other individuals are objects to him or in his
> experience; and he becomes an object to himself just as other individ-
> uals are objects to him or in his experience; and he becomes an object
> to himself only by taking the attitudes of other individuals toward
> himself within a social environment or context of experience and
> behavior in which both he and they are involved.
>
> (Mead 1974: 138)

At first sight a tension seems to arise between the intersubjective dimension of identity and the emphasis on the ideal of authenticity implicit in the *authenticity-thesis*. In fact, the identity originating from the process described by Mead might seem a perfect example of an *inauthentic* identity – an identity developed through the internalization of social expectations. Such an impres-sion is dispelled, however, by what Mead adds in paragraphs 25 and 26 of *Mind, Self and Society*. Here he states:

> Both aspects of the "I" and the "me" are essential to the self in its full
> expression. One must take the attitude of the others in a group in order
> to belong to a community; he has to employ that outer social world
> taken within himself in order to carry on thought. It is through his
> relationship to others in that community, because of the rational social
> processes that obtain in that community, that he has being as a citizen.
> On the other hand, the individual is constantly reacting to the social
> attitudes, and changing in this co-operative process the very commu-
> nity to which he belongs.
>
> (Mead 1974: 199–200)

We can describe a certain individual as a "conventional" individual whose ideas "are exactly the same as those of his neighbors": in such a case the person, continues Mead, "is hardly more than a 'me'." On the other hand, we can conceive of an individual who has a "definite personality" and "replies to the organized attitude in a way which makes a significant difference." In this case "it is the 'I' that is the more important phase of the experience." Thus, Mead concludes,

> the fact that all selves are constituted by or in terms of the social process, and are individual reflections of it . . . is not in the least incompatible with, or destructive of, the fact that every individual self has its own peculiar individuality, its own unique pattern; because each individual self within that process, while it reflects in its organized structure the behavior pattern of that process as a whole, does so from its own particular and unique standpoint within that process, and thus reflects in its organized structure a different aspect or perspective of this whole social behavior pattern from that which is reflected in the organized structure of any other individual self within that process.
>
> (Mead 1974: 201)

All identities arise from interaction, but *authentic* identities have a distinctive quality. In Greek "authentikós" derives from "eautón" and "theto," where "theto" is etymologically related to "thesis." Thus "authentic" refers to individuals who "posit themselves" or, more freely, "set themselves as a thesis." Such an act of "positing oneself," however, must also be understood along intersubjective lines: namely, as the capacity to express that *uniqueness* which has been socially constituted through the singularity and uniqueness of the formative contexts but which no formative social context as such can enjoin us to express. Such capacity is what distinguishes *authentic* identities from other kinds of individual identities. For example, in certain contexts it is appropriate to speak of a *role-identity*. In such cases, the question to which the identity constitutes an answer – "Who am I and who do I want to be?" – appears peculiarly dimidiated. For the premodern social actor who acts in a "traditional" way, in fact, the second part of the question is redundant. Knowing who one is – where "knowing" means to know one's station in social life, one's role, perhaps even one's personality – implicitly means to know who one might want to be. We can speak of an *autonomous identity* only when the individual does not limit himself or herself to enact an ascribed identity but also develops the *project* of an identity – of an identity, as Habermas has appropriately put it, "in eigener Regie behauptete."[22] For an identity to be *authentic*, however, it does not suffice that the actor articulate by himself or herself a project concerning who he or she wants to be. It is also required that such a project should possess certain properties – namely, the properties that the categories spelled out in Chapter 5 are designed to capture – which make of it a particularly illuminating example of what can be done

15

starting from a certain social predicament. In other words, for an identity to be *authentic* it must not only be *autonomously* willed; it is also necessary that its project-like moment ("Who I want to be") should fit in an exemplary way its diagnostic moment ("Who I am"), where the expression "to fit" does not mean that it depends in a mechanical way on it, but rather that a relation of mutual relevance is created or maintained between these two moments.

These last considerations lead me to discuss the second sense in which the *authenticity-thesis* presupposes an intersubjective perspective. There is no such thing as an authentic identity which does not presuppose a moment of recognition on the part of another. While it is possible for me to imagine that the person I intend to become, my life-project, might be meaningless for certain people, I cannot bring together within a meaningful picture the idea that my identity rests on a sensible project and the idea that such a project cannot be recognized as sensible by any other human being. An identity which no one can ever recognize is not a felicitous human identity. Yet, an identity constructed and pursued for the purpose, among other things, of being recognized by others is not an authentic identity – it is merely the attempt to imitate a model. What does it mean, then, for an individual to possess an authentic identity? It means to pursue a project in which a *willed uniqueness* is expressed, and to will that others should recognize this unique person whom we want to become. Two considerations are relevant in this respect.

First, there must be a priority of willing that "such unique project" should be recognized, over what we might call the mere fact of recognition. A recognition which does not take exactly what we want to be as its object, but which addresses itself to a project different from the one to which we intend to orient ourselves, is no recognition at all. The test for the authentic quality of an identity lies in the risk, which the actor is willing to take, of not having his or her identity recognized at all, in order to preserve the chance of having recognition directed precisely at the *intended* project – hence the rhetoric of "resoluteness" so caustically ridiculed by Adorno in *The Jargon of Authenticity*. Nothing is more inauthentic than an identity constructed with a view to recognition. Or, drawing on Kundera's *Immortality*, the authenticity of an identity can be understood as a certain outcome of the "reincarnation test." Assuming hypothetically that an actor has control over his or her next reincarnation, the actor has an authentic identity who would choose to have once again, in the next life, the same project he or she entertains now.

Second, it is important to understand what exactly "recognition" means, and what its object is. Axel Honneth is developing an interesting perspective based on the notions of "recognition" and "struggle for recognition" – a perspective in moral and political theory which tries to steer a course between the formalism of deontological theories of justice and the dubious perfectionism of communitarian conceptions.[23] Underlying Honneth's theory of recognition is a notion of self-realization formulated entirely from within an intersubjective perspective. Self-realization – understood also by Honneth as an equivalent of the good life

or *eudaimonia* – presupposes satisfying three standards. These formal requirements of self-realization are three properties of the relation of persons with
themselves: *self-confidence*, *self-respect* and *self-esteem*. Drawing on Hegel and
Mead, Honneth understands these three modes of relation as sedimentations of
three kinds of successful relation of reciprocal recognition: they are the
outcome, respectively, of adequate relations of parental *love*, of relations of *legal*
recognition and of relations of *solidarity* within which the cultural identity of
the person becomes the object of recognition.[24]

A fourth kind of relation of reciprocal recognition needs to be added to these
three, in my opinion – a type of relation which in the context of modernity
branches out from the third type described by Honneth. In this fourth type of
relation the object of recognition is not the inviolability of the bodily self, the
legal person or the cultural dignity, but the uniqueness of the project which
constitutes the individual and makes him or her distinguishable from the back-
cloth of their culture. In fact, without positing this fourth type of relation of
reciprocal recognition it is very difficult to articulate the distinction between
(1) recognizing the dignity and worth of another person from the standpoint of
what that person *shares in common* with the other members of a culture, and (2)
recognizing the dignity and worth of that person from the standpoint of what
distinguishes him or her from everybody else and makes them unique.

Finally, the idea of validity as authenticity assigns a central role to reflective
judgment and, within it, to the judgment of taste taken as a model for the kind
of judgments in terms of which we evaluate the degree of appropriateness of a
course of action, or of a life-project, to an identity. This kind of judgment is
inherently intersubjective, as Kant points out in paragraph 40 of the *Critique of
Judgment*. It is a kind of judgment that resembles a sort of *sensus communis*, of
sensibility, a kind of "critical faculty which in its reflective act takes account (*a
priori*) of the mode of representation of every one else."[25] When we make use of
this critical faculty, Kant argues, we do so:

> by weighing the judgment, not so much with actual, as rather with the
> merely possible, judgments of others, and by putting ourselves in the
> position of every one else, as the result of a mere abstraction from the
> limitations which contingently affect our own estimate.
>
> (Kant 1986: 151)

This means that it is impossible for anyone to exercise the judgment of taste or
reflective judgment if he or she fails to satisfy the following three requisites: (1)
to possess the ability to think *for themselves* – here we find in yet another form
the idea that autonomy is but a first step toward authenticity; (2) to possess the
ability to think *from the standpoint of everyone else*; and (c) to possess the ability
to think *consistently*.[26]

While a priori synthetic judgments – the building blocks of our knowledge of
the world – and moral judgments can be formulated, according to Kant, with

17

reference to one's own sense data ordered through the transcendental categories or by orienting oneself to the categorical imperative, in the case of reflective judgment the intersubjective dimension is part and parcel of our judgment from the outset. To assess the congruency of a symbolic whole, be it a work of art, a text or an identity, always presupposes the ability on our part to look at it alternatively through the eyes of others as well as our own.

These three aspects – the intersubjective origin of identity, the need for recognition encoded in any project for self-realization, and the intersubjective nature of reflective judgment – indicate that the *authenticity-thesis* cannot be accused of constituting yet another restatement of the philosophy of the subject, this time couched in a jargon of interiority. What still remains in need of clarification, however, is the relation of the *authenticity-thesis* to that *communicative paradigm* which represents the most complete and influential version of the intersubjective perspective thus far. For all that the *communicative paradigm*, which is part of the broader intersubjective perspective, and the *authenticity-thesis* share in common, there remain two basic points of divergence that distinguish these two approaches. The first consists of a different attitude that they presuppose toward the "project of modernity," the second concerns the different idea of validity embedded in them.

The first point of divergence does not require much comment. The *communicative paradigm* has been presented by Habermas as an attempt to *bring the project of modernity to completion*, by purifying it from a doctrine of the subject which represents, as he rightly points out, a residue of metaphysics. In its own way also the *authenticity-thesis* represents a radicalization of a movement of thought initiated by modernity: it takes seriously the subjectivization of reason and validity and brings it to its ultimate consequences. But a characterization of the *authenticity-thesis* in these terms would be misleadingly superficial. For it would obscure three senses in which the idea of validity as exemplary authenticity clashes with essential features of the project of modernity, implies a radical rethinking of it and thus comes into tension with the *communicative paradigm*. First, to the extent that the project of modernity presupposes a systematic connection between validity and demonstrability, even in the weaker form of the consensus-deserving quality of the best argument, the *authenticity-thesis* is discontinuous with it. Furthermore, the *authenticity-thesis* rejects the idea, underlying the nexus of validity and demonstrability, that the statements and norms paradigmatically valid are the ones generated by determinant judgment. Also, the *authenticity-thesis* cannot accommodate within itself the pre-Wittgensteinian idea of a neutral language of commensuration within which the testing of statements and norms generated from provincial contexts could be carried out without loss of meaning – an idea which at times surfaces again within the communicative paradigm.[27] The "presuppositions of argumentation" constitute no exception in this respect. They are just another attempt to come up with some context-transcending framework capable of neutralizing the particularity of local frameworks. Finally, the *authenticity-thesis* cannot accommodate a domesticated view of the aesthetic as the sphere specialized in expressiveness. Rather, it takes the aesthetic as a realm in which a specialized sphere of cultivated expressiveness coexists with a "principle of validity" whose relevance encompasses the whole spectrum of decentered Reason, including science, morality, law and politics.[28] These three aspects suffice to render the relation of the *authenticity-thesis* to modernity significantly different from the one entertained by the *communicative paradigm*. More on the nature of this relation will be said in the concluding remarks, after I have discussed a number of other aspects of the *authenticity-thesis*.

As regards the second point of divergence, Habermas's *communicative paradigm* can be summed up in the proposition that the modern idea of autonomous subjectivity was flawed by the one-sided and reductive notions of action and rationality that it embedded. More specifically, the autonomy of the subject came to fruition only in the form of instrumental or strategic rationality and of action inspired by this kind of rationality. This reductive conception of subjectivity, in turn, allowed only the pessimistic and apocalyptic interpretation of modernization to be found in *Dialectics of Enlightenment*, according to which the rationalization of action cannot but give rise to new forms of alienation, loss of meaning and weakening of individuation. Furthermore, from within this modern view of subjectivity it is impossible to generate any plausible account of the rise of intersubjectivity. The *communicative paradigm* is designed to avoid these difficulties. Habermas develops the idea of a communicative form of rationality, anchored to basic structures of language, and suggests that communicative rationality realizes itself in a form of communicative action which in turn is indispensable for the reproduction of the symbolic aspects of the social order. The articulation of the standpoint of communicative rationality, according to Habermas, allows one (1) to identify the progressive aspect of modernity at the level of modalities of identity and of social relations and (2) to conceive of reason and rationality as properties of a social relation rather than of a subject.

One of the main difficulties of the *communicative paradigm* concerns the theoretical level at which the problem of validity can be most appropriately posed. The consensus or communicative understanding of validity – according to which the validity of a proposition or of a norm derives from the rational consensus of the actors who evaluate it under "idealizing suppositions" – seems to oscillate between the two opposite dangers of formulating the notion of "consensus" in terms too close to the empirical (but most likely distorted) conditions of communication and, on the other hand, of formulating it in terms of conditions of communication so idealized that it then becomes difficult to recognize the concrete features of the real actors who face the practical dilemma out of which the necessity to test the proposition or the norm first arose. Historically the *communicative paradigm* has tended more toward the latter, formalistic side, partly due to the personal propensities of its founder, but today we observe the emergence of bits and pieces of a *new* intersubjective paradigm which puts a greater emphasis on the notions of judgment (Wellmer), of the "concrete other" (Benhabib) and of recognition (Honneth).

Furthermore, while on the one hand the strong point of the consensus-theoretical approach is the reconstruction from a *third-person perspective* of our intuitions regarding validity, on the other hand this approach leaves us impotent when it comes to a *first-person perspective* on validity. When we are faced with a number of alternative ways of solving a given practical or theoretical dilemma and we have to deliberate, we certainly cannot invoke, as a justification for our choice, the rationality of a consensus not yet formed. We have to choose on *some other* basis in order to contribute, through our choice, to the very formation of that rational consensus. One of the strong points of the *authenticity-thesis* lies, in my opinion, precisely in its providing an account of this alternative basis on which we rest our choices and deliberations.

Finally, the *communicative paradigm* continues to emphasize that nexus of validity and demonstrability which constitutes the seal of early modern universalism. It continues to pursue the ideal of a strong demonstrability of the validity of our theoretical and moral judgments. It understands such demonstrability in terms of standards – "presuppositions of communication," "idealizing conditions" or "strong idealizations" – which select models of rationality and judgment, and these standards, in turn, are difficult to reconcile with the renunciation of Archimedean points of which the defenders of the intersubjective paradigm make public profession. Also in this case the *authenticity-thesis* seems more in line with the postmetaphysical assumption of a plurality of language games or conceptual schemes.

The above remarks complete this initial outline of the main argument developed in this book. The Babel metaphors through which the cultural situation of our time is often depicted begin to appear under a different light if we recognize that underneath the plurality of subcultures, lifestyles, value orientations and moral outlooks that compose the canvas of contemporary complex societies there begins to be detectable one shared view of well-being or *eudaimonia* understood as authenticity or self-realization and one way of understanding validity – both theoretical and practical – that shifts the emphasis away from the generalizable and toward the exemplary. Judgment is the *organon* of this newly emerging conception of validity.

In the following two chapters I will reconstruct and discuss two major sources for the notion of singular and exemplary validity that is associated with the *authenticity-thesis*: Aristotle's conception of *phronesis* and Kant's theory of *reflective judgment*. In Chapter 4 various versions of the concept of authenticity will be reconstructed and contrasted with "reflective authenticity." Also, Simmel's contribution to the development of a notion of singular and exemplary universalism will be discussed. Chapter 5 picks up were the reconstruction of Kant's notion of reflective judgment had left off. In the context of discussing four constitutive dimensions of authentic subjectivity I implicitly try to spell out the grounds of universality for reflective judgment in terms compatible with the fact of pluralism and the Linguistic Turn. In Chapters 6 and 7 I discuss the relevance of the dimensions of fulfilled or authentic subjectivity to three domains other than individual identities: namely collective identities, the interpretation of texts and aesthetics. Finally, in Chapter 8 I address the relation of the *authenticity-thesis* to the "project of modernity" and take up, in a reflexive turn, the question concerning the justification of the authenticity view of validity.

2

POSTMETAPHYSICAL
PHRONESIS

In a seminal essay published over a decade ago, when postmodernism, post-structuralism and deconstructionism were still in their embryonic stage, Richard Bernstein characterized the intellectual climate of the day in terms that are still useful. At the center of his reconstruction was the contest between, on the one hand, the *objectivist* attempt to identify an invariant – though no longer ontological or transcendental or bound up with the notion of reason in history – basis for all judgments of validity and, on the other hand, a new *relativism* which takes the form of an anthropologically and sociologically informed contextualism.[1] In this chapter I want to argue that the notion of *phronesis*, usually thought to belong in the skeptical and contextualist camp, bears no necessary relation to relativism, but constitutes one of the conceptual tools that can help us formulate a notion of validity capable of embedding some form of universalism while being consistent with the Linguistic Turn and the fact of pluralism.

In the first section of this chapter I will review some of the reasons for the increasing attention that *phronesis* and a number of related concepts such as *wisdom*, *prudence* and *judgment* have recently received and will address some perplexities generated by the use of the concept of *phronesis*. In the second section, I will offer a characterization of *phronesis* which is designed to make this notion fit the coordinates within which we understand the exercise of theoretical and practical deliberation in a context defined by the fact of pluralism. In the third section, by relying on a reading of Aristotle which presupposes no allegiance to any specific Aristotelian doctrine, I will highlight some continuities that link my reformulated concept of *phronesis* with the classical notion.

The relevance of *phronesis*: consonances and dissonances

The concept of *phronesis*, as well as the related notions of wisdom, prudence, judgment and taste, has acquired a new relevance over the past few years. The reasons for this increasing intellectual popularity go well beyond the fortunes of the German strand of moral and political philosophy called the *Rehabilitation der praktischen Philosophie* and of Gadamer's reading of Aristotle in *Truth and Method*. Indeed, the internal vicissitudes of quite a number of diverse intellectual traditions have concurred in setting the stage for a comeback of this notion which, throughout the history of philosophy, cannot be said to have suffered from overexposure. Let me mention the cases that most readily come to mind. During the last three decades the once-prevailing empiricist project of devising a priori methods for the acceptance or rejection of scientific theories has suffered fatal blows. The work of Thomas Kuhn and the other post-empiricist philosophers of science has shown (1) that serious theory-testing only occurs in the context of the competition between two or more paradigms; (2) that any theory can be immunized practically against any kind of anomaly; (3) that the comparison of competing theories always involves some effort at translating incommensurable concepts and statements, and also that scientific translations, as all translations do, represent mere approximations of the original meanings; and (4) that all assessment of competing paradigms is inevitably bound up with the weighing and prioritization of scientific *values*.[2] Consequently, one of the insights generated by the philosophy of science of Kuhnian descent has been that at least at three junctures of scientific practice we find a moment of *phronesis* which escapes all accounts in terms of rules, deductive inferences or methods. The first of these junctures is faced by all scientists who are in a position of having to decide if the number and quality of the anomalies of a theory justify its abandonment. The second occurs when scientists have to determine whether certain theoretical terms can be considered equivalent across competing and incommensurable theories. And the third is constituted by those predicaments in which scientists have to determine which among several scientific values (for example, accuracy or theoretical scope or elegance) deserves priority in the context of a given paradigmatic choice.

Furthermore, contemporary proponents of a deontological approach to questions of justice and morality, such as Habermas, insist on separating norms or rules about which universally binding moral judgment can be passed, from broader value-orientations about which they wish to retain a pluralist position. Regardless of whether Habermas succeeds in showing convincingly that judgments about the justness of norms or institutional arrangements can be detached from notions of the good, *phronesis* seems to enter moral judgment, as conceived from a deontological perspective, in at least four respects: (1) insofar as the moral actor must determine how norms apply to the situation; (2) insofar as the moral actor must decide if an action fulfills a prescription; (3) insofar as different interpretations of a norm exist, which are rooted in competing values and call for choice; and (4) insofar as actions are *interpretations* of doings and depending on the interpretation the same doing can have different ethical implications.[3]

Third, some of the difficulties inherent in critical theory have also contributed to draw sympathetic attention to the concept of *phronesis*. For Habermas the truth of propositions and the rightness of norms rest on rational consensus, and rational consensus is consensus generated within a dialogical argumentation conducted under idealized conditions. Under the heading of "idealized conditions" or "strong idealizations," however, we find a collection of at least four distinct requirements: unrestricted participation, equality of status, equality of chances to continue or terminate discourse, equal degree of truthfulness and cooperative motivation. In the (obvious) absence of a hierarchical and a priori ranking of these requirements the strong idealizations can serve their purpose of helping us to evaluate the rational quality of consensus only if we tacitly assume that the evaluator is also endowed with a competence like *phronesis* which enables him or her to assess which combination of factors represents the best approximation of the ideal conditions for generating rational, validity-warranting consensus.

Furthermore, Habermas's view of modern rationality as differentiated in a cognitive, a moral and an aesthetic sphere, each governed by independent standards of validity, raises the problem of determining the kind of rationality-standard relevant for solving a given dilemma, a problem more recently compounded by the tripartition of the practical realm into a moral, an ethical and a pragmatical domain. To be sure, we cannot fall back on the current social definition of a scientific, practical (moral, ethical or pragmatical) or aesthetic problem without thereby falling into relativism. Nor can Habermas envisage a rational "metadiscourse" within which to argue on how to assign dilemmas to spheres of rationality or domains of the practical sphere, without thereby contradicting the idea of a decentered rationality. Again, some notion of *phronesis* or judgment must be invoked.[4]

Before introducing a postmetaphysical version of such a notion and discussing its relation to Aristotle's own concept of *phronesis*, however, I would like to consider a number of objections raised by Herbert Schnädelbach. In his paper "Was ist Neoaristotelismus?" (1986), Schnädelbach criticizes the conservative and skeptical implications of what he calls the "ideology of *phronesis*." Neo-Aristotelianism, portrayed by Schnädelbach as an ideology of sophisticated neoconservatives for whom "to be enlightened as to the end of Enlightenment is the ultimate enlightenment" (Schnädelbach 1986: 41), can be characterized with reference to three oppositions: *theory* versus *praxis*, *praxis* versus *poiesis*, and *ethics* versus *ethos*.

As far as the opposition of *theory* and *praxis* is concerned, Schnädelbach draws attention to the fact that the historically enlightened neo-Aristotelian cannot but bid farewell to principles, "take distance from the Kantian ethic of duty as from the Platonizing ethics of values, abandon the study of practical prudence to the social sciences, and rid himself of all normative claims" (Schnädelbach 1986: 45–6). As regards the opposition of *praxis* and *poiesis*, Schnädelbach takes issue with the neo-Aristotelian use of the concept of praxis for criticizing the modern image of *homo faber*. Those who invoke praxis, attracted by its relation to "eupragia" and the good life, argues Schnädelbach, are faced with the difficulty of having to specify what the good life is without contradicting the modern idea that legitimate normativity can only be self-imposed. This difficulty leads the consistent neo-Aristotelian to deemphasize the normative aspects of praxis and thereby to feed conservatism. With reference to the *ethics* versus *ethos* dichotomy, Schnädelbach argues that neo-Aristotelianism implies a "systematic harnessing of ethics to the yoke of some kind of existing ethos." More specifically, the neo-Aristotelian position entails a "critique of utopia" and a "rejection of ultimate ethical foundations" (Schnädelbach 1986: 51). Such diffidence *vis-à-vis* ideal images of the Good or a priori principles of justice rests on the conviction "that the good is already in the world" and the problem is only to recognize it. Today, the sophisticated neo-Aristotelian replaces Aristotle's "static" notion of ethos with the task of identifying the presence of Reason in history. However, since we can no longer subscribe to the Hegelian idea of a logic of history, the neo-Aristotelian attempt to grasp the presence of Reason in history turns into a search for Reason in tradition. Finally, Schnädelbach accuses the ethics of ethos of containing merely *hypothetical* imperatives, i.e. "situation-bound rules of prudence, which Kant or Fichte would have never called moral" (Schnädelbach 1986: 53).

Against the ideology of *phronesis*, Schnädelbach also raises two objections of a more general tenor. First, the notion of *phronesis* can be relevant to our modern context only if we overlook the colonization of the life-world by purposive rationality and the preeminent position that *poiesis* and *techne* have acquired in the modern world. Instead of appealing, somewhat nostalgically, to the idea of *phronesis* as the counterimage of *techne*, according to Schnädelbach one had better take up the challenge of "overcoming the limits of techne by its own means" (Schnädelbach 1986: 55). How a merely technical attitude can be overcome from within, through technical means or a technical mentality, is left unexplained.

Second, for Schnädelbach the ideology of *phronesis* is linked to the renunciation of all universalistic claim. For the ethic of ethos moral universalism means no more than a concrete, historically situated or "merely pragmatic universalism" (Schnädelbach 1986: 56). The only way to rescue the notion of *phronesis*, according to Schnädelbach, is by reconstructing the concept from within the Kantian perspective as *practical judgment*. Only then would the pragmatic-universalist element of *phronesis* be linked with the "real," i.e. *principled*, universalism of Kant's practical reason.

All in all, it is hard to avoid the impression that Schnädelbach's argument is plausible relative to the German context and to the meaning that neo-Aristotelian themes have acquired in it. It is equally hard to see any "inevitable" conservatism in the idea that the true, the good and the beautiful are constantly being produced in the world though they often go unrecognized, or in the idea that validity is concrete and singular, as opposed to general and a priori, or in the emphasis on commonsense over expert knowledge. Furthermore, I do not see any "inevitable" affinity of *phronesis* and relativism or, worse, traditionalism. After all, the Kuhnian scientist who revolutionizes a received paradigm, the Weberian politician who reconciles the claims of competing values and principles, or the Hegelian world-historical individual who recognizes what is timely and acts on his intuition, can all be seen as exercising judgment or prudence in the service of *innovation*. Above all, in dismissing all accounts of validity based on singular judgment as relativist and therefore conservative, Schnädelbach seems to forget that it is the crisis of objectivistic and procedural modes of thought which is largely responsible for the present resurgence of interest in Aristotelian themes and not the other way around.

Moving on from interpretive to systematic considerations, a case could be made for rescuing the notion of *phronesis* in quite different terms than the ones suggested by Schnädelbach. Granted that the affinity between Kant's theory of judgment and Aristotle's account of *phronesis* is worth exploring, the project of reconstructing *phronesis* as a kind of *applied practical judgment*, in the guise that Habermas once thought would complement the discourse ethics, strikes me as quite reductive. On the contrary, the notion of *phronesis* seems capable of playing a much broader role if we de-ethicize it and conceive it as a *general* competence which plays a crucial role in the solving of *all* transschematic, transparadigmatic and cross-cultural dilemmas, regardless of their ethical, cognitive, political or aesthetic nature. Furthermore, instead of endowing *phronesis* with a vicarious universalism at the cost of turning it into a mere applicative appendix to some principle of generalization as suggested by Habermas and Schnädelbach, more promise seems to be carried by an investigation of the specific kind of universalism inherent in prudential judgment itself.

Phronesis revisited

By the term *phronesis* I understand the competence to choose between conceptual schemes which embed incompatible or differently ranked values in situations where no a priori standard can be invoked.[5] From the vantage point of scientific practice, *phronesis* designates the competence to choose correctly between rival paradigms or research-programs which embed a roughly similar balance of anomalies and strong points. With respect to post-conventional moral judgment, *phronesis* designates the ability of the moral actor to choose between conflicting value-orientations and action-interpretations to which he or she is exposed in the context of a differentiated and pluralist life-world. In relation to Habermas's communicative paradigm within critical theory, the term *phronesis* designates the ability of the actor to evaluate the rationality of consensus, i.e. to assess the extent to which the presuppositions of argumentation embedded in the strong idealizations of the discourse theory of validity are realized in an actual context of discussion. Finally, from the perspective of the Wittgensteinian theory of language games, *phronesis* designates the ability of actors not simply to follow the rules of a given game, but to pass judgment on the desirability or worth of a game as a whole, and to choose the game to be played in a given situation.

The four perspectives mentioned above – despite the diversity of their central concepts: paradigms, cultures, contexts of argumentation, language games etc. – place a common demand on the actor. Since paradigms, cultural horizons, life-worlds and language games embed hierarchically organized values, to choose between them requires that the actor should assign priorities to values and then assess the worth of the competing conceptual schemes in the light of these priorities. These approaches, however, all fail to indicate how values can be correctly assessed and a choice between them made. Kuhn shies away from the issue of cross-paradigmatic validity; Habermas relegates evaluative questions within those second-order arguments for which the term "discourse" is inappropriate, whereas Wittgenstein and his followers give up entirely on the question and embrace various forms of relativism.

This predicament poses the challenge of reconstructing a competence which all human beings more or less possess and use when faced with theoretical or ethical dilemmas. Such competence, designated in ordinary language by expressions such as judgment, good judgment, soundness of judgment, prudence, consideration, sound understanding, common sense, wisdom, sensibleness, sagacity, discernment, insight etc., is the capacity to rank competing values in the absence of general guidelines or criteria. Some aspects of the capacity for choice in the absence of guidelines have been discussed in the past by Aristotle and by Kant under the headings of *phronesis* and of *aesthetic judgment*. Yet, unfortunately, both Aristotle and Kant have restricted this capacity to a scope narrower than necessary (respectively, the domains of ethics and aesthetics) and both have understood it as a sort of "natural" faculty of humanity. Their reflections provide a good starting point, but we must go beyond their accounts by recognizing the importance of judgment or prudence in *all* human activities, including science, and by reconstructing the *inner structure* of *phronesis* also from a *psychological* standpoint as well as the *social conditions* which favor its rise.

As far as the inner structure of *phronesis* is concerned, it is possible to think of all choices between rival conceptual schemes as ultimately resting on value-choices and to link conceptually the question "Which value deserves priority in a given situation?" with the question "Which needs are more crucial for a given identity?" The analogy between assigning priority to values and recognizing the salience of inner needs for an identity rests on the fact that in both cases it is a matter not so much of determining whether one "has" a need or if a single value is worthy *in general*, but rather of placing the various needs or values into what might be called (in a sense yet to be clarified) "the right order." If the conceptual bridge between values and needs can be built, then we can account for the validity of transparadigmatic, transschematic and cross-cultural judgments without falling back into metaphysical claims. In fact, questions about the primacy of needs cannot be answered a priori and in general, as various kinds of substantive ethics of value maintain,[6] because which needs are central to an identity depends not on the general characteristics of the identity – what one shares in common with all other human beings – but on what is unique to it, on the specific and unique equilibrium of its components. At the same time, there is a sense in which some needs are more crucial, more *objectively* crucial, than others. Psychoanalytic practice offers an example of the competence, on the part of the analyst, to assess the cohesion of an identity and its dependency on the satisfaction of a unique configuration of needs. Although it cannot be objectivated in a method, such competence can be taught and evaluated, as the practice of having prospective analysts undergo didactic analysis suggests. If a value-horizon is conceived as the equivalent of a configuration of needs at the level of a collective identity, we could then decide between values and cultural aggregates of values, without resorting to an external yardstick which would contradict our pluralist intuitions and would be quite difficult to ground.

Let me now try to spell out this basic idea of establishing an order of needs without invoking a priori criteria on which the ability for value-choice is supposedly parasitic. The archetypal version of this operation is the understanding of the psychological needs of an individual's identity, as it takes place in contexts of everyday life. From this basic ability, which we all possess to various degrees, derive the more refined and specialized versions of *phronesis*, including the balancing of values in the making of policy when matters of collective identity are at stake, the aesthetic evaluation of works of art, the choice between rival paradigms on the basis of the scientific values that they embed, the interpretation of the patient's neurotic patterns in therapeutic practice, and the balancing of conflicting motifs in the interpretation of a text or in the evaluation of a translation. More generally this ability amounts to recognizing whether and how a symbolic element fits the whole of which it is a part.

The possibility of translating the question "What do we do when we assign priority to values?" into the more tractable question "How are judgments on the integrity of an identity possible?" rests on the analogy between judgments regarding values and judgments regarding needs. But how can we make a case for that analogy? *Prima facie*, needs and values seem to belong to the incommensurable realms of the *Sein* and the *Sollen*. Needs are associated with necessity, values with the will. One "has" a need regardless of one's intentions, desires and awareness, whereas one cannot "have" certain values unless one so desires, though not all desires are conscious.

On closer inspection, things appear less neat. Needs are three-place predicates. One needs something *for* something or *in order to* do something. Even absolute or primary needs are needs for survival. Thus every need-statement presupposes, at some level, the desirability of something valuable – a purpose, a state of affairs, a feeling – for the sake of which we need what we need. To this extent needs are also, however remotely, related to the will. On the other hand, when we value things – even abstract things such as liberty, justice or equality – we feel *pressed* to decide as we do, i.e. we feel that we are recognizing some kind of necessity and, like Luther, "can do no other." Perhaps needs and values at their upward limit converge in the notion of the good life.

The relation of needs and values can be clarified also with reference to a psychoanalytically based conception of identity and of the dimensions of its flourishing which will be outlined in greater detail in Chapter 5. Identities, individual and collective, are symbolic representations generated by the Ego which include at least: (1) some perception of continuity of the self or the collective in question; (2) a configuration of various kinds of needs and urges; and (3) an ideal projection of a desired self. Any prospective action must thus be checked by a competent actor not only against its instrumental efficacy and normative acceptability, but also against: (1) its potential for enhancing or disrupting the sense of continuity of the self; (2) its relation to the inner needs of the identity; and (3) its contribution to the attainment of the ideal self. For individual identities continuity takes the form of an unbroken and meaningful biography, a life-course which can be cast in the form of a coherent narrative. Collective identities experience continuity in the form of narrated history and cultural tradition.

The core of an individual identity can be conceived as a structure of needs linked with the inner world of object-relations, with the quality and aims of the person's libido, with the regulation of self-esteem and with the person's "character," i.e. a combination of defense mechanisms and interactive styles typically used by the person. The equivalent component in the case of collective identities consists of processes of cultural reproduction, social integration and socialization which stabilize the content of the collective representation as well as produce a sense of historical continuity. Central to these processes is the transmission, reproduction and maintenance of values.[7] Collective action and policy decisions must continuously be checked against this set of communal values which, like the needs embedded in an individual's identity, cannot be violated or neglected for long without endangering the cohesion and even the existence of a collective identity.

Finally, all individual identity includes an anticipation of the ideal self that the person wishes to become. This ideal self is the product of early identifications with significant figures and, later, of the internalization of social images. It must bear a realistic relation to the past selves and to the needs embedded in the central component. It is part of a sound identity to posit an ideal which can be attained by the real self. Collective identities also embed the image of a collective ideal self which can be more or less consonant with the actual possibilities of a group. At this level we have a thematization of central values of a society and their assessment in relation to the past history and the perceived potential of the present.

From this view of the analytical components of identity we can derive a number of evaluative dimensions that, jointly working, orient all judgments concerning the relative appropriateness of our assignment of a priority both to needs and to values. Again, more on this subject will be said in Chapter 5.

A non-rationalistic rationality

Insofar as clinical judgments on the integrity or authenticity of identities concern single cases but nonetheless claim a broader significance, it is possible to capture some of their properties by reference to an Aristotelian concept of *phronesis* reformulated along postmetaphysical lines. Although for Aristotle *phronesis* is essentially an ethical concept,[8] his doctrine of *phronesis* carries broader implications. What makes a course of action the right one, or rather – as we should say – *a* right one, is not its being to the immediate advantage of the actor, nor its meeting the expectations of the community, nor its accordance with moral principles or rules, but rather its being "conducive to the good life [*eudaimonia*] generally" (Aristotle *Nichomachean Ethics*: 1140a24–b12; 1953: 209). Thus, to understand what *phronesis* in the Aristotelian sense is requires that we understand what can be meant by the expression the "good life" and that we see how *phronesis* relates in a particular way to the good life.

The term *eudaimonia*, used by Aristotle in order to designate the good life, is frequently translated as "happiness." Yet it refers to a very special kind of happiness. In using this term, Aristotle had in mind three rival conceptions of the good life influential in Athens at the time. On the first of these views, a good life is tantamount to a life spent in the successful pursuit of pleasure, on the second the good life is a life in which we achieve honor, on the third the good life is a life spent in contemplation. Aristotle decidedly rejects the first two and takes an ambiguous attitude toward the third view. The good life cannot be reduced to the pursuit of pleasure or honor, because while we pursue honor and pleasure for the sake of our happiness, "we always choose it [happiness] for itself, and never for any other reason" (Aristotle *Nichomachean Ethics*: 1097a15–b2; 1953: 73). Specifically, Aristotle denies that the good life can be equated with the pursuit of honor. We receive honor because we are good, so goodness, insofar as it is that quality the possession of which is rewarded by honor, has primacy over honor. Furthermore, because honor is conceded to us by others, if we sought honor we would be dependent on those who recognize us as honorable. We are then left with the somewhat vague statement that the good life is a life spent in trying to achieve the good for man. But what is the good for man?

In Book I of his *Nichomachean Ethics* Aristotle defines the good as the "activity of the soul in accordance with virtue" (1098a8–27; 1953: 76), but in Book X specifies that the activity in which "happiness" consists is mainly "contemplation" (1177a25–b13; 1953: 329). The first thing to be noticed here is the idea that happiness is an activity (*energeia*) rather than a state. Activity is a term obviously related to *praxis*, which means not only to act but to *act well*. In this context, Aristotle means that happiness is not something that one possesses, like a quality of the mind or a trait of character, but includes the active exercise of certain powers and dispositions. Second, "soul" is to be understood as "character" or "personality"[9] or more simply as "being animate." Third, we must clarify the meaning of the expression "to act in accordance with virtue." *Areté* is the abstract noun for *agathòs*, good, which always means *good at something*. *Areté* is the property of being good at something, of excelling in some activity, but to be *agathòs* means also that the something at which one is good is in some sense "typical" of the kind of being one is. Thus, an *agathòs* archer is one that aims and shoots precisely, an *agathòs* vessel is one that fares well, an *agathòs* plow is one that plows well, an *agathòs* knife is a sharp-edged one which can cut well. In the case of man, then, to act in accordance with virtue means to perform well, over a period of time, the task which is most typical of man in general. If there is a plurality of typically human tasks, as seems to be the case, then to act in accordance with virtue means to excel at the most perfect among the typically human tasks.[10]

Then the question emerges: What is distinctively human among the many activities in which human beings engage themselves? Aristotle is thought to waver between a more comprehensive and a narrower answer. According to the reductive version, the most distinctively human ability is *contemplation*; according to the more comprehensive version, the good life has to be conceived not just in terms of intellectual contemplation, but rather as connected with "the full range of human life and action, in accordance with the broader excellences of moral virtue and practical wisdom."[11] The latter version is the one more relevant for our purposes. One way to rethink *phronesis* along postmetaphysical lines, in fact, is to interpret *eudaimonia* or well-being in terms of a philosophical theory of the identity of the human self. Then the good life can be seen, with Aristotle, as the *telos* at which the best human conduct aims but, differently than Aristotle, as a *telos* not preordained to the individual but immanent to the vicissitudes of one's psychic life. To act in accordance with virtue for us moderns cannot mean to perform well the task most typical of the human being *in general*, but to perform well the task of maintaining the integrity of one's identity in the plurality of situations one encounters and of expressing the salient traits of one's identity in a unique biography. Although this task confronts every person, its content varies from individual to individual and cannot be known a priori.

The good life or *eudaimonia* in a post-modern sense is then a life-course in which one is able to enrich the main plot of one's life-narrative with the largest possible amount of episodes and sub-plots compatible with the preservation of a sense of overall unity. The ability to unify one's biography into a coherent narrative is a good which plays a similar role to *eudaimonia* for Aristotle. On the one hand, it is a good which we seek for the sake of no other good. Rather, all other goods are pursued in order to attain the realization of one's identity, even though we often make mistakes and pursue goods that are not conducive to this purpose. On the other hand, self-realization is also a good whose lack diminishes the meaning of all the other goods that we may possess – as the case of Tolstoy's Ivan Illyitch teaches.

From this vantage point we can make sense of the nature of the virtues and of the special place of *phronesis* among them. A virtue is a disposition or trait of character which can be expressed in action and is an ingredient of a lifestyle conducive to *eudaimonia* or well-being. Aristotle characterizes the virtues in terms of the unfortunate doctrine of the mean, i.e. as the right proportion of a certain quality which lies between two excesses. Thus, for instance, courage lies between rashness and cowardice, liberality between prodigality and meanness. Laden with problems as it is, this characterization nonetheless can help us to understand the special role of *phronesis* among the virtues. As already stated, actions are always interpretations of doings relative to a context. The same act could count as an instance of courage in one context and of cowardice in another, and perhaps of rashness in a third. To attend a funeral can count as an act of cowardice if it means for a public official of a small Sicilian town to pay homage to a powerful mafia boss or as an act of courage if performed in order to pay homage to an opposition leader in an authoritarian regime. Thus no virtue can be exercised unless one possesses the capacity to appraise how different situations confer different meanings on our acts. This capacity, along with the capacity to place the various goods in the order that is most conducive to the good life, constitutes *phronesis*. Being an indispensable requisite for the acquisition and exercise of all other virtues, *phronesis* is thus the fundamental virtue.[12]

This reconstruction of Aristotle's view of *phronesis* goes in a direction different from the interpretation suggested by the protagonists of the *Rehabilitierung der praktischen Philosophie*. According to Vollrath, for example, *phronesis* is a virtue that relates solely to the choice of means and not to the choice of our ends.[13] He points out that in positing *eudaimonia* as the highest good, Aristotle assumes that *phronesis* is merely the virtue through which we can identify the best means for attaining the highest good in a concrete context. At the same time, however, Aristotle conceives of *phronesis* as a virtue distinct from a *merely* instrumental ability to calculate the effects of our acts – the ability of which *techne* consists. The exercise of *phronesis* then, argues Vollrath, presupposes a given conception of the good. More specifically, it presupposes a kind of knowledge of the ultimate ends which can be thought of as differentiated in two distinct types of knowledge hierarchically superior to *phronesis*, the first of which is theoretical-ontological knowledge of human nature and the second of which is a kind of ethical-practical insight into the ends that, on the basis of the first type of knowledge, are worth pursuing. Above all, it is not up to *phronesis* to decide that "the end of the human being and of the polis is happiness." The domain of *phronesis* must remain limited to judgment and deliberation on "which actions are useful and conducive to the attainment of that end" (Vollrath 1977: 86).

Against this interpretation both a philological and a systematic objection can be raised. There exist two possible versions of philological objection, formulated respectively by Otfried Höffe and Helmut Kuhn. In the first version, the objection concerns the implications to be legitimately drawn from the peculiar qualities of knowledge about *eudaimonia*. Because *eudaimonia* is not one end among others or merely an end of broader scope, but the end for the sake of which we pursue every other end,[14] *eudaimonia* is like a transcendental condition which *constitutes* or makes the other ends possible.[15] This special status of *eudaimonia* changes the picture also as far as *phronesis* is concerned. If the good only exists in a particular, actual form, as *this good*, then when *phronesis* guides us in attaining a certain specific good, it does not provide us with a means but rather with a *way* of attaining the good.[16] Thus, as Cortella suggests:

> while in the case of *techne* the means is chosen in light of an external end and has relevance only in relation to that end, in the case of *praxis* the means already counts as a realization of the end. It constitutes an instantiation of the universal principle of the good, in the guise of a particular good. The *means* is thus a *way* of realizing the good in given circumstances.
>
> (Cortella 1987: 53)

The other version of the objection – put forward by Helmut Kuhn and by Alasdair MacIntyre – calls our attention to the fact that in the practical sphere, to reflect on the means always presupposes making sense of the end to which they are means, and thus inevitably reflection on the means leads to a reflection on the ends. Unlike the attempt to determine the location of an oil deposit, the quest for the good is not the same as the search for something whose nature is fully known in advance. Rather, the quest for the good is the search for something which is known only vaguely and generally – otherwise we could not search for it – but whose constitution becomes more specific as we repeatedly compare it with what supposedly is a local and temporal instance of it in a given context.[17]

Both versions of the objection, however, run against a difficulty. Over and over again Aristotle reaffirms that means are something quite different from ends and that *sophia* is the only virtue that has to do with knowledge about the good. Ultimately we cannot overlook Aristotle's continuous insistence on the "subordination of ethics to metaphysics and of *phronesis* to *sophia*." [18]

The systematic objection, instead, hinges on the different implications of two competing projects. The first is the project of rescuing some aspects of the Aristotelian concept of *phronesis* in a profoundly transformed context in order to respond to the challenge posed by our contemporary sense of "groundlessness." The other project consists of a thorough reconstruction of the whole *doctrine of phronesis* – a project that makes sense only as part of the larger intent to "rehabilitate" Aristotelian philosophy as a more general philosophical option. From the standpoint of the first project – the one pursued here – the inability, on the part of *phronesis*, to deliberate on ends ceases to constitute a problem once we leave behind all foundational perspectives which, from a transcendental or *geschichtsphilosophisch* or any other perspective, assume the existence of some privileged access to an uninterpreted reality. Paradoxically, the closer our reconstruction of *phronesis* remains to Aristotle's *metaphysical* assumptions, the more this outstanding model of a non-rationalistic rationality loses in relevance for us. On the contrary, any effort to reappropriate the suggestive fruitfulness of this model must start from and come to terms with the contemporary modern postulation of a plurality of competing conceptions of the good. In light of this assumption, the notion of *eudaimonia* or well-being comes to acquire a formal quality and to be understood as that end for the sake of which we pursue all other ends. *Eudaimonia* in our sense – in a "post"-modern though not "postmodern" sense – remains then a horizon constitutive of praxis, but no *sophia* can capture its meaning once and for all. In a contemporary or "post"-modern context, in fact, the meaning of *eudaimonia* is up for every and each human being to specify in a unique way though not independently of a given culture. This specification can be more or less felicitous in the same way that each work of art has its own way of being "felicitous" or "well-formed." Within a constellation marked by the acceptance of the "fact of pluralism," of the intersubjective genesis of subjectivity and of the Linguistic Turn, to rethink *phronesis* along postmetaphysical lines not only allows, but actually requires, that we conceive of it as including not only the identification of means and strategies, but also the specification of the concrete meaning of *eudaimonia* or well-being for a single human life lived in a unique context – a specification that can be effected, in turn, only if we assume that *phronesis* also includes the ability to reconcile or select (as it may be the case) competing views of the good without falling back on any modern substitute of *sophia*.

In a postmetaphysical context, also Aristotle's more general point, mentioned by Vollrath, that "the end of the human being and of political association is happiness" cannot be presented as a philosophical certainty derived from practical knowledge or from metaphysical insight, but must be understood as that way of conceiving the human being and political association which it is *prudent* for us – us moderns of the end of the twentieth century – to embrace. Even the thesis that *eudaimonia* is the ultimate end of the human being and that it has to do with well-being or happiness understood as self-realization cannot be presented as a truth, but must be presented more modestly as the best thesis concerning the ultimate ends of human action that *phronesis* urges us to choose from among the set of available theses on that subject.

The relation of subordination of *phronesis* to *sophia* not only ceases to be defensible in a context where access to uninterpreted reality is no longer believed to be possible, but actually undergoes a reversal of direction. Now it is practical knowledge, the substance of *sophia*, to the extent that we can still speak of a practical *knowledge* – at least in the minimalist sense in which some authors insist on the possibility of an ethical *cognitivism* – that depends on *phronesis*, in the sense that it appears valid to us insofar as *phronesis* selects it as the best among all the competing reconstructions of our moral intuitions that are available to us.

Finally, if we examine the relation of *phronesis* to the intellectual virtues mentioned by Aristotle in Book VI of the *Nicomachean Ethics*, we can notice a number of similarities to the qualities attributed by Kant to the judgment of taste. In contrast with *techne*, which remains external to the personality of the expert, *phronesis*, just as the ability to judge, can neither be learned through a method nor forgotten. *Phronesis* and the capacity for judgment can only be cultivated through exposure to exemplary cases of good judgment as provided by someone already endowed with superior ability in this respect. Differently than with *episteme*, and again in analogy to the judgment of taste, the conclusions suggested by *phronesis* cannot be demonstrated but only shown and made plausible. In fact, *phronesis* has to do with deliberation and, argues Aristotle, no one deliberates about things that are universal or necessary. *Phronesis* is different from intuition or *nous* in that intuition apprehends *general definitions* which cannot be logically demonstrated, whereas *phronesis* apprehends objects which also cannot be the object of demonstrations, but are *particular*.

The greatest divergence between Aristotle's notion of *phronesis* and Kant's notion of the judgment of taste concerns the place of this competence in the overall picture of the human faculties. While for Aristotle *phronesis* is the crucial human ability in the realm of the practical, and political science represents its highest realization, for Kant the relevance of the judgment of taste is limited to the aesthetic realm. Although he acknowledges that politics and morality both require some degree of prudence (*Klugheit*), he directs his efforts to the search for principles of choice (the categorical imperative, the principle of publicity) that can reduce to a minimum the importance of reflective judgment.[19] Aristotle and Kant are again at one, however, in denying any relevance of prudence or taste in the sphere of cognition.

To sum up, though neither Aristotle nor Kant provides us with a theory of *phronesis* or judgment directly applicable to the contemporary context, nonetheless their accounts offer insights that remain of great relevance for us. For instance, both operate with an implicit distinction, which will have to be part also of a *postmetaphysical* notion of *phronesis*, between a basic level of judgment, close to common sense (*sunesis* or understanding for Aristotle, taste for Kant), and a superior type of judgment which includes motivation and the ability to translate judgment into action (*phronesis* for Aristotle, genius for Kant). Kant offers also a phenomenological account of this higher form of judgment, when he connects the performance of genius with the ability to set the play of all our mental faculties in motion and with the falling short of our expressive powers *vis-à-vis* the meanings thereby created.

What is not to be found in Kant or Aristotle is the distinction between *ordinary* and *exceptional*, *normal* and *abnormal* contexts of choice, i.e. between problems that arise *within* a conceptual scheme, paradigm, life-world etc. and problems that *cut across* conceptual schemes, paradigms or life-worlds. The latter problems cannot be solved, in principle, without recourse to *phronesis* whereas the former are usually "tackled" successfully through the application of some algorithm or standardized procedure. If we neglect this distinction we generate the misleading impression that dramatic acts of judgment are the norm in social life and that *phronesis* is what keeps the wheels of social interaction turning.[20] On the contrary, in everyday life we usually do substitute rules of thumb, received social expectations, or sheer habit for judgment proper. Judgment of the kind investigated here, instead, occurs only at exceptional moments in personal and social life, when all the available conceptual schemes somehow fall short of doing justice to various aspects of some complex dilemma – when "the wind of thought" has blown away the untenable crystallizations of received words and images, we suspend routines and "the stakes are on the table," as Hannah Arendt reminds us.[21]

3

FROM KANT TO KANT

A normativity without principles

Of all the modern philosophical classics, Immanuel Kant partakes of a unique destiny. His thought features on both sides of an ideal equation. On the one hand Kant's philosophy is part and parcel – indeed, it constitutes one of the founding moments – of that early modern philosophy of the subject which has become highly problematical to us. One need just recall Kant, the author of the *Critique of Pure Reason*, fascinated by the method and the promise of cumulative progress which he sees embedded in the natural sciences of the time, deeply convinced that the universal validity of the results generated by that method rests on the universality of the categories by way of which all human beings in all times and places apprehend reality. Kant the moral philosopher comes to mind next, to whom we owe the idea that to act justly means to follow, honestly and consistently, the right rule, the idea that the right is morally more significant than the good and is a matter of hypothetically generalizing rules of conduct – Kant the strenuous defender of the notion that "ought implies can," convinced as he is that there exists one and only one correct solution to each moral dilemma and that moral conflict is thus inherently the conflict between a correct alternative and one alternative that only seems so; Kant the modern Platonist who only has eyes for the conflict between good and evil and remains blind to that much more devastating kind of moral conflict which is the conflict between good and good.

On the other hand, however, Kant is also the author of the *Critique of Judgment* and in that capacity he constitutes an ineludible starting point for rethinking the aporias of modernity and reformulating the question of the nature of universalism, cognitive and ethical, in a new way capable of avoiding, if not solving, these aporias. His most precious legacy for us, on which more will be said in this chapter, consists in his outline of a kind of normativity – that inherent in reflective judgment – independent of methods and general principles, undemonstrable and yet universalistic. After the echoes of two momentous resurgences of Kant's thought in this century fade away – one linked with the question of the relation of science to values, the other linked with positing generalizability as the core of the moral point of view – it might not be a bad idea to look once again at Kant's work as the source of inspiration. Once again, he can speak to our concerns.

The question and the answer

It does not take much imagination to say that the twentieth century will go down in history as a skeptical one, a century in which more philosophical theories and paradigms have been shattered down than built up. Among the most illustrious victims of its critical spirit are the interrelated concepts of rationality, subjectivity and validity which we associate with modernity.

The new form of universalism, if there will be one, will bear traits quite different from the one to which modernity has accustomed us and which has fallen under the critical lens of Wittgenstein and Heidegger and their postmodern followers. Above all, it will have to measure up to the challenge raised by a transformation which has changed the face of the philosophical world in which we have lived for centuries: the "Linguistic Turn." I understand what goes under the name of the "Linguistic Turn" as a cultural *Gestalt switch* consisting essentially in the awareness of the formative, as opposed to instrumental, function of language and of the inescapable dimension of *contextuality* that surrounds all our theoretical and practical claims. Such awareness of contextuality amounts to the awareness that the truth of propositions and the justness of norms and actions can be claimed, assessed or contested only against the background of shared conceptual schemes, and that there exists an *irreducible* plurality of such conceptual schemes.

The first formulation of this awareness can be traced back to Dilthey's view of history. For Dilthey, the contexts to which the contextuality of our validity claims responded were historical totalities, historical epochs. The same idea can be found later developed along anthropological lines in Malinowsky, Evans-Pritchard and almost every major anthropologist. Within the phenomenological tradition it was the Husserlian notion of the *life-world* that provided the focus for similar considerations on the context-boundness of knowledge and normativity. Within the analytic philosophy of language a similar role is played by the concept of the *background* introduced by John Searle, and within hermeneutics by the notion of *tradition* developed by Gadamer. Within the philosophy of science it was Kuhn's concept of *paradigm*, within social theory that of *symbolic universe* coined by Berger and Luckmann, that played an analogous role. There is virtually no major theorist of the twentieth century in whose work this idea does not occur in one variant or another. The most felicitous formulation, however, is perhaps the one provided by Wittgenstein's image of a plurality of *language games* all existing side by side as symbolic totalities structured as sets of rules and containing their own independent, incommensurable conditions of validity.

Such awareness of the contextuality of valid assertions and norms imposes powerful restrictions on anyone who addresses the problem of validity. As Richard Rorty has pointed out in *Philosophy and the Mirror of Nature*, the awareness of contextuality rules out all search for an "ultimate framework" designed to constitute a metalanguage of universal commensuration into which all local languages will then be translated. Equally unacceptable is any restoration of figures of thought and "ultimate frameworks" that constitute the legacy of early modern thought, be they ultimately amenable to the model of the rationality of an abstract subject (like, for example, the paradigms of the theory of rational choice or of game theory) or to the model of the rationality inherent in the developmental path of a macro-subject. At the same time, unless we draw from the premise that issues of validity can be addressed only from within a conceptual scheme the erroneous conclusion – as Rorty does – that nothing meaningful can be said about the validity of conceptual schemes and consequently about our theoretical and practical decisions to operate within one or another scheme, the question concerning the foundations of validity remains to be answered: What can it mean for us, who inhabit a "post-linguistic turn" or "postmetaphysical" philosophical universe, to speak of the *trans*contextual, though not *context-free*, validity of an assertion or a practical norm?

To be sure, in our answer, whatever it will be, we will have to renounce all reference to a priori and general standards of truth and justice. Contrary to what Habermas and other contemporary theorists claim, however, the universalistic and anti-skeptic spirit can and will survive this renunciation just as, at the onset of the modern age, it has survived another major renunciation: namely, the abandonment of all attempts to ground the truth of our descriptions in their mirroring of essences and the rightness of our moral norms in their reflecting divine will or human nature. Indulging in the suspect activity of building narratives, the predicament in which we are could be conceived as one in which the subjectivization of reason comes to completion. The dimidiated subjectivization carried out by modern thought – whereby truth and justice are part of the human mind and not of the furniture of the universe, yet part of an abstract or in any case super-individual human mind – is about to come to fruition in the contemporary notion that the only requisites that can be accepted as bases of a new universalism consistent with the Linguistic Turn are the requisites of the well-being or *eudaimonia* of a concrete identity – individual or collective. Paraphrasing Kant, we could say today that the only thing which can count as unconditionally *good* is a good identity, i.e. a *fulfilled* identity.

The relevance of Kant in the twenty-first century consists, then, not so much in his ethical doctrine – whatever the fortune that it might have had within late-twentieth century liberalism and critical theory – as, rather, in his combining a certain kind of question that he raised in a context similar in some respects to ours with a certain direction in which he looked for an answer.

On the one hand we can borrow from Kant a certain philosophical attitude, a certain way of philosophizing in an epoch of interregnum as his, like ours, was – an epoch when all philosophical certainties (Aristotelian and medieval metaphysics for Kant, the modern philosophy of the subject for us) appear doomed and hollow but no new constellation is yet in sight. Kant reacted to this predicament by looking at the internal operation and philosophical presuppositions of a practice – modern Newtonian natural science – that from its beginning stood in opposition to the metaphysical outlook and appeared to be capable of a cumulative progress. Kant observes the fact that even though it is based on experience this new discipline generates a kind of knowledge that appears as solid and uncontroversial as the deductive theorems generated by formal logic, and raises the question: which conditions make it possible? The answer to this question, as we all know, contains a new concept of validity, no longer ontological but transcendental. In his phrase "a priori synthetic," which qualifies the kinds of judgments on which the new science is built, Kant brings together for the first time what in the classical world had always remained split apart: he manages to bring together into one consistent formula "what comes from experience" and "what is absolutely certain" – at the cost, of course, of deflating "what is absolutely certain" to "what is absolutely certain for us."

Today we witness what might well be the final crisis of this *answer* to the question concerning the meaning of validity, but that crisis leaves intact the relevance of Kant's way of posing his *question*, namely in the guise of a reconstruction of the conditions of the possibility of certain types of *judgments* that inhere in certain practices of exemplary significance. The practices that possess exemplary significance for us – who are not looking for cumulative progress but rather for a way of reconciling *universalism* and *pluralism* – are practices that belong in one capacity or another to the aesthetic sphere.

Two of these practices are psychoanalysis and art criticism: they produce judgments respectively on the integrity of an identity and on the well-formedness of a work of art which possess some characteristics important for our concern. They are judgments which do not subsume the individuality of the object under laws or principles external to it. Wellformedness and integrity must be assessed in a holistic way and cannot be reduced to the sum total of a finite number of qualities or conditions. At the same time the judgments found within these practices are not arbitrary. Neither can they be reduced to the status of projections of subjective preferences. Rather, they embed a universalistic claim *sui generis*: they anticipate the general consensus of those who possess the necessary *expertise* for passing judgment on the matter. Such *expertise* cannot be objectivated in the form of a method or a technique, but can be taught through exposure to exemplary instances of its exercise, can be institutionalized in degrees of learning and proficiency, and can reflexively be made the object of evaluation and supervision. Finally, because the kind of validity claimed by this kind of judgment does not rest on fulfilling standards external to the object being evaluated, the problem of the incommensurability of conceptual schemes is not overcome but *defused*. In fact, if our judgment takes as its object the congruence of a work of art or an identity with its own internal normativity, with its own "individual law," then the impossibility of exhaustively translating one vocabulary or conceptual scheme into another ceases to constitute an obstacle against the universality of judgment. Psychoanalysis is a modern creature, and a child of the Enlightenment, but the discourse of art criticism has existed for centuries under conditions of pluralism. There has always been a pluralistic understanding of validity in the aesthetic realm, and this genuine acceptance of the fact of pluralism has never prevented aesthetic discourse from performing universalistic judgments concerning the merits of works of art. Going back to the philosophical attitude with which Kant formulates *his* question, we can then raise *our* question: How are valid judgments of this kind possible at all?

The contemporary relevance of Kant lies, however, also in his providing the beginning of an answer to this question in his analysis of the internal constitution of aesthetic judgment and of its universalistic basis. To a reconstruction of his *answer* we will now turn.

The normativity without principles of the judgment of taste

In the *Critique of Judgment* Kant characterizes *pure* aesthetic judgment, or judgment of taste, by opposition to *empirical* aesthetic judgment, or judgment of sense. Both these types of judgment belong in the larger category of *aesthetic*, as opposed to *teleological*, judgments, and in turn teleological and aesthetic judgments are instances of *reflective*, as opposed to *determinant*, judgment. Judgment generally concerns, for Kant, the inclusion of a particular into a universal. In the case of determinant judgment, the universal – be it a law of nature, a principle of reason, such as the categorical imperative, or a principle of logical inference – exists prior to and independent of the particular. In the case of reflective judgment, instead, the universal must be found at the very same time as we attribute the particular to it.[1] Let us return to the distinction of judgments of taste and judgments of sense. They are both reflective and aesthetic but differ in that judgments of taste concern the *beauty* of artistic or natural objects, whereas judgments of sense concern the *agreeableness* or *disagreeableness* of objects.[2]

In Paragraphs 32 and 33 Kant illustrates two peculiarities of the judgment of taste. First, all judgments of taste raise an implicit claim to universal consensus. This is possible because the judgment of taste does not attribute mere agreeableness to the object (e.g. by virtue of its smell or its colors in the case of a flower) -- which could be a matter of arbitrary preference – but, rather, attributes beauty to the object by virtue of its spontaneous adapting to our cognitive faculty. Second, although it raises a universalistic claim, a judgment of taste cannot be *proven* valid:

> The judgment of others, where unfavorable to ours, may, no doubt, rightly make us suspicious in respect of our own, but convince us that it is wrong it never can. Hence there is no empirical *ground of proof* that can coerce anyone's judgment of taste.
> (Kant *Critique of Judgment*: Paragraph 33; 1986: 139–40)

In fact, argues Kant, the judgment of taste "is invariably laid down as a singular judgment upon the Object" (Kant *Critique of Judgment*: Paragraph 33; 1986: 140). The possibility of a judgment which on the one hand concerns the individual's feeling of pleasure and on the other claims that everyone ought to feel pleasure in taking notice of a certain object is just what needs to be explained. That this claim is made a priori and with no reference to concepts compounds the problem. In the subsequent paragraphs Kant discusses the issue at greater length. At one point he suggests that the pleasure which the judgment of taste claims to be linked with the mental representation of an object

> must of necessity depend for every one upon the same conditions, seeing that they are the subjective conditions of the possibility of a cognition in general, and the proportion of these cognitive faculties which is requisite for taste is requisite also for ordinary sound understanding, the presence of which we are entitled to presuppose in everyone.
>
> (Kant *Critique of Judgment*: Paragraph 39; 1986: 150).

Two aspects of this answer come into tension with our postmetaphysical sensibility. On the one hand, Kant's thesis implies a cognitive naturalism which reduces the shared basis of human cognition, on which rests the possibility of intersubjective agreement, to a *natural* endowment of man. On the other hand, Kant asks us to subscribe to the whole of his analysis of the categories of cognition in the *Critique of Pure Reason* in order to understand how pleasure arises from the congruence of perceived objects with our cognitive apparatus in the absence of interest.

Perhaps a different account of the universality of the judgment of taste can be found if we proceed from the assumption that every person develops his or her identity through interaction with others and if we try to understand the fulfillment of an identity in analogy to Kant's notion of an *aesthetic idea*. In Paragraph 49, Kant starts out by characterizing *soulless* works of art as products in which "we find nothing to censure . . . as far as taste goes" but which leave us uninspired and unmoved. Lack of soul means here the lack of a certain "animating principle of the mind [*Geist*]." An aesthetic idea, instead, is capable of setting "the mental powers into a swing that is final, i.e. into a play which is self-maintaining and which strengthens those powers for such activity" (Kant *Critique of Judgment*: Paragraph 49; 1986: 175). Through their capacity for stimulating a never-ending play of all our mental faculties, aesthetic ideas provide a tangible instance of the overwhelming of language by thought and of thought by being. In Kant's words,

> the aesthetic idea is a representation of the imagination, annexed to a given concept, with which, in the free employment of imagination,

such a multiplicity of partial representations are bound up, that no expression indicating a definite concept can be found for it.

(Kant *Critique of Judgment*: Paragraph 49; 1986: 179)

This leads us to the concept of *genius* as the ability needed in order to create aesthetic ideas. For Kant genius is the ability "to find out ideas for a given concept, and, besides, to hit upon the *expression* for them" so that they can be communicated.[3] More specifically, genius is characterized through: (1) the fact that it is a talent for art, not for science, politics or morality; (2) the fact that it presupposes both understanding and "a relation of the imagination to understanding"; (3) the fact that it "displays itself, not so much in the working out of the projected end in the presentation of a definite *concept*, as rather in the portrayal, or expression of *aesthetic ideas* containing a wealth of material for effecting that intention"; and (4) the fact that it presupposes an accord between the imagination and the understanding "such as cannot be brought about by any observance of rules, whether of science or mechanical imitation, but can only be produced by the nature of the individual" (Kant *Critique of Judgment*: Paragraph 49; 1986: 180–1).

The project of reconstructing Kant's theory of judgment in order to account for how actors choose among competing conceptual schemes runs into other difficulties as well. Let me briefly mention three of these difficulties. For example, it has been stressed by Gadamer that while Kant assumes a primacy of taste over genius – the inventiveness of genius must be submitted to the discipline of taste and in case of conflict it is taste that should prevail – in the domain of art, taste is best understood as being "only a *limiting condition* of the beautiful" which does not contain the *principle* of beauty. As Gadamer suggests, it would be more appropriate for Kant to ground his aesthetics on the notion of genius, which "fulfils much better than does the concept of taste the requirement of being changeless in the stream of time."[4]

Second, Kant tries to separate beauty and perfection. Paragraph 15 is devoted to showing that "beauty, as a formal subjective faculty, involves no thought whatsoever of a perfection of the object." According to Kant, the notion of perfection implies the representation of an end for which the object is deemed "perfect" and thus contradicts the purely "formal subjective finality" of beauty. This distinction need not be so crucial as he suggests. On one hand, it is hard to imagine identities as objects that are good for some purpose – perfection here seems entirely synonymous with beauty – and, on the other hand, it is not clear why Kant would need to deny all cognitive content to aesthetic judgments, provided that the cognitive aspect, amenable to determinant judgment, does not prevail.[5]

Third, in Paragraphs 22 and 40 Kant stresses the *social* nature of taste. Every act of reflective judgment requires us "to think from the standpoint of every one else." This has rightly been seen as a more promising approach to validity than the monological perspective of the other two *Critiques*, which remains entangled in the "philosophy of the subject."[6] Two considerations are in order here. Paragraph 40 is the juncture at which *communication* enters the picture of judgment. For it is possible to "think from the standpoint of every one else" only insofar as one is able to actively participate in exchanges with others regarding the subject matter of judgment. Communication, in turn, rests on the peculiar relation of the object of judgment to community and *sensus communis* – another notion that plays an important role in Paragraph 40. But what is the relation of *sensus communis* to "common sense" and thus to a concrete community? *Sensus communis* cannot be understood as synonymous with what happens to be believed in the community to which the actor belongs. The agreement of others that one courts or "woos" in rendering one's judgment is not the agreement of those who belong in a given and limited community, but the general agreement of those who are capable of taking the enlarged standpoint. Hannah Arendt has rightly underscored the role that this normative notion of humanity as a larger object of loyalty – an idea whose consequences for moral theory only now begin to be worked out – has for Kant's understanding of the validity of judgment: "It is by virtue of this idea of mankind, present in every single man, that men are human, and they can be called civilized or humane to the extent that this idea becomes the principle not only of their judgments but of their actions. It is at this point that actor and spectator become united" (Arendt 1982: 75).[7]

It must also be noted that the social dimension of taste is considered by Kant only from the standpoint of the *justification* of the judgment of taste, not from the perspective of its *genesis*. Although it can be refined and cultivated, taste remains for Kant a *natural* faculty of man, not a social competence. Furthermore, in keeping with his view of practical reason primarily as a law-testing faculty, taste is conceived by Kant as a critical, rather than productive, faculty.[8] This leads attentive critics such as Beiner to view Kant's position as relevant only to a third-person account of prudential judgment and in need of a complementary first-person perspective, best represented by Aristotle's notion of *phronesis*. To be fair, Kant does have a first-person, productive moment of judgment, one found not in taste but again in genius. The problem, once again, is that genius is naturalized and examined merely under the derivative aspect of *artistic* genius. On the one hand, Kant's restrictive use of the term genius for artistic performance makes sense only under the assumption that in activities such as science, morality or politics, reflective judgment plays no significant role and can be almost entirely replaced by methodology, rules, principles and the like. On the other hand, there is no awareness in Kant that artistic genius is but a special case of the broader capacity to understand what best suits the inner balance of a symbolic whole.

Once again, as it is the case also with Aristotle's conception of *phronesis*, if we want to appropriate the most valuable aspects of Kant's theory of judgment, we have to translate his position into a perspective which takes the related notions of *identity* and of the fulfillment or authenticity of an identity into account. We can tentatively equate aesthetic ideas with the quality of a cohesive and well-balanced identity, and Kant's notion of a soulless work of art with a fragmented or shallow identity. Aesthetic ideas and balanced identities share a quality of self-congruency and self-containedness. Their components appear to be at the proper place with respect to the symbolic center. The overall harmony resulting from the combination of elements stimulates the imagination and elicits a sense of pleasure, self-enhancement and awe. On the other hand, soulless works and inauthentic identities share a certain appearance of rigidity and unnaturalness, the opposite of grace. Sometimes they exhibit an obvious disproportion between certain elements; at other times while there is no flamboyant disproportion the whole yet remains unmoving and uninspiring, as though the combination of its elements were obvious and uninformative. From the perspective of action, what Kant calls genius is *phronesis*. Just as genius is the ability to create aesthetic, as opposed to soulless, ideas, so *phronesis* is the ability to choose courses of action and assign priority to values in a way that results in an authentic, as opposed to shallow or fragmented, identity. *Phronesis*, like genius for the work of art, requires a special relation to the *imagination*, in order to create a well-balanced and cohesive identity.

Drawing on Freud's implicit view of a healthy and non-neurotic psychic life, we can see the capacity to let our mental representations circulate from one ambit of our inner life to another, so that the insights gained in one area of experience can be readily applied to another, as the key component of both *phronesis* and genius. Conversely, the compartmentalization of mental life into rigidly insulated areas, typical of the neurotic person, is at the basis of uninspiring and soulless identities or works of art. Kant introduces the distinction between taste and genius in order to account for the fact that the ability to recognize beauty in a work of art does not include the capacity to produce one. Similarly, the capacity to recognize which needs are crucial to the equilibrium of an identity cannot be equated with the capacity to pursue self-realization effectively, although it constitutes a condition of it. Thus *phronesis* stands out from mere good judgment, on which it nonetheless rests, in that it incorporates a special form of integrity on the part of the actor, which I have called *authenticity*.[9] Good judgment plus authenticity equals *phronesis*. Furthermore, through their capacity for stimulating a never-ending play of all our mental faculties, aesthetic ideas and innovative actions provide a tangible instance of the universalism *sui generis* inherent in the experience of authenticity. On the nature of this universalism I will offer some comments in the remaining section of this chapter.

Oriented reflective judgment

In order to appropriate the most valuable aspects of Kant's theory of judgment, we have to account for why it is that something exemplary, like the products of genius, can still be valid in the universalistic sense of the term, i.e. exert some kind of influence beyond the context from which it arose. Again, such account can be based on the notions of identity and authenticity.

Let me start by recasting Kant's definition of judgment in the vocabulary of identity and authenticity. Then I will proceed to show that we can draw from the text of the *Third Critique*, in an immanent way, a quite different answer to the question concerning the basis for the universality of judgment than the one explicitly offered by Kant and mentioned above. Judgment in general – understood by Kant as an instance of "thinking the particular as contained under the universal" (Kant *Critique of Judgment*: Introduction; 1986: 18) – is about the appropriateness of some element to an identity, namely about whether something, be it an action, a norm, or whatever, fits or not with the whole of a relevant identity. Authenticity or the integrity of an identity, what is best for its flourishing, is the regulative idea that makes judgment function. In a number of passages concerning the nature of the special pleasure afforded by the aesthetic experience of things beautiful, Kant, by using the term "feeling of life" in a way close to what is here designated by authenticity, implicitly comes to endorse this view.

In Paragraph 1 of the *Critique of Judgment* Kant denies the presence of any cognitive content in aesthetic judgments. Rather, aesthetic judgments involve the awareness that the representation of a certain object is accompanied by a "sensation of delight." Such representation, continues Kant, "is referred wholly to the Subject, and what is more to its *feeling of life* – under the name of the feeling of pleasure or displeasure – and this forms the basis of a quite separate faculty of discriminating and estimating that contributes nothing to knowledge" (Kant 1986: 42, my emphasis).[10] In a subsequent passage (Paragraph 23) Kant further specifies what he means by "delight": "the beautiful is directly attended with a feeling of the *furtherance of life*" (Kant 1986: 91, my emphasis). In this passage lies the possibility of a different, less cognitivistic and more hermeneutic, interpretation of what Kant understood to be the basis for the universal claims raised by aesthetic judgments.

As we will recall, the problem of the universalistic dimension of judgment, as stated in Paragraph 36, contains an explicit reference to the aspect of "pleasure":

> How is a judgment possible which, going merely upon the individual's *own* feeling of pleasure in an object independent of the concept of it, estimates this as a pleasure attached to the representation of the same object *in every individual*, and does so *a priori*, i.e. without being allowed to wait and see if other people will be of the same mind?
> (Kant *Critique of Judgment*: Paragraph 36; 1986: 145)

If we consider the answer offered by Kant in the subsequent two paragraphs, we can notice again that explicit reference is made to the relation of aesthetic judgment to pleasure. First, argues Kant, we are "justified in presupposing that the same subjective conditions of judgment, which we find in ourselves are universally present in every man" (*Critique of Judgment*: Paragraph 38; 1986: 147). Second, given that in aesthetic judgment we assess the ability, on the part of our representation of an object, to engage both the imagination and the understanding "in their freedom in an harmonious employment" and thus to generate pleasure, such pleasure, observes Kant, "must of necessity depend for every one upon the same conditions, seeing that they are the subjective conditions of the possibility of a cognition in general" (*Critique of Judgment*: Paragraph 39; 1986: 150). This is the reason why he who judges with taste "can impute the subjective finality, i.e. his delight in the object, to every one else, and suppose his feeling universally communicable, and that, too, without the mediation of concepts".

Now, if by pleasure we understand the ability, on the part of a representation, to arouse in ourselves the feeling of the *furtherance of our life*, we obtain a less naturalistic and more hermeneutically oriented answer to the question concerning the universality of judgment. The assumption that human beings possess a perceptual apparatus that naturally makes them perceive the same thing given the same stimulus – an assumption which enters into tension with our idea of the formative role of language and culture – loses relevance and becomes indeed superfluous. But how can I anticipate that the experience of an object that I judge as beautiful will not just translate into the "furtherance of my life," namely in the advancement of my own unique life-project, as the flourishing of my identity or the enhancement of my authenticity, but will translate into an equal feeling of the furtherance of *anyone's* life?

We can make better sense of how this is possible if we introduce at this point a distinction between *pure* reflective judgments and *oriented* reflective judgments – a distinction which constitutes one of Makkreel's contributions to the interpretation of Kant's theory of judgment.[11] As Makkreel points out, Kant presents his own notion of "orientation" in the 1786 essay "What is Orientation in Thinking?" and cursorily or implicitly refers to this notion in the *Critique of Pure Reason* and in the *Critique of Judgment*. In its most elementary sense, "orientation" refers to the ability, on the part of the actor, "to proceed from one quadrant of her field of vision to the other three which make up her horizon" (Makkreel 1990: 155). My ability to bring what I see in front of me into a relation with the other quadrants originates in the imagination – the ability to instantiate what is not present to the senses – and rests on the immediate bodily feeling bound up with the left and right distinction (see Makkreel 1990: 155). At a more mediated level, Kant mentions the possibility of a "mental orientation of the thinking self to the transcendent realm" (Makkreel 1990: 155–6), and in the *Critique of Judgment* mentions the principle of "finality" as a concept potentially capable of "orienting" reflective judgment. In the latter case, we relate to the manifold phenomena of nature *as if* the laws which regulate them would add up to a unity, not because so is required by a principle of nature or by a principle of freedom, but because this "transcendental principle of a finality of nature . . . represents the unique mode in which we must proceed in our reflection upon the objects of nature" (Kant *Critique of Judgment*: "Introduction";

1986: 23) *if* we want to get a "thoroughly interconnected whole of experience." As Makkreel suggests, we can further distinguish a notion of "aesthetic purposiveness" (namely, "an aesthetic orientation that evaluates the world on the basis of the feeling of life") and a notion of "teleological purposiveness" understood as a "teleological orientation that interprets culture on the basis of common sense or the *sensus communis*" (Makkreel 1990: 156).

It goes to Makkreel's credit to have cast light on the intrinsic connection that binds together the notion of the *enhancement* or *furtherance of life* or *authenticity*, the notion of "orientation" and the universality *sui generis* of reflective judgment. Writes Makkreel:

> The mental feeling of the enhancement of life in aesthetic pleasure and that of its diminution in displeasure involve immediate discriminations analogous to the direct bodily feeling of the distinction between left and right that orients us in space. Aesthetic discrimination relates to reflective judgments about the world as the spatial feeling of right and left relates to determinant judgments about nature. Both are subjective, but constant, feelings that provide the necessary orientation as the imagination moves from what is directly given to what is only indirectly given.
>
> (Makkreel 1990: 156)

Our question concerning the nature of the universalism of judgment can then receive a non-cognitivist and non-naturalist answer, which still remains quite in line with Kant's own view of judgment. The universalism of judgment, on this interpretation, rests neither on the biological set-up of the sense apparatus nor on the contingent sharedness of certain cultural forms. It rests on a commonality of orienting factors which cannot be reduced to the biological and yet is not merely cultural, namely on the fact that – independently of the culture we inhabit, and just by virtue of simply existing, in the way human beings exist, with a body, a mind, a consciousness of the self and of its finiteness – we all have an intuitive sense of what it means to enhance and further, or to constrain and stifle, our life. In a different vocabulary, we all have a sense of what it means for our identities to flourish or to stagnate. Cultures articulate this basic feeling of well-being or flourishing and stagnation in different vocabularies, to be sure, and there exist local variations that emphasize one aspect over another.

If we elaborate further on this point, we could say that for us the feeling of the "furtherance of life" must be understood in terms of *self-realization* or the attainment of an *authentic* relation to the self. The expression "authentic relation to the self," in turn, designates an optimal congruency of an identity with itself. In Chapter 5 I will probe further, by drawing on psychoanalytic theory, into the dimensions that are constitutive of such notions of a fulfilled or realized identity and which can thus play the same "orienting" role for our reflective judgment that Kant attributed to the notion of finality.

Certainly, the psychoanalytic vocabulary is but one among many possible vocabularies with which we may try to reconstruct our intuitions concerning what it means for a human identity to flourish or attain authenticity. However, insofar as we have reasons to believe that at least some of these intuitions may be common to other cultures we have also a way of making sense of how a judgment which invokes no principles or concepts and tells us about the potential, inherent in something, for enhancing or furthering our life, can claim universality after all.

From this vantage point, in fact, judgment and the exemplary action inspired by it are capable of exerting an influence on us who are not within its context of origin, by virtue of their ability to realize, within the horizon of an action or of a life-course, an optimal congruity between the deed and a certain inspiring motive underlying it — a congruity which in turn resonates with us by tapping the same intuitions concerning authenticity that the work of art is capable of tapping. Exemplary actions and exemplary acts of judgment guide us not as schemata, principles or rules do, but as well-formed works of art do, namely as outstanding instances of congruency capable of educating our discernment by way of exposing us to selective instances of the feeling of the furtherance of our life.

4

REFLECTIVE AUTHENTICITY
AND EXEMPLARY
UNIVERSALISM

In the preceding two chapters I have reconstructed and discussed the potential, inherent in Aristotle's notion of *phronesis* and in Kant's notion of *reflective judgment*, for providing us with a concept of validity compatible with our intuitions about the plurality of language games and the impossibility of a non-linguistic access to uninterpreted reality. Neither of the two notions is immediately applicable to our context, but both contain important elements that can be included in the authenticity approach to validity. The crucial challenge, in both cases, has taken the form of the need to insert, at the relevant structural locus, a thoroughly new understanding of the basis on which the universalist valence of prudential and reflective judgment rests. Neither the Aristotelian idea of a set of ultimate ends for all human beings – whatever its substantive specification might be – nor the Kantian notion of a universality of perceptual responses will do. Before taking up this challenge in Chapters 5, 6 and 7, however, I need to go back to the general outline of my view and to further unpack the authenticity view of validity. In this chapter I will further specify the notion of authenticity that underlies it, by contrasting it with other concepts of authenticity, and will reconstruct Simmel's attempt to work out a view of normativity based on authenticity and judgment, an attempt that this time originates within the sociological tradition.

Authenticity as a normative category

Why talk about authenticity today? It is a question to be posed in the most serious way, a question urged on us, among other things, by the following "philosophical facts." First, the polemical force of the term "authenticity" seems to be somehow exhausted. On the one hand, the connotations which opposed it to a certain view of moral *autonomy* and of *autonomous* agency provide a contrast with these notions which is less and less sharp. Today, who defends *autonomy* in the strict Kantian sense of self-legislation *guided by universal principles*? When they – implicitly or explicitly – speak of autonomy, moral and political philosophers such as Habermas, Rawls, Dworkin, Ackerman, Nagel or Scanlon speak of a process of self-determination guided by a *situated* understanding of the *good* – a self-determination kept in check by principles that the actor believes, and "you and I" believe, that no one could reasonably reject.[1] On the other hand, many of the notions of autonomy being proposed today, for example Axel Honneth's notion of "decentered autonomy," do include so many references to authenticity-related dimensions – such as a careful attending to the uniqueness of one's identity and of the internal needs ensuing therefrom, and empathy or receptivity to others[2] – that the gap with the concept of authenticity becomes only a terminological one.

Second, the use of the notion of authenticity is not free of philosophical costs. For example, in order to reconcile it with that *intersubjective* understanding of subjectivity which has now become almost commonplace, one has to extricate the notion of authenticity from the existentialist framework within which it has become enmeshed in our century, and in particular from the Heideggerian heritage.[3] Thus the very use of the term "authenticity" without quotation marks or other markers of distance might seem problematic. The existentialist tradition, from Jaspers to Sartre, has imbued the term "authenticity" with essentialist, individualist and "humanist" connotations; as a consequence, if used without quotation marks the term might at first sight convey the impression that the relation of validity to subjectivity is, once again, articulated along the lines of the philosophy of the subject, namely as the neo-Romantic view according to which "all that is inside" is *tout court* the cornerstone on which all forms of normativity are based. The same function which in the early modern philosophy of the subject was assigned to the subject's capacity to *reflect* on its own action would now be exerted, in an equally solipsistic way – according to this existentialist interpretation of the *authenticity-thesis* – by the subject's capacity for *introspective reflection*. If this were the case, both the culture of authenticity and the *authenticity-thesis* would be more than continuous with the early modern culture of autonomy. In fact, earlier under the heading of *possessive* individualism, now under the heading of *expressive* individualism, the same idea would underlie both the culture of autonomy and that of authenticity – namely, the idea that the social order can be evaluated from the standpoint of an isolated individual who assesses the benefits it affords and the costs it exacts.

Another problematic aspect of the concept of authenticity is that it seems to convey the suggestion, read into it by many of its critics, that the self possesses an essential core. This fundamental core is thought to determine what is good or befitting for the self in matters of social interaction, without being itself determined by social interaction. The essential core of the self would function as the source of all normativity while itself being just a brute fact. The *authenticity-thesis*, however, as it will become clear from the rest of this book, could not be further removed from such a conception. It has nothing to do with what Adorno called the "jargon" of authenticity – it is not a jargon of authenticity with a neo-Romantic gloss instead of an archaizing one.[4]

Finally, it is not immediately clear what authenticity has to offer in the realm of political philosophy and political theory that contemporary competitors like "difference" cannot offer.[5] In this case, the claim is that the category of authenticity, broadly understood as the congruity of the self or of a collective identity with itself – a congruity not reducible to consistency – carries a superior potential for helping us to bring together different aspects of the "practical realm" (including our understanding of justice), and to throw light on the interconnections between them. Authenticity can help us to account even better than autonomy and difference for what it is that cultural rights, multiculturalism and the right to privacy are meant to protect,[6] for what we understand today by "human dignity," for the *integrity* that Hercules presupposes and exercises in adjudicating constitutional hard cases,[7] and for the meaning of Rawls' statement to the effect that what justifies justice as fairness ultimately:

> is not its being true to an order antecedent to and given to us, but its congruence with our deeper understanding of ourselves and our aspirations, and our realization that, given our history and the traditions embedded in our public life, it is the most reasonable doctrine for us.
>
> (Rawls 1980: 519)

In the case of Habermas, as mentioned above,[8] things are more complex and I cannot discuss in greater detail here the place of the notion of authenticity within his discursive theory of justice and deliberative politics.[9] Sometimes political versions of the notion of authenticity resurge in the form of a neo-Romantic emphasis on commonality of tradition, culture, language, history – briefly, as a "politics of identity." More interesting, however, is the emergence of a discourse of authenticity along *radical* lines, in the tradition that George Kateb has called "democratic individualism."[10] The idea of authenticity, finally, is evidently at work in the notion of social criticism developed by Walzer in *Interpretation and Social Criticism* and in his more recent *Thick and Thin*.[11] The ability of social critics to convince the unconvinced, often in the presence of vigorous apologetic defenders of the *status quo* who try to undermine or minimize the impact of what the critic has to say, and in the absence of general "thin" principles accepted by both parties and capable of deciding the issue, can best be explained by the fact that good criticism embeds a greater potential for an *authentic* self-relation of the collective identity than its apologetic counterparts. We, whoever the "we" are, become more "ourselves" as an effect of accepting what correct criticism suggests.

In order for the concept of authenticity to fully reveal its special fruitfulness for helping us to make sense of the general direction toward which our intuitions about validity have changed in this century, however, we have to move some steps further from the elementary notion of "being oneself," "realizing oneself" or establishing a certain congruency between conduct and identity. In other words, we must make our notion of authenticity more specific. To this task I will now turn, and then, in the last section, I will try to highlight the relation of "reflective authenticity" to a certain kind of exemplary universalism.

Models of authentic subjectivity

The *authenticity-thesis* does not commit us to one specific version of the concept of authenticity. Much as the notion of autonomy presupposed by Locke differed from those of Kant, Descartes or Hegel, so today we have several distinct concepts of authentic subjectivity. Let me begin with what is shared in common by all conceptions of authenticity. All *normative* conceptions of authenticity share the assumption that a life in which the deepest and most significant motifs that resonate within us find expression is somehow not just a fortunate contingency which happens to grace the lives of some "happy few," but is rather a kind of "ought" which binds all of us. Furthermore, all conceptions of authenticity share an aversion to the reason-centered view of subjectivity typical of the Western tradition and especially to the hierarchical structuring of human subjectivity into a higher rational component and a lower one, constituted by the realm of affects, emotions, feelings and the passions. Their point of convergence is in the emphasis on the affective dimension of rationality and the rational dimension of affect. The conceptions of authentic subjectivity that we can reconstruct from an interpretation of modern philosophy, however, differ in many other respects. I suggest that at least four distinctions should be considered if we want to make our notion of authenticity more specific.

The first distinction to be considered contrasts *substantialist* with *intersubjective* conceptions of authenticity, depending on their resting respectively on a *substantialist* or an *intersubjective* view of the self. This divide separates the existentialist understanding of authenticity of Jaspers and Sartre from the one that I am suggesting here. This distinction, however, should not be confused with the opposition between a "centered" and a "decentered" conception of authentic subjectivity. In fact, we can have views of authenticity which are centered and yet intersubjective, such as the one put forward by Charles Taylor,[12] or we can have views of authentic subjectivity that are decentered and yet non-intersubjective, like the one implicit in Nietzsche's writings. Substantialist perspectives, such as the existentialist version of authenticity espoused by Sartre or Jaspers, embed the assumption that every human self possesses an essential core, a kind of psychological DNA, which it tries to assert *through* its interaction with others: in the most sophisticated philosophical versions such core is conceived as an essential tension toward self-transcendence. The intersubjective moment of relating to the other, instead, plays a role for Sartre only in a formal sense, namely for the acquisition of the certainty of being a subject like any other, but for the rest is conceived mainly as a negative limit on the possibilities inherent in the self.[13] All social institutions and roles, then, appear as mere sources of reification – for no social role exists which does not to some extent enjoin us to adapt, to become slightly "other" than we are, to channel our uniqueness along lines that are more common than unique.

The conception of authenticity defended here, instead, is fully, and not just formally, intersubjective. First, because the category of *identity*, central to it, must itself be understood along intersubjective lines. Second, because the equally central category of *self-realization* presupposes the notion of *recognition*, which in turn holds centerstage within certain views of the intersubjectivity paradigm. And third, because the model of universalism presupposed by the perspective of *authenticity* rests on the notion of *reflective judgment*, and reflective judgment, as Kant has shown, is inherently intersubjective.

These three aspects of an intersubjective view of authenticity have been discussed in Chapter 1 and here we need only recall them briefly. The idea of an "authentic identity" to which we moderns of the late twentieth century subscribe presupposes, among other things, Mead's idea that to possess an identity means to be able to see oneself through the eyes of another – a presupposition, however, which does not exhaust the meaning of the expression "authentic identity." All identities, in fact, authentic and inauthentic, are equally rooted in interaction. What distinguishes the authentic ones is something else, namely, the capacity to express a *uniqueness* which has been socially constituted through the interplay of the singularity of the formative contexts and the singularity of our responses to them.

The second sense in which my view of *authenticity* presupposes an intersubjective perspective is through its paradoxical relation to *recognition*. On one hand recognition is presupposed by authenticity, on the other it cannot be constitutive of it. As anticipated in Chapter 1, I can certainly imagine that my life-project might be meaningless for certain people, but I cannot consistently think of the project underlying my identity as a sensible one and yet as one doomed to rejection, as opposed to recognition, by every other human being. For we cannot consider an identity which no one can ever recognize as a felicitous human identity. On the other hand, to select a life-project for the purpose, among other things, of having one's identity recognized by others does not mean to strive toward authenticity – it means to follow a model.

Finally, as we have seen, the perspective of authenticity takes reflective judgment as a model for the kind of judgments in terms of which we evaluate the degree of appropriateness of a course of action, or of a life-project, to an identity, and this kind of judgment is inherently intersubjective, in that it "takes account (*a priori*) of the mode of representation of every one else."[14] While in science and morality, according to Kant, we can formulate valid judgments by relying on bases – one's own sense data ordered through the transcendental categories or the categorical imperative – located entirely within the subject, in the case of reflective judgment the *inter*subjective dimension is part and parcel of our judgment from the outset. It is impossible for us to assess the congruency of a symbolic whole, be it a work of art, a text or an identity, if we do not possess the ability to look at the object of our judgment not only through our own eyes but also through the eyes of others, "by putting ourselves in the position of every one else."[15]

While these three aspects – the nature of identity, its need for recognition and the nature of the judgment of taste – define the intersubjective quality of the view of authenticity that I am defending, they do not exhaust all the relevant aspects of authenticity. Further dimensions are relevant for adequately specifying our notion of authenticity.

Consider, as a second distinction, the opposition between *antagonistic* and *integrative* conceptions of authentic subjectivity. Some view authenticity as primarily linked with breaking free from the constrictions of an entrenched social order, whereas other notions of authenticity carry no such implication. For example, some authors affiliated to aesthetic modernism (Baudelaire) or to *Lebensphilosophie* (notably Nietzsche) tend to understand authenticity as something to be attained "*in opposition* to the demands of society" and of culture, whereas in the writings of authors such as Rousseau, Schiller, Herder, Kierkegaard and others we find a recognition (with very different degrees of awareness and explicitness) of the fact that social expectations, roles and institutions cannot be understood as playing a merely constraining, "disciplinary" or repressive role but also somehow constitute the symbolic material out of which authentic selves and authentic conduct can be generated. In the opposition between these two ways of understanding authenticity we find a contemporary echo of the modern opposition of the *sublime* and the *beautiful* as leading aesthetic ideals. Both the sublime and antagonistic authenticity by definition stand against the established order and the powers that be. On the other hand, beauty and integrative authenticity, from the vantage point of the sublime and of antagonistic authenticity, appear as the enervated and non-oppositional equivalent of a fully-fledged expression of the self. Furthermore, the responses elicited by these conceptual pairs could not be more different: while beauty and integrative authenticity, as Edmund Burke points out in his *Enquiry into the Origin of our Ideas of the Sublime and the Beautiful*, elicit love and reconciliation, antagonistic authenticity and the sublime inspire a kind of awe and *terror*.[16]

In the psychological realm also we find representatives of these two versions of authenticity. We need only recall R.D. Laing's understanding of schizophrenia as a response to the imposition of an inauthentic life and of "madness" as resistance to the irregimentation of mental life, or Lacan's formula "*Là où je suis je ne suis pas, et là où je ne suis pas, là je suis.*" On the other hand Kohut's psychology of the self and Winnicott's notions of "creative living" and of the "true self" are the most obvious representatives of an integrative version of authenticity within the psychoanalytic tradition.

Finally, the integrative and antagonistic versions of the concept of authenticity presuppose different attitudes *vis-à-vis* the modern differentiation of the value spheres. All the authors who understand authenticity along "antagonistic" lines understand the paradigmatically authentic act of breaking free of established normativity as the only kind of conduct endowed with *real*, as opposed to distorted or derivative, meaning. From Schlegel to Novalis, from Baudelaire to Artaud and Breton, from Nietzsche to Foucault, action inspired by value-spheres other than the aesthetic – for example, action motivated by the quest for truth or by the moral point of view – is devalued to the mere semblance of action: it is merely covert manipulation or a self-deluding manifestation of self-assertion or, in Nietzsche's vocabulary, a distorted reflection of the will to power. By contrast, the authors who understand authenticity along "integrative" lines understand authentic action as action which brings into play *all* the three complexes of modern rationality and thus, in a sense, *without dedifferentiating them*, brings to fruition all the interconnections between the modern value spheres.

A third distinction, anticipated before, contrasts a <u>centered</u> and a *centerless* or <u>decentered</u> view of authentic subjectivity. Far from considering as exemplarily authentic a life-course which can be summed up as a coherent narrative, some consider *narratability* as the epitome of inauthenticity. For every narrative assumes that there is order in the material to be narrated. In his reflections on the notion of "limit-experience," for example, Foucault, continuing a tradition which he associates with the names of Nietzsche and Bataille, equates the paradigmatic kind of fulfilled subjectivity with the one undergoing a "limit-experience" – namely, the kind of experience capable of " 'tearing' the subject from itself in such a way that it is no longer the subject as such" or of making it "completely other than itself so that it may arrive at its annihilation, its dissociation."[17] From a variety of *lebensphilosophisch*, aesthetic modernist, post-structuralist, therapeutic and postmodernist vocabularies, theorists of *decentered* authenticity oppose all attempts to restore an internal hierarchy between what is central and what is peripheral to a life-project, a personality, an identity. By contrast, all authors who propound a *centered* notion of authenticity do wish (1) to maintain some kind of orderly stratification of the layers of an identity, (2) to continue to speak of a core and a periphery, and (3) to make sense of the plurality of experiences, detours, and side-narratives to a life-history as variations on a unique theme. Authentic subjectivity, understood along these lines, neither renounces unity and coherence in favor of an unstructurable self-experience nor seeks a coercive coherence stemming from principles external to the self.[18] Rather, it aims at reconciling all the constitutive moments of the self under the aegis of a unique life-project, which retains the status of a normative construct in the light of which the quality of the life-course can be assessed. The archetype of this way of understanding authenticity is constituted by Schiller's view of the *beautiful soul* as a human identity capable of reconciling *grace* and *dignity* and thus of obeying reason with joy[19] – namely, as a kind of human subjectivity capable of integrating cognitive rationality, moral reason and feelings without sacrificing any of them.

If we bring together the last two distinctions (between *antagonistic* and *integrative*, *centered* and *decentered* authenticity), we obtain an interesting typology of concepts of authentic subjectivity. If on one of the axes, drawing on Weber, we put the two basic attitudes of "world affirmation" and "world negation" and on the other axis, drawing on Nietzsche, we distinguish "Apollonian" and "Dionysian" conceptions of subjectivity, we can observe new partitions and overlappings in our conceptual map. For example, the model of authentic subjectivity underlying Herder's view that "Each human being has his own measure," Schiller's "beautiful soul" or Winnicott's notion of "creative living" shares with the anti-hierarchical, decentered and quasi-Dionysian model of subjectivity typical of Rameau's nephew, of the "man without qualities," or of Rorty's "ironic liberal," a non-antagonistic, affirmative attitude toward the social world. In contrast, the Marxian notion of subjectivity no longer alienated shares with late-nineteenth century avant-garde not simply an aversion to the bourgeois order, but also the idea that the affirmation of the self necessarily entails a challenge against the powers that be.

On the other axis, instead, we can notice that Romantic nationalism, Sartre's view of authentic subjectivity and Kierkegaard's notion of the individual who has "chosen himself," for all their diversity, share the idea that self-realization presupposes individuation, and individuation in turn presupposes the internal structuration of subjectivity in terms of a center and a periphery. Or we can notice how, despite their different ways of relating to the world of established normativity, Rameau's nephew and Barthes's "écrivain," Baudelaire's poet as "albatross," Deleuze and Guattari's "machine désirante," Zarathustra and the characters of *Endgame*, all share a certain view of subjecthood as illusory – a view which, however, seems to presuppose some privileged standpoint, from which the judgment as to the illusory quality of unitary and centered subjectivity is formulated.

However, a fourth distinction, relevant to current debates in feminism and political theory, is more interesting than any of the preceding ones. Today political versions of the notion of authenticity resurge once again along nationalistic lines, as an expressivist and neo-Romantic emphasis on commonality of tradition, culture, language, history. We also witness the emergence of a public discourse of authenticity along *radical* lines, as a *politics of difference* or *identity-politics*, endowed with an appeal and mobilizing potential which contributes to the increasing fortune that the related terms *difference* and *identity* enjoy in the public culture of the advanced industrial societies. Now, the relation of authenticity to *difference* can be characterized in two ways.

First, the notion of difference cuts across our previous distinction between integrative and antagonistic authenticity. On the one hand, in fact, those social movements which understand themselves in terms of "difference" also tend to think of their communal action as contributing to the construction of an authentic communal identity – their own – as well as contributing to secure expressive space for that identity within the public arena. In this sense the politics of difference remains within the perspective of the integrative version of authenticity. On the other hand, however, there exists an elective affinity between certain versions of *authenticity as difference* and the antagonistic understanding of authenticity. In contemporary feminism, for example, we often find a critique of centered (male) subjectivity coupled with an emphasis on authenticity understood as pure difference and resistance. To affirm difference then means basically to undermine an established symbolic order rather than to try to inscribe one's own modality of self-expression within that symbolic order.[20]

Second, the distinction between authenticity and difference can be elucidated with reference to two conceptions of what it means for individuals "to realize their uniqueness." According to the first view – let me call it the authenticity of "*immediate* uniqueness" – the uniqueness worth realizing, or deserving recognition, is the sum total of the features that set us apart from the rest of our fellow human beings, or that set one people apart from all the other peoples of the earth. Of course these features will possess various degrees of significance, ranging from the relatively insignificant uniqueness of our fingerprints (which becomes relevant only if one is involved in a criminal trial) to the utmost relevance of the uniqueness of our formative experiences in childhood, but the existence of a broad range of variation is secondary with respect to another feature of this view of authenticity. Important is the fact that "uniqueness" is here the result of a metaphorical subtraction – uniqueness equals the sum total of our being minus what is shared in common with others. This is the view of authenticity with which "difference" and Heidegger's "Eigentlichkeit" are truly synonymous.

According to the second version – the authenticity of "*reflective* uniqueness" – worth realizing or deserving recognition is not the *factual* uniqueness of certain traits, from fingerprints to formative experiences, but the unique way in which an individual brings together his or her "difference" with what is shared, the "thick" with the "thin," the universal with the particular aspects of an identity. This view of *reflective authenticity*, anticipated by Rousseau's moral thought as it can be reconstructed from *Emile* and from *La nouvelle Heloise*,[21] brings together normativity and singularity without sacrificing one to the other in a way that its competitors – "difference" and "Eigentlichkeit" – cannot easily match.[22] In our century such reflective understanding of authenticity has been articulated by Georg Simmel in a way which best illustrates the relation of authenticity as a normative category to a new kind of non-generalizing universalism. In the following section such view of authenticity in its relation to judgment will be reconstructed. Before doing so, however, we have to consider one alternative view of the authenticity of immediate uniqueness – namely, Stendhal's view of "le naturel" as reconstructed by Charles Larmore.[23]

Stendhal's conception of authenticity is an extreme version of the authenticity of immediate uniqueness, which goes so far as to emphasize *immediacy* over uniqueness. The opposite of authenticity is *la vanité*, defined as conforming to the expectations of others and ultimately "being like someone else" (Larmore 1996: 86). From this perspective authenticity becomes radically opposed to reflection or "l'esprit de l'analyse": "Authentic passion is a kind of *folie*, driven not by the more or less clever calculation of interest but by the imagination" (Larmore 1996: 87–88). The best example of the contrast between reflection and authenticity is Julien Sorel, the hero of *Le rouge et le noir*, who kills his lover Mme. de Rênal in an act of blind destructive passion that sets him free of a life of calculating reflection. To be sure, many problematic implications haunt this conception: to mention just the most obvious one, authentic action is set in opposition not just to "inauthentic" action, but to *social action* as such, which by definition presupposes that we take the expectations of others into account. Yet Larmore's attention is drawn to three elements that apparently possess so much relevance as to make him willing to grapple with the attending difficulties of Stendhal's conception of authenticity. First, the notion of authenticity becomes severed from the value of *originality* and is consequently "de-aestheticized": "Being truly ourselves is a matter not of being different from others but of ceasing to guide ourselves by others" (Larmore 1996: 91). Second, authenticity becomes independent of any essentialist notion of a preexisting real self to which to be true. Third, the unreflective view of authenticity is not vulnerable to the objection, developed by Valéry and later by Sartre, that the conscious project of being authentic is self-defeating in that it is contradictory. If one consciously pursues the project of being oneself, argues Sartre, one is doomed to fail, in that "as soon as we posit ourselves as a certain being, by a legitimate judgment, based on inner experience or correctly deduced from *a priori* or empirical premises, then by that very positing we surpass this being – and that not toward another being, but toward emptiness, toward *nothing*" (Sartre 1966: 106). In the end one of the most precious aspects of the legacy of Romanticism, according to Larmore, consists of this notion of *unreflective* authenticity, which "disabuses us of the idea that life is necessarily better the more we think about it" (Larmore 1996: 95). Fortunately, none of the reasons that militate in favor of adopting a concept of authenticity that exacts such costs as setting authentic action in opposition to social action apply to the notion of reflective authenticity developed here. First, while a parallel is established between the normative significance of the congruency of an individual identity and the congruency of a well-formed work of art, at no point is it suggested that uniqueness has to be conceived in terms of "originality" or "innovativeness" as these notions are commonly understood in aesthetics. Furthermore, the intersubjective quality of the notion of authenticity defended here has no difficulty being reconciled with the idea that there is no essential self to be true to. Finally, the contradictoriness rightly attributed by Sartre to the notion of consciously pursuing the project of becoming who one is applies only to an extremely cognitivistic understanding of that project, namely if one understands "being authentic" as knowing consciously all that lies "inside" – a view that in such crude form existed only in the early stages of Freud's thinking. If we change the leading metaphor from "transparency" to "governance" the objection falls away. If living authentically is understood as bringing conduct into line with a chosen guiding framework that embeds a certain constellation of values, much as the multifarious activities of government and the ordinary legislators have to be brought into line with a constitution that embeds a constellation of *political* values, the objection that we cannot at the same time be identical with the sum total of our psychic contents and aware of this coincidence loses all relevance.

Reflective authenticity does not presuppose a total transparency of the self or the conscious grasping of all the contents of the mind, a state – as even Freud came to acknowledge – that if possible at all, would not be desirable. To this extent, it remains as unaffected by Sartre's objection as Stendhal's view, without generating such counterintuitive implications.

Exemplary universalism: Simmel's lesson

For a long time the social sciences have been, and in a sense continue to be, conquest lands in which major philosophical paradigms perpetuate by proxy their centuries-old confrontation. Social theory, in particular, has always been internally divided along lines underneath which we can still see the profiles of the two main philosophical conceptions of the individual: the atomistic paradigm inaugurated by Hobbes and Locke and the "man-as-a-social-being" paradigm which finds its most illustrious defenders in Aristotle and Hegel. According to the former (and for us more familiar) paradigm, human beings come to this world endowed with two attributes that are essential to them: they are self-interested and at the same time rational. Human beings are self-interested in the sense that all of their motivations, even the most complex, can ultimately be derived from two basic ones: to seek pleasure and to avoid suffering. While these two basic motives guide all humans in their relation to other humans, the human being, however, is also rational, in the sense that he or she always tries to achieve his or her goals with the minimum possible expenditure of effort. Thus human beings are also ready to consider whether it wouldn't ultimately be more expedient, after all, to accept the limits set by a social order on their own selfishness, if the benefits to be gained by participating in it were reasonably to outweigh the costs. The normative force of the social order and its ability to reproduce itself over generations is thus explained by authors so diverse as Hobbes, Locke, Smith, Spencer and Freud by pointing to the fact that the benefits provided by it outweigh the costs generated by the constraints emanating from it. The Aristotelian and Hegelian paradigm, instead, takes a radically different assumption as its point of departure. Human beings are intrinsically social beings. So natural to humans is society that the idea of a being that is fully human and yet stands, even hypothetically, outside society in order to weigh the pros and cons of joining the division of labor is regarded as contradictory. Rationality and self-interestedness, according to this alternative paradigm, are certainly part and parcel of human motivations, but they are to be understood as motives and abilities produced by society. Under several banners and rallying cries – methodological individualism, holism, symbolic interactionism etc. – these two paradigms have waged an intellectual warfare whose sociological heroes have been Smith, Spencer, Pareto, Homans and Boudon in one camp, Rousseau, Comte, Durkheim and Parsons on the other side, with such a key figure as Weber being torn between the two sides.

In our century sociology's role as a conquest land has acquired a new facet, linked with the debate on modernity and postmodernity. Also in this context the most original and innovative arguments – for example, those concerning the end of "Grand Narratives" and the Linguistic Turn – have been formulated within the philosophical discussion, and whatever arguments have been developed within social theory have not influenced the philosophical picture in any appreciable way.

More recently, however, a new revisitation of the classics of sociological theory has begun, spurred partly by the British debate on postmodernism. Authors such as Anthony Giddens, Scott Lash, Mike Featherstone, Roland Robertson and others have been reading again some of the canonical authors of the sociological tradition – Simmel and Weber, mainly, though Durkheim's work certainly deserves the same degree of attention – with a new sensibility. The names of Weber and Foucault have been brought into an intellectual relation concerning the theme of eroticism and modernity. An interest in the relation of Weber to Nietzsche and Simmel to Nietzsche has come to replace the older relevance accorded to Weber's position in the debate on neo-Kantianism.

This changing sensibility in the interpretation of the classics of sociological theory carries the promise of rebalancing the net tradeoff of influence between social theory and philosophy. In Simmel, in Weber and in Durkheim, in fact, we find important traces and anticipations, located at different junctures of their work, of a possible model of exemplary universalism based on reflective judgment that can be counted as a quite original contribution, on the part of the sociological tradition, to a solution for the present difficulties of philosophy in articulating a sensible notion of transcontextual validity consistent with the fact of pluralism and the Linguistic Turn. Such new sensibility provides the backdrop for my analysis of Simmel's critique of Kant's *moral* universalism presented in this section, but similar considerations on the relation of validity to authenticity and judgment could be drawn from a discussion of Weber's notion of the ethic of responsibility or from Durkheim's conception of divinity and of the sacred.

Simmel's 1913 essay "Das individuelle Gesetz" ("The Individual Law") provides an original view of the relation of universalism to singular exemplariness which remains thus far one of the most interesting proposals for justifying an understanding of *normativity* compatible with "the fact of pluralism" and for grasping the *moral*, and not merely ethical, relevance of authenticity. Some passages of the essay reflect themes already anticipated in "The metropolis and mental life" (Simmel 1967). Among them, let me recall the concept of "Wechselwirkung," a kind of reciprocal influence of all social phenomena, actions and institutions with one another that Simmel sets in opposition to the positivist notion of a strictly causal relation among variables and posits as the key concept for a correct understanding of the social. The task of the sociologists, according to Simmel, is neither to *explain* social phenomena as though they were things, nor to understand the meaning of social action, but rather to *identify correspondences* between different aspects and moments of the same social context – for example, between the size of a group and its effect on the individuality of its members, or between the metropolitan dimension of modern life and its cultural and psychological consequences for the individual. Another theme, somehow related to the idea of "Wechselwirkung," is the notion of "Vergesellschaftung," understood by Simmel as a process of sociation in the sense of social structuration – where "sociation" means the coalescing and sedimentation of processes of interaction within which a multiplicity of individuals enter relations of reciprocal influence. Simmel calls our attention to the processes whereby from the fluidity of interaction sediments of structure emerge. There is certainly a non-accidental *Wahlverwandtschaft* between Simmel's perspective in both his essays and the attention with which Freud, in the same years, called our attention to the sedimentation of psychic structure out of the fluidity of drives and their vicissitudes.

In his 1913 essay, Simmel approaches these themes from a somewhat narrower perspective: he focuses on the relation of the universality of the moral law to the individuality of the individual, but his point holds just as well for the kind of collective individuality that we assign to communal identities, cultures, subcultures, communities and the like.

Simmel's polemical target is Kant's *Critique of Practical Reason*. Simmel objects – and the contemporary relevance of his argument could not be greater, if we think of the debate about the liberal theories of justice which are the natural heirs to Kant – to a certain way of connecting (1) the distinction between "particularity" and "universality" with (2) the distinction between what is "real" and what is "ideal" or, in a language closer to us, "facts" and "norms." Not everything that is individual is merely factual and as such *particular*, argues Simmel, and not everything that is normative has necessarily to be *general*. Ironically, argues Simmel, it is the universality of Kant's moral law that fails to be adequately accounted for by the model of generalizing universalism underlying the *Critique of Practical Reason*: "In fact, paradoxical though it may sound, also the universality [of the categorical imperative] is something particular insofar as it stands over against individuality" (Simmel 1987: 179).

In other words, if and to the extent that the moral law enjoins me to become another and thereby sets itself over against my own uniqueness, it fails to be truly *universal*. Because it certainly fails to include *me*, it appears to be just another "particular" of a size larger than my own subjectivity. Thus by setting up an irreducible opposition between the normative universality of the moral law and the factual singularity of the individual, Kant, according to Simmel, ends up missing his object and undermining the very universality of the law.[24]

An alternative path, still consistent with the determinant-judgment model of universality underlying the *Second Critique*, could be followed. This path would include two steps. First we could try, continues Simmel, to reconcile the universality of the law and the particularity of action by "tracing for each action a universal law that takes into account the whole complex of its partial aspects and the determinations stemming from the life context in which it occurs" (Simmel 1987: 179). Subsequently, as a second step, by bringing together all these contextualized moral laws, we could generate – just as it is the case in physics with the parallelogram of component forces – a *moral resultant* susceptible of accounting for the singular moral duty relevant for a given moral actor. According to Simmel, however, this attempt to rescue the model of universalism underlying Kant's moral philosophy also leads to a dead end.

The reason why it ultimately self-defeats consists in the fact that, as Simmel puts it,

> Each object, even the simplest, contains such an infinity of qualities and relations that no imaginable series of concepts and thus of laws could exhaust it: we should then be content with onesided and partic-ular determinations of the object which leave out innumerable aspects of it.
>
> (Simmel 1987: 179–80)

Furthermore, continues Simmel in one of the most classical restatements of the central point of all *Lebensphilosophie*: "if we want to master reality *through concepts*, we must reduce the continuities and the uninterrupted correlations within and between things to separate multiplicities, we must render discontin-uous that which is continuous and stop the infinite flow of relations" (Simmel 1987: 180, my emphasis). In other words, we must petrify life if we want to make a moral theory based on the model of determinant judgment work. Here we touch on another limitation of Kant's moral philosophy.

Kant considers the moral value of isolated actions – actions that are consid-ered apart from the complex and the texture of the life-conduct and the identity of the actor. Kant, in the *Critique of Practical Reason*,

> separates the action – lie or truth-telling, goodhearted acts from cruel acts – from the actor, treats it as a logical and free-floating material for moral considerations, and then raises the question concerning its permissibility. Its permissibility is then determined on the basis of the intrinsic meaning of the action per se and not on the basis of its meaning for the actor who performs it.
>
> (Simmel 1987: 182)

In this context the *lebensphilosophische* perspective that Simmel shares with Bergson and Nietzsche emerges with greater clarity than in his essay on the metropolis. In a passage that echoes the Bergsonian theme of *durée* without echoing the Bergsonian emphasis on *conscience*, Simmel writes:

intrinsically life does not consist in the summation of a lie, then of a
courageous decision, then of a debauched extravagance, then of a good
work, but in a continuous flow, within which each moment represents
the totality that unceasingly forms and transforms itself. Within life as
a totality no part is separated from any other by sharp boundaries and
each part shows its meaning only within the totality and when considered from the standpoint of it.

(Simmel 1987: 188)

The universalism of the categorical imperative, instead, can be purchased only
at the cost of reductively understanding moral duty as taking classes of isolated
actions – breaking a promise, appropriating a deposit, telling a lie – as its object.
The generalization test at the basis of Kant's ethics only functions, however, if
we take a reductive view of human action and overlook the fact that the same
act acquires different moral valences in the context of two different lives. The
test is not reformable. If we tried to immanently improve Kant's approach to
morality by including the *lebensphilosophisch* holistic account of the meaning of
moral action, continues Simmel, the generalization test would put us in the
absurd position of wondering whether we may want that "the totality of one's
life" should be generalized and become a law for everybody else or, in other
words, whether we may want that everybody else should become "us."[25] The
outcome of an attempt to reform the Kantian approach by hermeneuticizing the
view of human action embedded within it would result in the extinction of the
individuality of the self-legislating moral actor. If each action acquires its
meaning in the context of the conduct of an entire life, how can I – in order to
effect the generalization test understood in new terms – will that the totality of
my life should lose its uniqueness and, via hypothetical generalization, give rise
to an infinite series of I's that are exact replicas of my own?

Simmel's critique of Kant's moral philosophy, as this brief reconstruction
suggests, implicitly rests on a normative concept of authenticity. In fact, the
overall direction of his argument can be best understood if we attribute to him
(1) a view of a person's identity as not being entirely at his or her disposal, (2)
a normative priority of the person's identity relative to any "ought" dimension
external to it and (3) a distinction between an inauthentic, and as such
destructive, autonomy and a form of authenticity which embeds a moment of
autonomy. Furthermore, a normative concept of authenticity is implicit also in
the critical dialogue that in the rest of his essay Simmel engages in with the
anthropology and the moral psychology underlying Kant's approach to moral
validity.

If we examine the crucial notion of "self-legislation," in fact, it emerges that
it is not the individual as a whole living being that acts as a moral lawgiver to
him- or herself, but merely that part of his or hers by means of which he or she
forms the representation of a superindividual reason. In this sense, continues
Simmel, Kant

64

by no means goes beyond the principle according to which what morally directs the individual must be something external to the individual. And since he rejects all heteronomy, he is forced to split the individual into a sentient and a rational part

(Simmel 1987: 199)

Kant must also postulate that the rational, *noumenal* part of the individual constitutes also the most authentic self of each of us. Against this view Simmel contends that the moral conduct of the individual should be guided by an *individual moral law* which is really a "principle of authenticity." Such law "is but the totality or centrality of this life that manifests itself as duty" (Simmel 1987: 203). Implicit in this passage is also a concept of human dignity considerably different from that of Kant. The dignity of the individual stems from his or her ability to represent and bring to realization within him- or herself "the whole of life – obviously not in its extension, but in its meaning, in its essence – and to do so in a specific, individual and unique way" (Simmel 1987: 207). For Simmel the epiphany of life within the life of each person – the epiphany which underlies what we call "dignity" – is not different from the manifestation of aesthetic value in every aspect of a great work of art:

every part of the work of art is what it is only by virtue of the fact that every other part is what it is and the meaning of each part somehow includes the meaning of the whole work of art.

(Simmel 1987: 209)

Incidentally, in this passage we find articulated from a theoretical point of view the roots of that *fragmentariness* which accompanies Simmel's thought as a unique cipher. From the standpoint of Simmel's conception of art and of life, the systematic quality of a conceptual position adds nothing to its value, but on the contrary carries the risk of a gratuitous dissipation of meaning. For the enlightening fragment contains *in nuce* all the facets of a complex reality. Hence the peculiar flavor of Simmel's implicit notion of authenticity as an expressive cipher of the personality enshrined in every single act of a person. Simmel's psychological holism leads him to suggest that "in every action the whole person is implicated" (Simmel 1987: 211).

Moving on to the *pars construens* of Simmel's essay, the main point of "The Individual Law" could not be farther removed from the attempt to formulate "a new moral *principle*." For the deontological opposition of moral duty and life Simmel substitutes a new opposition between an "ought" (an "ought" which can be universal just as well as individual) and "reality" or "facticity" (again, a "reality" or "facticity" which could have an individual just as well as a superindividual nature) in which both aspects – the "ought" and "reality" – are both part of *life*. From this point of view *life as it ought to be* will no longer appear to us as something to which we have access in any significantly different way from our mode of perceiving life *qua* reality or facticity. And because life comes to fruition only in the individual, also moral normativity will have to be traced, according to Simmel, at the level of the individual.

This is not to say, however, that the "ought" with which every individual must come to terms is determined entirely by the opinion that the individual has of it. In the last section of the essay Simmel is extremely careful in drawing the other boundary of the notion of authenticity – the boundary which separates the subjective and the non-subjective dimension of authenticity – and at this juncture his position helps us to sort out a view of authenticity as mere *difference* or as "Eigentlichkeit" from a view of authenticity which includes reference to a *normative* standpoint.[26] The individual law which should inspire our conduct is not given by the uniqueness of one's life as perceived by the moral actor. The actor's perception is but one element among many. For the internal access to the meaning of one's life does not preclude the possibility of committing an error, according to Simmel, when one has to sort out what is central and what is peripheral. The "ought" of the individual moral law must, rather, be anchored in a judgment which possesses a kind of objectivity *sui generis*. As Simmel puts it:

> if a life individualized in a certain way exists, also its corresponding ought [Sollen] exists as objectively valid, and we can conceive of true and false representations of it on the part of both the subject of such life and other subjects.
>
> (Simmel 1987: 217)

The other moral actors are only in a less favorable position for assessing what the moral law requires of the moral subject. They lack direct and immediate access to the life aspects that constitute the "backdrop" of the subject's conduct, a deficiency which makes it more difficult but not impossible for them to grasp the specific content of the individual law. On the other hand, the moral subject's direct and immediate access to the circumstances of his or her life does not in and of itself guarantee the validity of his or her appraisal of the individual law.

The insistence on the relative independence of the individual law from the moral subject's subjective representation of it serves for Simmel the purpose of distinguishing his ethics of authenticity based on the individual law from all sorts of hedonistic self-indulging or from the avant-garde ideal of living one's life as a work of art. In fact, an ethic of authenticity, as he points out, may be even more demanding than an ethic based on general principles. Far from legitimating any extenuating circumstances that might ease off the hold of the moral law on us, the ethic of the individual law, by virtue of its finetuning its requirements on the individuality of our being, is likely to result in casting our actions under a light that makes them appear much more serious than if they were considered separately from our whole personality. Certain minor infractions and certain misdemeanors of seeming little consequence can, if appraised in connection with and as indicative of our personality, acquire a much larger moral import.[27] In fact, our recognition of the fact that a fragment of our life-conduct reflects the whole of our life cannot but increase our sense of being responsible for every moment of our life: "Included in the moral requiredness of each single action is a responsibility vis-à-vis our whole life-history" (Simmel 1987: 228).

This strong normative, albeit individual, quality of the moral law is illustrated by Simmel with reference to the example of a committed pacifist being drafted into the army. The ethics of the individual law concurs with the deontological solution to the ensuing conflict of conscience that Simmel hypothetically attributes to Kant – the pacifist's ethical (*sittlich*) convictions must eventually give way to the moral duty to defend the integrity of the homeland – but on different grounds.

According to Simmel, arguments revolving around the notion that the security of the State and the *salus publica* require mandatory military service are not cogent unless they can appeal to something *internal* to the life of the pacifist. The pacifist's *moral* obligation to serve in the military must be grounded, consistently with the perspective of the "individual law," on the fact that the pacifist's "individuality" or identity is not "ahistorical, indifferent to substantive and material determinations, or merely constituted by the so-called 'character'" (Simmel 1987: 218–19). Rather, it includes among other things the fact of being a citizen of a given State. From the uncontested fact of being a citizen follows "the duty to serve in the military" (Simmel 1987: 219) – a duty, points out Simmel, whose cogency is independent of the subject's recognition of it but is, rather, linked with the presence of an actual relation between citizenship and the life of the individual.

While the presuppositions of Simmel's argument remain linked with the historical constellation of 1913, and thus appear quite dated today, the example maintains its relevance, in that it shows the intention, on Simmel's part, to take distance both from the modern and Enlightenment idea that the worthiest aspect of the human being is the rational core (understood in this case as responsiveness to principles) common to all members of humankind and, on the other hand, from the modernistic and Romantic idea that the worthiest aspect within each of us consists in what factually distinguishes each of us and renders him or her unique. Both of these conceptions in the end equally fail to do justice to one important aspect of the human being, and prove equally onesided. The modern and Enlightenment view devalues the internal configuration of psychic structures, needs and motivations which makes us unique as mere contingency. The modernistic and Romantic view devalues those internal competences and dispositions that enable us to share something with all other human beings as irrelevant or, worse, repressive. Simmel's implicit conception of individuals, instead, locates them beyond this narrow alternative, in an area which we can characterize as the overlapping of the traditions of *integrative*, *centered* and *reflective* conceptions of authenticity. "The individual," as he writes, "is the whole person, not the rest which is left after subtracting what is shared with others" (Simmel 1987: 223).

At the same time Simmel wishes to distinguish his ethics of the individual law from what he understands as a "hedonistic ethics of self-realization." Happiness – not even happiness understood as the fulfillment or realization of one's personality – is not as such the ultimate end presupposed by the individual law. To equate the duty prescribed by the individual law with the pursuit of one's happiness or one's self-realization would amount to what Simmel calls "a naive lack of differentiation" (Simmel 1987: 226). Anyone who conceives of the individual law in these terms misses the fact that the fulfillment or realization of one's personality represents just one kind of objective value, and a single substantive object of duty, next to which other moral requirements may co-exist.[28] For example, nothing can in principle prevent the individual law from enjoining a given individual to commit him- or herself to altruistic, spiritual, artistic or social endeavors that actually result in a *sacrifice* of the self. It must be observed, however, that in this context Simmel uses an extremely "experience near" and unreflective concept of self-realization. The possibility of a contrast between the individual law and the pursuit of authentic self-realization disappears as soon as we move to a notion of self-realization that includes the objectivation not just of one's needs and inclinations but also of the rest of the determinations of one's identity, including normative contents. Even the choice to renounce one's "self-realization," if made and executed with reflective awareness, is a choice *for* self-realization.

If we accept Simmel's contention that the "individual law" is endowed with the same normative cogency as any "superindividual" law, even though it applies to one case only, then it becomes clear that the notion of authenticity can be relevant also for grasping the nature of modern normativity as such.

One of the clearest accounts of the relation of authenticity to normativity is offered by Luigi Pareyson, Umberto Eco's and Gianni Vattimo's mentor, when in his *Estetica* he writes that:

> The work of art is as it should be and should be as it is, and has no other law than its own. . . . The work of art is universal in its very singularity: its rule holds for one case only, but exactly in that it is universal, in the sense that it is the only law that should have been followed in its making.
>
> (Pareyson 1988: 140–1)

Pareyson's point applies beyond the realm of aesthetics, just as Simmel's case for the "individual moral law" applies beyond ethics. We could paraphrase Pareyson's sentence in the following way: The good society (i.e. the society which is good for us) is as it should be and should be as it is . . . The good society has universal significance in its very singularity: its rule (the constitution, or its underlying conception of justice, if we consider it from the standpoint of *political* philosophy; the mechanism of social reproduction, from the standpoint of *social* philosophy) holds for one case only, but exactly in that it is universal, in the sense that it is the only (or perhaps we should say the best) law that should have been followed in its making. The plausibility of the point being made here does not diminish as we vary the field of application of the notion of an individual law from aesthetics to ethics to politics and so forth.

Going back to the predicament of social theory in its relation to philosophy, these cursory notes suggest that Simmel's reflections on ethics constitute – along with Weber's notion of an *ethic of responsibility* discussed in Chapter 1 – one of those junctures in the development of the sociological tradition at which a conception of singular or exemplary normativity can be found. Although still in an embryonic stage, this conception carries the promise of delivering us from the problem of incommensurability and finally providing us with a kind of universalism consistent with the fact of pluralism and the Linguistic Turn. In the next chapter a central element of the internal structure of this new universalism will be explored in depth, namely the dimensions that we implicitly refer to when we speak of the authenticity of an individual identity.

5

POST-MODERN *EUDAIMONIA*

Dimensions of an authentic identity

Many of the paths followed thus far have led us to the same crossroad. The *authenticity-thesis* was shown to contain a methodological claim centered on the notion of the "self-congruency of a symbolic whole" – a notion which can be partially explicated with reference to the notion of the congruency of a life-history. In that context "congruency" was claimed not to be reducible to a mere aspect of *consistency*, but to include other dimensions, which were not spelled out any further. In Chapter 2, postmetaphysical *phronesis* has been defined as the ability to choose between conceptual schemes embedding incompatible or differently ranked values in contexts where no a priori or external standard can be invoked. And while *phronesis* reconstructed along these lines thus appeared to be ultimately about the weighing of values, it has been argued that the weighing of values is conceptually linked with the furthering of the authenticity of the identity in whose service it is carried out. Also in this case we have been left in need of a further specification of what the expression "authenticity of an identity" might mean and what dimensions it may include. In Chapter 3, the discussion of the normativity without principles presupposed by Kant's notion of reflective judgment once again pointed to the notion of authenticity or integrity of an identity, understood from this angle as the regulative idea that enables reflective judgment to operate. It was argued that by reformulating Kant's idea of the "furthering of life" in terms of self-realization or of the attainment of an authentic relation to oneself we gain access to a more hermeneutic and less naturalistic understanding of the nature of the universalism embedded in reflective judgment. Yet, the constituents of an authentic relation to oneself remained to be spelled out and the suggestion was offered that such specification should be carried out in the vocabulary of psychoanalytic theory.

It is now time to explore this crossroad in a more detailed way. Before we enter *in medias res*, however, it might not be inappropriate to situate the object of our discussion not just with respect to the arguments that have led us to it, but also with respect to broader coordinates. As the title suggests, such object is in a sense the good – "in a sense" because a lot of topics traditionally associated with the good will be neglected. For example, no mention will be made of the moral-theoretical distinction between the good and the right or of the conflict,

70

much more tragic than the conflict of good and evil, which sometimes opposes the good to the good – namely, conflict of value. The aim of my argument is simply to present a tentative reconstruction of one view of "the good for a human life" which in my opinion can, with some degree of plausibility, be said to meet our intuitions.

The case for a postmetaphysical notion of *eudaimonia*

There exist, in my opinion, at least three additional reasons – aside from the need to spell out, for the sake of completeness, the presuppositions of the argument about authenticity developed above – for taking up the task of formulating a postmetaphysical notion of the good. First, the hope that an approach to normative validity based on a sharp distinction between the context-transcending and universalistic nature of fairness, justice or impartiality and the context-boundness and particularistic nature of our conceptions of the good would be easier to ground than one that included a more nuanced distinction between the right and the good has proven overly optimistic. Rawls's retreat from "rational choice" to "overlapping consensus" as the terrain on which to defend his theory of justice as fairness,[1] as well as Habermas's difficulties in convincingly responding to the many critics of his discursive approach to normative validity, provides evidence for this point.[2] On the other hand, a postmetaphysical eudaimonistic ethic is intrinsically free of the task, so taxing for all deontological ethics, of explaining the *motivational* appeal and efficacy of moral insights. For it rests on the idea that it is happiness that generates virtue rather than the other way around.

Second, no real reconciliation of universalism with what Rawls has called "the fact of pluralism" can be effected, unless one does take up the challenge of reconstructing our intuitions about what makes a certain choice between competing vocabularies, paradigms, traditions or conceptual schemes *better* than another. However, since the conflict between rival vocabularies, paradigms, traditions or conceptual schemes always includes, in some respect, a conflict between value-stances, and values are about the good, there seems to be no way, within an adequate theory of normative validity, to avoid the task of reconstructing certain common intuitions regarding the good.

Third, the only kind of universalism that can "defuse," if not "solve" or "overcome," in the traditional modern sense, the problem of incommensurability is the universalism *sui generis* that inheres in *phronesis* or *judgment.* If we apply Kant's model of reflective judgment to identities, individual or collective, confronted with value-choices, the question that emerges is not whether an act of choice satisfies some external criterion of rationality, but whether and to what extent a given choice satisfies the inner normativity of an identity. Then the impossibility of exhaustively translating one vocabulary into another ceases to be an obstacle to the universality of judgment. For we no longer have to *translate* one vocabulary into another, but simply to assess the degree of self-congruency of an identity in its own terms. Of course the kind of universalism that we can thus hope to obtain is of a peculiar kind, *exemplary* rather than methodologically *cogent*, *singular* rather than generalizing, and not susceptible to *demonstration*.

In sum, today's philosophical predicament is one in which our awareness of the difficulties connected with grounding the deontological approaches to justice, our realization that the "fact of pluralism" imposes on us the task of assessing competing weighings of values and, finally, our suspicion against all attempts to retraditionalize our moral life concur in creating a demand for ethical theories that do embed a *formal* or *thin* theory of the good and somehow try to bridge the gap between the deontological inspiration of the neo-Kantian accounts of justice and the flipside teleological priority of the good typical of communitarian and neo-Aristotelian approaches.

One way of formulating a formal theory of the good is to anchor it to a view of the good understood as the fulfillment of an identity. Our intuitive ideas about the fulfillment of an identity – an individual identity in the first place, a collective and a symbolic identity in a derivative sense – seem to rest on experiences that can be conceptualized in the vocabulary of psychoanalysis as the experiences of psychic symbiosis and separation, of narcissistic exhibitionism and idealization, of self-acceptance and shame, of Oedipal rivalry, of emotional ambivalence and affect splitting, of sovereignty over the self and of the fear of being emotionally overwhelmed. From the writings of Freud, Melanie Klein, Harry S. Sullivan, W. Ronald D. Fairbairn, Donald W. Winnicott, Edith Jacobson, Margaret Mahler, Otto Kernberg, Heinz Kohut and other psychoanalytic theorists it is possible to reconstruct an implicit vision of a fulfilled identity which in my opinion constitutes one of the credible candidates, in a postmetaphysical context, for that role of the *common ground* which Kant attributed to the categories of cognition and Aristotle, in his *Nicomachean Ethics*, attributed to an ontological notion of human nature. Such reconstruction of the dimensions of authenticity against the background of the psychoanalytic view of the fulfillment of an identity is based on three assumptions.

The first assumption is that today we understand the good for a human life in *psychological* terms, as self-realization or as the fulfillment of an identity. Kant once wrote, in the *Groundwork of the Metaphysics of Morals*, that the only thing which "we" – by which he understood "we Western moderns of the eighteenth century" – can regard as unconditionally good is a "gute Wille," namely a will oriented to the categorical imperative. To paraphrase him, the only thing which for "us" – Western (post)moderns of the late twentieth century and early twenty-first – counts as unconditionally good is the possession of a "good identity," a fulfilled identity. "Unconditional" does not mean, here, that one's own self-fulfillment is all that counts in matters ethical. On the contrary, there are many other considerations, including concern for justice, that count and set limits on, or somehow must be figured in, my conception of the good for me. In this sense, "unconditional" does not mean "absolute." It means something else.

Try to think of something, of anything, *for the sake of which* we might wish to have a good or fulfilled identity. If you find it hard to come up with anything, then such difficulty clarifies the sense in which I have used the term "uncondi-tional." Self-fulfillment is "unconditionally good" for us in that it meets the Aristotelian test of the good life. It appears, at least *prima facie*, to be that special good for the sake of which all other goods, including justice, are sought.

The second assumption is that self-fulfillment bears no direct relation to the notion of *pleasure*. The irreducible diversity of levels at which the two concepts are located is best illustrated by the existence of scores of people who, despite severe frustration of their needs, despite severe deprivations, losses and conflicts, do manage to maintain a sense of direction, purpose and meaning in their lives. On the other hand, it is also illustrated by the existence of lots of people who, while blessed with high levels of gratification of their needs, while blessed even with socially sanctioned gratifications, nonetheless experience their lives as empty, purposeless and fruitless. Even if we understand pleasure in the broadest terms possible as the satisfaction of the sum total of one's desires, fulfillment appears to be something more complex and at the same time quite unrelated to it. As Kohut writes:

> Even death and martyred passivity can be tolerated with a glow of fulfilment. And, in reverse, survival and social dominance can be bought at the price of the abandonment of the core of the self and lead, despite seeming victory, to a sense of meaninglessness and despair.
>
> (Kohut 1977: 117)

A somewhat similar view of the good for an identity has been present for a long time in the tradition of thought that coalesces around the notion of an "ethic of authenticity." For example, in *Either/Or* Kierkegaard formulates one of the sharpest versions of the distinction between pleasure and fulfillment to be found in the history of Western moral thought. According to Kierkegaard:

> The richest personality is nothing before he has chosen himself, and on the other hand even what one might call the poorest personality is everything when he has chosen himself; for the great thing is not to be this or that but to be oneself, and this everyone can be if he wills it.
>
> (Kierkegaard 1959: Volume 2, 181)

From the standpoint of this conception of authenticity or fulfillment, even the possession or acquisition of a good character is irrelevant unless one "chooses oneself" or, in Freud's terms, unless one "cathects one's self" or, in ordinary language, one fully accepts the reality of one's own self. This distinction between the plane of drive-satisfaction or drive-frustration and the plane of the realization or stifling of the potentials of the self, as we will see, underlies the work of many psychoanalytic theorists, including Winnicott, Fairbairn, Mahler,

Jacobson and, of course, Kernberg and Kohut. The lack of this distinction, instead, haunts Freud's argument in *Civilization and its Discontents*. In fact, the motivational requirements of the maintenance of the social order represent a limit for the individual's happiness, as well as a source of constraints, only if we understand happiness or the good as the gratification of drive-related needs or as *pleasure*.[3] On the contrary, if we understand the good as fulfillment, then the relation between society's claims and the individual's drive-related needs appears in a different light. The notion of the good as fulfillment, in fact, bears more than an elective affinity with an intersubjective conception of the individual, according to which only in the medium of social relations – i.e. in the medium of relations of reciprocal recognition – can the human individual become who he or she is and approximate that elusive fulfillment which can never be fully specified in an affirmative way but can best be reconstructed *a contrario*, from our sense of what it means to fail to attain it. Far from constituting a mere limit-condition, a kind of toll to be paid on the road to a post-modern version of *eudaimonia*, these relations, along with the requirements of their reproduction, become then a condition of the possibility of attaining the good life. This is the entry point, incidentally, for discussing the relation of the right to the good from a eudaimonistic perspective. If I am interested in my own good, understood as fulfillment, I am also thereby interested in justice as the sole condition that can preserve those relations within which alone the good can be attained.[4]

The third assumption concerns the status of the "post-modern *eudaimonia*." The dimensions of the authenticity of an identity articulate a common ground that all concrete lifeforms can be said, until empirical evidence to the contrary is brought up, to share. I do not use the phrase "bring to expression" because such common ground cannot be conceived as preexisting the lifeforms in which it inheres, but rather evolves with them and is a precipitate of their existence. Nor can this common ground be conceived as a kind of deep-seated "internal reality." Rather, I understand the common ground for which I suggest the ironic name of *post-modern eudaimonia* as a regulative idea that we presuppose (1) whenever we *want* to make sense of the subjective experience of *necessity* that we associate with taking a considered and authentic stance in a dilemma – the "Here I stand. I can do no other" of Luther; (2) whenever we anticipate a *consensus omnium* on our judgment concerning the fulfillment or authenticity of a concrete identity; and (3) whenever we are exposed to, and successfully recognize, instances of self-fulfillment in cultures other than our own.

Individual identity and self-fulfillment

Authenticity, self-fulfillment, self-realization and integrity have thus far been treated as properties of an identity. Embedded in the *authenticity-thesis* is the claim that roughly the same set of dimensions can capture our intuitions concerning what authenticity or fulfillment means for an individual, for a collective or for a symbolic identity – where by symbolic identity I mean disembodied but by no means less effective identities such as those of texts, works of art, traditions and disciplines. In this chapter, however, only the dimensions of fulfillment of individual identity will be addressed, whereas the points of intersection with the fulfillment of collective and symbolic identities of various kinds will be explored in the following chapters. Some further elucidation is then needed concerning the meaning of the term "individual identity" – provisionally characterized in Chapter 2 as a representation which in the case of the individual includes at least (1) some perception of continuity of the self, (2) a configuration of various kinds of needs and urges and (3) an ideal projection of a desired self. At the same time, one more word of preliminary clarification is called for by my choice of the vocabulary of psychoanalytic theory. Any understanding of the dimensions of the post-modern *eudaimonia* must obviously be couched in a language and a vocabulary. Substance and language, however, are here intertwined. As we will see, to formulate a reconstruction of the common ground at a *psychological* level carries certain advantages over other possible choices.

The notion of individual identity with which I am concerned here must be distinguished from three distinct alternative notions. For example, unlike the purely logical or formal theories of identity, the authenticity approach (despite its addressing the general properties of individual, collective and symbolic identities which are fulfilled) is aimed at preserving a strict relationship with the subjective experience (the *Erlebnis*) of identity-fulfillment – and here, as well as in other respects, the resources of the psychoanalytic vocabulary constitute a significant asset. In the course of my reconstruction of the dimensions of a fulfilled or authentic identity I will thus not be concerned with the abstract features which allow an individual to remain the same across different possible worlds,[5] nor will I be concerned with the problem of the identity of the self across time and the related theme of the "closest continuer,"[6] or with the formal relation of the theory of identity to the notion of survival of the body or the brain,[7] or with the relation of identity to a series of interconnected selves in Parfit's sense.[8] Common to all these approaches is a misguided attempt to account for the self-sameness of individual identity from an external standpoint, as it were, namely to understand it as the product of cognitive and perceptual processes that in principle are as accessible to an observer as to the bearer of the identity. Such an attempt is misguided in that it is my possessing an identity which is a necessary condition in order to recognize a sequence of experiences as mine, and not an inference that follows from an "objectively" observed series of cognitive and perceptive acts.

Second, the view of identity presupposed here differs from purely psychodynamic theories of identity – such as Kohut's "psychology of the self," or Jacobson's view of the relation between the self and its objects, or Mahler's theories of individuation – in that it considers certain psychodynamic properties of individual identity only as a *point of departure*. The descriptive categories used in order to characterize individual identity are chosen with an eye to their possible application to an account of collective and symbolic identities.

Third, the view of identity outlined in the present reconstruction of the dimensions of authenticity differs from the social-psychological theories of identity – such as symbolic interactionism, Parsons's, Keniston's, Slater's or Erikson's theories of identity[9] – in that it does make reference to "depth-psychological" processes and in that, although it considers identity not a *primum* but a result of interaction, it does not approach identity as an expression of the broader fabric of shared values, meanings and orientations which underlie the cohesion of a social group but, rather, seeks to characterize identity at a deeper level. Once again, the anchoring of the reconstruction of today's notion of *eudaimonia* in psychoanalytic categories offers certain advantages. In this case, it attenuates the impact of the *social* and *cultural* factors which remain determinant in the social-psychological approaches to identity developed by symbolic interactionism, by Parsons, by Erikson, by Slater or by Keniston. To be sure, other psychological vocabularies could have been chosen, but psychoanalytic theory stands out for its superior degree of differentiation.

Finally, I wish to distance my theory of identity from Habermas's thesis of an ontogenetic and philogenetic evolution of identity through the stages of natural identity, of role identity and of ego identity.[10] According to Habermas, at the stage of "natural identity" only an awareness of the demarcation of the body from the surrounding environment and of its continuity in time exists. At the stage of "role identity," typical of premodern and early modern societies, the sense of one's identity centers around one's place in the division of labor. Finally, at the stage of "ego identity," typical of advanced industrial societies, the individual anchors his or her identity at a level deeper than social roles, i.e. in the unity and uniqueness of his or her personality. Such a theory, if empirically plausible, would shed light on the evolutionary process which has led individual identity to possess the characteristics which today we attribute to it, but would not tell us much about the conditions which define the fulfillment of an identity and guide our value judgments.

Furthermore, the meaning of the term identity can be illustrated by contrasting it with a number of neighboring notions. First, identity should not be confused with the self. The identity of a person is only one component, albeit a crucial one, of a person's self. In fact, while it makes sense to speak of unconscious aspects of the self, it is meaningless to speak of unconscious aspects on an identity. For an identity is a *representation* of the self as perceived by the person.

Such consideration brings us back to the question "What is the self?" if we consider it disjoined from a self-*representation*. Many authors within the psychoanalytic tradition question the legitimacy of the concept of the self, if understood in any sense other than as a representation located in the ego. Kohut's theory of narcissism, often referred to in the following pages, enables us to understand the sense in which aspects of the self can exist that are not immediately part of the representation of the self with which an actor operates. For instance, Kohut's self is constituted by a pole of ambitions, genetically linked with the stage of grandiose narcissistic exhibitionism, a pole of idealized goals, genetically linked with the relation to an idealized self-object, and an intermediate area which includes those talents and abilities which can be mobilized in the service of the ambitions and ideals. Of course any and all of these aspects of the self may remain hidden to consciousness and thereby exert a covert influence on the identity of the person. Thus the term identity is here used in a different sense than in Kohut, who employs it basically in a social-psychological sense.

Second, the term identity must be distinguished from the related notions of *personality* and *character*. Just as in relation to the notion of self, also in relation to personality, identity can be described as a component. What is then the difference between the self and personality? The self constitutes the center of the personality but does not exhaust it. For personality includes a *periphery* as well. For example, the characteristic flavor of a personality derives from the relative weights of the different components of the self within it. Within the spectrum of normality we can see personalities characterized by an idealizing, a self-expressing or a sociable flavor. Another difference between the self and personality is constituted by the diversity of perspectives from which either can be described. Whereas the self can be best described in psychodynamic terms, the personality of an individual can be described in experience-nearer terms. A personality or a character is fundamentally a *style* of interaction typical of a self. Thus personality is causally related to certain features of the self, but in other respects it possesses a certain independence from the self. For instance, a self weakened by serious empathic failures on the part of the self-object during the exhibitionistic-grandiose phase may later on, on the basis of different formative and cultural experiences, give rise to an authoritarian personality or to a personality leaning toward nihilism, to a withdrawn and introverse personality or to an extroverse personality characterized by a compensatory exuberance. In other words, the self is a concept situated at a "deeper" level (in the sense given to the term "deep" by the psychoanalytic tradition) than personality. The difference between the two notions can best be perceived from the perspective of pathology. Whereas the defects of the self generate pathological configurations such as borderline syndromes, narcissism, autism, paranoia and schizophrenia, the defects of the personality may coincide with these configurations, but may also result in lesser distortions and especially in distortions linked with very specific symptoms and patterns of conduct. From the standpoint of the theorists of narcissism, and particularly of Kohut, it makes sense to talk of neurotic personalities, meaning by that something quite similar to what Freud meant by the term neurotic, but it is utterly meaningless to talk of a "neurotic self." For a personality which is "merely" neurotic in the classical sense is a personality that includes at its center a basically cohesive self.

With regard to the relation of personality to identity, it must be emphasized that while it is self-contradictory to say that to a weak or ill-constituted self corresponds a fulfilled identity, certain negative characteristics of a personality or character – those characteristics, for example, recorded in the classical moral vocabulary under the name of such vices as stinginess or prodigality, rashness or fearfulness, arrogance or servility, and so on – do not, in and of themselves, prevent an identity from reaching its own fulfillment.

Another way of drawing a distinction between the concepts of identity, of self and of personality is to think of the description of an identity as an answer to the question "Who am I and who do I want to be?", of the description of a self as an answer to the question "What drives me and what guides me?", and of the description of a personality or character as an answer to the question "What is peculiarly distinctive of my way of interacting with others?" This way of distinguishing the three notions does not coincide with the distinctions drawn by the authors who, within the psychoanalytic tradition, have most closely been concerned with the theme of identity, namely Erikson, Jacobson and Kohut. Kohut, for example, defines identity as "the point of convergence between the developed self (as it is constituted in late adolescence and early adulthood) and the sociocultural position of the individual" (Kohut 1978: 472). This definition enables Kohut to characterize the diversity of personality types on the basis of the relation of the self to the identity within the person. There exist individuals with a firm and cohesive self, acquired during infancy, who are led by external vicissitudes (e.g. immigration, social mobility, war, traumatic events etc.) to develop a weak and diffuse identity. This type of personality tends to be associated with a number of positive characteristics. While the relative fluidity of identity favors the ability to relate empathically to the diversity of other people, the cohesion of the self protects the personality against fragmentation. At the opposite end of the spectrum, for Kohut, there exist individuals with a weak and uncohesive self – a self whose precariousness must be buttressed by an identity strong and rigid. This is, typically, the case of individuals with an authoritarian personality.[11]

Kohut's equation of identity with social identity raises some questions. On the one hand, there exist specifically *psychological* aspects of any individual identity, which can be captured through those dimensions of the fulfillment of an identity that form the object of this chapter. On the other hand, the interrelation of self, identity and personality which Kohut wishes to point out can be conceived equally accurately in terms of a multi-layered notion of identity, which includes a phenomenological, a sociological and a psychological level of the description of an identity. The same holds for Erikson's distinction of "personal identity" and "ego identity," as well as for Jacobson's distinction of "Self" and "self-representation" or "identity."[12]

Finally, three different perspectives on identity should be distinguished. It is possible to look at an individual identity from a *phenomenological*, a *psychodynamic* and a *sociological* perspective. The *phenomenological* perspective is the standpoint of what is immediately experienced, the depth-psychological perspective directs our attention to those aspects of identity which are linked with defensive and unconscious dynamics, and the sociological perspective elucidates the intersubjective aspects of identity. These three standpoints or perspectives cannot be reduced to one another but can, in combination, generate the plurality of approaches to identity actually found in the social sciences. Erikson's, Slater's or Keniston's approaches, for instance, represent different mixed models in which a sociological and a psychodynamic perspective are combined.

From a *phenomenological* perspective, the minimal constituents of an individual identity are: (1) memories and recollections which together amount to a coherent biography that can be narrated; (2) a configuration of needs and drives distributed across the center and the periphery of the identity; and (3) some kind of ideal projection of a future and desired state of the self. From being the main actor of a more or less coherent life-story the individual derives a sense of continuity in time which, as we will see, is part of any conception of the authenticity or fulfillment of an identity. Such fulfillment is also a function of the degree to which the central needs of the identity are satisfied or frustrated as well as of the degree to which they are accessible to consciousness. Finally, the anticipation of an ideal self which the person intends to become, if commensurable to the real potentials of the self, provides the individual with a sense of purpose in life as well as with a confident expectation of future fulfillment.

From the standpoint of a *psychodynamic* and, more specifically, *psychoanalytic* theory of identity an individual identity consists of a more or less adequate representation of the inner reality of the self – namely a representation (1) of a motivational core constituted by needs for fulfillment and for mirroring, (2) of a configuration of idealized goals and (3) of a set of talents and abilities which make the reaching of these goals and the satisfaction of these needs possible.

From a *sociological* perspective the minimal constituents of an individual identity are (1) the possession of cultural roots (i.e. the inclusion of one's biography within the context of a broader history of which it partakes), (2) a network of goals and (3) the participation in one or more socially recognized roles. From being embedded within a shared, though by no means necessarily societal in scope, horizon of meanings the individual derives a sense of belonging, a sense of being part of larger entities (communities, traditions, nations, professions etc.) whose destiny he or she comes to share. As far as the second constituent is concerned, no social actor exists who does not orient his or her action toward consciously pursued goals. The complexity or undifferentiated quality of this network of goals produces a sense of purposefulness or aimlessness in the individual, whereas the degree to which these goals are autonomously posited produces a sense of accountability. Finally, the presence and intense quality of the participation in a set of roles generates a confident expectation of social recognition.

Dimensions of the authenticity of an individual identity

Within the history of the psychoanalytic tradition we can observe a broad convergence among authors as diverse as Freud, Sullivan, Melanie Klein, Fairbairn, Winnicott, Edith Jacobson, Margaret Mahler, Kernberg and Kohut on the salience of four dimensions of the authenticity, well-being or fulfillment of an individual identity: *coherence*, *vitality*, *depth* and *maturity*. Actually, each of the four dimensions is a complex of subdimensions and aspects that only in the last analysis, and not without some Procrustean conceptual twisting, can be grouped together under the heading of coherence, vitality, depth or maturity. Evidence for the relevance of these basic dimensions for the evaluation of the fulfillment of an identity can be found in three areas. First, most influential theorists of the object-relations schools, and also a large number of theorists who keep closer to the classical drive model, *presuppose*, and some of them explicitly underscore, the importance of these dimensions for the understanding of single clinical cases as well as for metapsychological theorizing. This convergence is all the more significant insofar as these authors openly and deeply disagree on many essential aspects of their approaches. Second, in one way or other the themes of coherence, vitality, depth and maturity appear in all debates on the termination of analysis, regardless of the theoretical perspectives considered. Finally, the relevance of these dimensions emerges also from most debates on the psychoanalytic curriculum and particularly on the selection of candidates. Let us now examine each of these basic dimensions of the authenticity or fulfillment of an individual identity.

Coherence

The dimension of *coherence* can be generally understood as the possibility of summing up the modifications undergone by an identity during the lifetime of its bearer in the form of a narrative. It includes the aspects of *cohesion* versus *fragmentation*, of *continuity* versus *discontinuity*, and of *demarcation* versus *indistinctness*. Cohesion refers here to the quality of being integrated, having unity, and feeling embodied as opposed to being fragmented, fearing being overwhelmed, flooded, disintegrated or falling forever, or spinning or being directionless or feeling disembodied. All the authors considered somehow view the cohesion aspect of coherence as an important ingredient of human well-being, though they account for it in different terms and obviously take very different attitudes toward it. For example, in *Civilization and its Discontents* Freud states: "Normally, there is nothing of which we are more certain than the feeling of our self, of our own ego. This ego appears to us as something autonomous and unitary, marked off distinctly from everything else" (Freud 1930: 65–6). The point that Freud is trying to make, in response to R. Rolland's theses on the sacred and the "oceanic feelings," is not important here. What is relevant is the fact that Freud takes for granted something which for the next generations of psychoanalytic theorists, from Sullivan to Fairbairn, from Winnicott to Kohut, becomes very problematic. Indeed, most of contemporary psychoanalysis is based on the premise that the presence in each of us of a sense of the self as a cohesive and well-demarcated entity should *not* be taken for granted. On this point Fairbairn and Sullivan concur and, coming from quite a different angle, Melanie Klein and Margaret Mahler, and also Winnicott and Jacobson. Cohesion also holds centerplace in the whole work of Heinz Kohut. Interestingly, even in Freud, who notoriously did not make use of a distinct notion of the self, numerous references to the subdimension of cohesion can be found – for example in the remarks on anxiety that can be found throughout his entire work, from the "Draft E" of 1894, to the *Interpretation of Dreams* (1900), to *Inhibitions, Symptoms and Anxiety* (1926). In Freud's early writings, for instance, anxiety is associated with the frightening perception of a disintegration of the self. The archetypal anxiety situation is the trauma of birth,[13] but anxiety is linked also with the experiences of flying, of riding a see-saw, of standing in high places and generally with situations which may induce vertigo. In his "Draft E," on "How Anxiety Originates" (1894), Freud explains anxiety as a damming up of excitation which cannot find an outlet and, more precisely, as the transformation of an accumulated sexual tension.[14] This explanation rests on the idea that the libidinal block generated by the inhibition of discharge increases the pressure exerted by the drive: anxiety results from a fear of being overwhelmed, flooded or submerged – precisely as a dam whose safety outlets are clogged while the water rises.

Also in his middle period Freud continues to link anxiety – now differentiated into *neurotic* anxiety (i.e. anxiety *vis-à-vis* the id), *realistic* anxiety (i.e. anxiety *vis-à-vis* the external world) and *moral* anxiety (i.e. anxiety *vis-à-vis* the superego) – with the ego's experience of impotence in relation to an increase of excitation, internal or external,[15] or in relation to a mortal danger,[16] and thus ultimately with the experience of a fear of being overwhelmed and disintegrated.[17] The subdimension of cohesion plays an important role also in Freud's theory of mourning, presented in "Mourning and Melancholia" (1917b). In this essay Freud focuses on a new nexus of cohesion and mourning. The function of mourning, in fact, consists in a reappropriation of the libido invested in an object now lost, and thus also in the restoring of a psychic unity which would be jeopardized if the libido remained attached to the object. In *Inhibitions, Symptoms and Anxiety*, Freud stresses how the ego's genetic roots in the sexual drive determine its imprinted tendency toward "synthesis" and the reconciliation of psychic contents. The ego is the prime psychic agency that strives for unity.[18] The materials that prove more recalcitrant to reconciliation are the repressed contents of the id. The aim of the psychoanalytic cure is to heal the splits of the psyche through the demolishing of these repressions.

Finally, in the fragment on "Splitting of the ego in the process of defence" (1938) and in *An Outline of Psychoanalysis* (1940) Freud examines a kind of defense that consists in the splitting of the ego – an ego understood as one of the psychic agencies and not as a self-representation. In the 1938 essay, Freud describes a case of fetishism: a child, caught while masturbating, is threatened with castration. The threat reactivates the visual memory of the female sexual organ and such mental image in turn makes the threat plausible. The alternatives are, at this point, either to renounce the drive-satisfaction provided by the act of masturbation or to deny reality in order to convince oneself that there is nothing to be afraid of. The defense adopted by the child, however, leads him to do neither. He substitutes a fetish for the penis which the woman lacks. In this way he has denied reality (the woman still possesses a penis), has protected his own penis from the threat of castration and at the same time has protected the possibility to continue to satisfy his libido.[19] Thus both contendents have had their way: the drive can continue to be satisfied and reality is paid its dues. Reality has been paid its dues because in the end the child has not deluded himself by hallucinating a non-existent penis, but simply has transferred "the importance of the penis to another part of the body" (Freud 1938: 277). However, "this success is achieved at the price of a rift in the ego which never heals but which increases as time goes" (Freud 1938: 275–6).[20]

Also in the case of Melanie Klein the subdimension of cohesion is linked with anxiety and with defenses against anxiety, such as *introjection*, *projection* and *splitting*, but the notion of anxiety takes on a more relational coloring than in Freud. Anxiety is connected with the fear of suffering retaliation from an object which has been the target of one's aggressiveness. The splitting of objects into good and bad aspects bears a complex relation to cohesion, in Klein's view. While it would seem at first sight that splitting, especially when applied to the self, should result in the opposite of cohesion,[21] on closer inspection it becomes clear that in fact the defensive splitting operates in the service of *coherence*. At first, anxiety leads the baby to constantly split objects and feelings, retaining the pleasant feelings and introjecting the good objects while expelling the bad objects and projecting the bad feelings. Subsequently, the libido is also projected onto an external object – the good breast. The desire arises in the child to incorporate the ideal object and to identify with it as a nourishing and protective entity, whereas the bad object and the parts of the self linked with the death instinct are kept at a distance. If these defenses fail entirely, then according to Klein a disintegration of the ego ensues. On the contrary, if positive experiences prevail over negative ones and if the person's identification with the ideal object grows stronger with time, the need for splitting decreases and the individual moves from the "schizo-paranoid position" to a "depressive position" in which he can relate to a whole object considered in its good and bad aspects and loved and hated at once. This transition enables the person to perceive the self as unitary and cohesive, and at the same time contributes, through the discovery of one's dependence upon an external object and of the ambivalence of one's feelings, to an awareness of objects as separated from the self. Furthermore, in Klein's essay "On Identification" (1955) an important distinction can be found between *splitting* and *fragmentation*. If splitting and projection apply not to whole parts but to already fragmented parts of the self, and if during the schizo-paranoid position negative experiences prevail, then the ego will be exposed to what Klein calls a "fatal weakening by dispersal" and will undergo a pathological process of *fragmentation*.[22] Finally, in "Notes on Some Schizoid Mechanisms," Klein explicitly mentions *integration* as the overarching goal of human development and as the key aspect of mental health.[23]

The account of cohesion offered by Margaret Mahler hinges on her notion of the process of *separation–individuation*. This process begins with a *normal autistic phase*, in which the infant has no awareness of external objects and experiences only a sequence of gratifications or frustrations (real or just hallucinatory) of his or her drive-based needs. The subsequent *normal symbiotic phase* includes: (1) a subphase of *differentiation*, in which the child begins to explore the world beyond the symbiotic orbit, to distinguish the mother from other people and to distinguish between internal and external stimuli; (2) a subphase of *practicing*, which culminates with the acquisition of the capacity to walk, the ensuing sense of exhilarating omnipotence and a primitive form of identity; and (3) the subphase of *rapprochement*, in which the previous feelings of omnipotence give way to the child's realization that he or she is indeed "a very small person in a big world," and separation anxiety reappears. Finally, at the end of the normal symbiotic phase, which occurs around the third year, the individual is set on a lifelong phase that consists in the approximation of *object-constancy*, where object-constancy means the acquisition of a stable representation of the self and the other, the acquisition of a sense of the other as an inner presence, the acquisition of intrapsychic separateness and the attainment of *object-constancy* in the twofold sense of the psychic permanence of the object despite its physical absence and of the integration of its good and bad aspects. Cohesion arises at the end of this process, as a function of the prevailing of centripetal over centrifugal drive-processes. Fragility of the ego, resulting in a fragility of identity as well, is the outcome, according to Mahler, of a development in which the centrifugal thrust of primitive aggressive drives is not adequately counterbalanced, in the presymbiotic or symbiotic phases, by libidinal cathexes directed onto the body.[24]

A somewhat different understanding of cohesion emerges from the writings of the more object-relation oriented theorists. While for Freud and Klein, and to some extent for Mahler and Jacobson, the threat to cohesion mostly comes from within, as a result of drive-based and drive-fueled processes, for Sullivan, Winnicott and Kohut the cohesion of the self is threatened essentially from without, as a result of faulty object relations (i.e. as a result of relations with insufficiently empathic caretakers). Anxiety plays a key role also in Sullivan's view of cohesion. For him the construction of the self proceeds from the need to avoid the recurrence of experiences marked by anxiety. Paradoxically, one of the ways in which the individual can prevent the resurgence of the "not-me" associated with the experiences of deepest anxiety is the *dissociation* of the motivational system – namely, the refusal, through the use of selective disattention, of flight dynamisms and of other defenses, to become aware of the aspects of the self more closely related to experiences of anxiety.[25] Now, this need to avoid anxiety makes sense only insofar as Sullivan presupposes a tendency, typical of the human psyche, to avoid fragmentation and to avoid the risk of disintegration connected with the states of acute anxiety. The need for security, crucial for Sullivan's explanation of pathological outcomes, originates in anxiety of anxiety. According to Sullivan, however, anxiety is a reaction not only to the threat of disintegration but also to lack of mirroring or recognition. To this extent the consequences of anxiety touch also on self-esteem and shame, and thus on the dimension of vitality.

According to Kohut, finally, a cohesive self is the outcome of an optimal object relation with empathic self-objects capable of satisfying the child's needs for both mirroring and idealization. The child's self – only a potential self at birth – "expects" empathic responses from the human environment in the same sense as his or her body "expects" to find an atmosphere with oxygen at the moment of detachment from the mother's body. A bipolar self – or tripolar, in the later Kohut – coalesces if the mother is able to include the baby within her psychic organization and to respond to his or her need to be recognized as an autonomous human being. She must respond to the baby and later to the child as to a whole person, namely by attributing will and responsibility to him or her and by accepting with spontaneous joy the expressions of the infantile exhibitionism and omnipotence. The development of a cohesive self goes through a second phase, however, which can compensate, if needed, for the faulty outcome of the former. A cohesive self can be established also through the optimal fulfillment of the need to idealize someone and to feel part of something great, calm and strong. If the self-object – in our culture this role is usually, but not exclusively, played by the father – accepts with joy to be idealized by the child, then the insufficient degree of mirroring which may have characterized the relation with the first self-object will not give rise to the exhibitionistic and narcissistic pathologies of the weak self.[26] The later Kohut has increasingly emphasized the importance, as a determinant of self-cohesion, of the experience of interacting with someone like us and *equal to us*, capable of entering an intrinsically egalitarian relation of mutual recognition.[27]

While, despite their divergences, Freud, Klein, Mahler and Kohut agree in seeing cohesion as the final outcome of an uncertain process, Fairbairn takes the opposite view. For him the potential ego (a term by which he actually means a self) is integrated and cohesive at the beginning of life and only as a result of unsatisfactory experiences in the first object relation splits into components which correspond to the frustrating, exciting and gratifying aspects of its relation to the object.[28] These components are: the *libidinal ego*, related to the exciting object in a continuous search for the pleasure inherent in satisfying relations; the *internal saboteur*, linked with the rejecting object, hostile toward all relational contact[29] and later renamed *anti-libidinal ego* by Fairbairn;[30] and finally the *central ego*, related to the ideal object, which represents the only portion of the ego available for mature and positive relations with real objects. The internal saboteur or anti-libidinal ego becomes the receptacle of aggressiveness, and in this sense Fairbairn keeps close to the Kleinian tendency to see libido as located in the ego and aggressiveness as located in the id.

In sum, while the three aspects of the ego or self serve a function of sources of intrapsychic conflict homologous to the role played in Freud's theory by the tripartite structure, cohesion is in a sense for Fairbairn the starting point and not the end point of psychic maturation. The final degree of cohesion of an identity, however, is a function of the degree of gratification or frustration experienced by the child in his or her relation to the mother. The more frustrating is that relation, the stronger is the gravitational pull exerted by the anti-libidinal ego within the adult person and, consequently, the more difficult it will be to integrate in with the central ego. The identity of the person, understood as the perception of the self, will accordingly show a quality of fragmentation.

In a second sense, closer to the understanding of identity in the philosophical literature, the dimension of coherence can be seen as the property of feeling a *continuity* in time. Winnicott understands continuity as a perception of *durée* in Bergson's sense, as a perception of the inner flow of one's psychic being or, in his terms, as the perception of one's "going on being" (Winnicott 1965: 38). Kernberg emphasizes that only a self in which all the bad and good images are integrated "is characterized by a continuity of the self experience" (Kernberg 1976: 316). Borderline personalities, instead, show a pathological dependency on external objects to which they attribute the function of maintaining, through their constant presence in the individual's thoughts and feelings, a sense of continuity which cannot be produced from within.[31] Also Kohut views the capacity to experience the *continuity* of one's being as a function of the cohesion of the self. In his discussion of the case of Mr. B in *The Analysis of the Self*, Kohut suggests that a weak self typically looks for a compensatory mirroring to be extracted from always different and immediately devalued objects, or pursues ideals and personifications of perfection which are promptly abandoned upon discovery of their less than perfect stature. To these ways of relating to others corresponds a tenuous sense of continuity and the recurring illusion of starting all over once again.[32]

Finally, the coherence of an identity includes a quality of *demarcation* of the identity from the self's internal objects, the opposite of which is identity-confusion or identity-diffuseness. We find interesting considerations on demarcation in Jacobson, Mahler and Kohut. The demarcation of an identity is genetically related, according to Jacobson, to aggressiveness and frustration. The experiences of deprivation, of frustration and of disappointment which every child inevitably undergoes give rise to intense feelings of ambivalence toward his parents. If such feelings, however, do not exceed a certain threshold of intensity and frequency, they contribute to the growth of a self well demarcated from the object world.[33] Hypergratifications, however, just as traumatic frustrations, tend to induce regressive fantasies of merger between the self and the love object and thus to delay the process of construction of firm boundaries between the self and the objects.[34] Interestingly, in her view of the importance of optimal frustrations Jacobson seems to postulate a kind of anti-individuating basic tendency which runs opposite to the quasi-instinctual tendency toward individuation at the center of Mahler's theory.

Demarcation is the aspect of coherence most strongly emphasized in Mahler's view of human flourishing – a view according to which flourishing ultimately requires that we find our uniquely correct mix of the two polarities of fusion and isolation.[35] The tendency toward individuation understood as demarcation is argued to arise out of an optimal symbiotic phase and a gradual and a not premature hatching.[36] While weak cohesion is argued to derive from a relation with a mother incapable of providing an adequate symbiosis, a child's relation with a mother who is incapable of adequately responding to her need for independence and exploration, but tries to keep the child within the symbiotic orbit, almost always results in a faulty demarcation of the self from the object world. All the more crucial appears the subdimension of demarcation if we consider the pathological effects of the distortion of the developmental processes described by Mahler. The psychotic pathologies that she examines all have to do with the individuation of the self. The *autistic* syndrome, for instance, typical of children whose mother is functionally non-existent, is understood by Mahler as an attempt at "undifferentiation and deanimation" – an attempt which includes an "obsessive desire to preserve unchangeability," a stereotyped preoccupation for few inanimate objects or for models of action, which are the only objects of the child's attention, a "total intolerance toward any change in the inanimate environment" and the "struggle against any request of human and social contact" (Mahler 1968: Ch. 3). At this extreme of the pathological spectrum there is a total closure of psychic life within a limited world populated only by inanimate objects from which the self cannot separate without risking disintegration. The *symbiotic psychotic* syndrome, instead, presupposes a more differentiated personality and the capacity to relate at least to partial objects. In infantile symbiotic psychosis, argues Mahler, "the mental representation of the mother remains fused, or is regressively fused with the self; that is, it is not separated and remains part of the delirium of omnipotence of the disturbed child" (Mahler 1968: Ch. 3). This type of psychosis appears much later. It is necessary that the differentiation of the ego and psychosexual development have already somehow drawn the child and his mother apart in order for this initial degree of separation to pose a threat to the illusion of symbiotic omnipotence. Such events as an illness, the birth of a sibling, or attendance in kindergarten can all potentially evoke a "hostile and threatening" world. Then the fragile ego of the symbiotic psychotic child is overwhelmed by separation anxiety and, as the case of Stanley shows, soon collapses if the autonomous ego functions grow much faster than the child is able to emotionally differentiate from the mother.[37]

Unlike the other authors, Kohut does not consider the sharp demarcation of the self from the world a univocally positive element, but evokes the image of a tension between the dimension of maturity, which will be discussed below, and the dimension of coherence understood as demarcation. According to Kohut the spontaneous tendency of the self toward cohesion can produce its positive effects, under certain conditions, even if both self-objects, the mirroring one and the idealized one, are empathically inadequate. The "gifted" child can try to give shape, cohesion and vigor to his or her self through compensatory structures built in the context of a creative activity. And in his discussion of creativity as an alternative route to self-cohesion Kohut offers some interesting considerations on the subject of the demarcation of an identity from the object world. The relation of the creative person to his or her object, suggests Kohut, bears a resemblance not so much to the relation of a parent to his or her child as to the still uninhibited and exhibitionistic narcissism of early childhood: "The creative individual, whether in art or science, is less psychologically separated from his surroundings than the noncreative one; the 'I–you' barrier is not as clearly defined" (Kohut 1978: 446–7).

In sum, despite the different angles from which the dimension of coherence is addressed, a common set of considerations seems to emerge. All the authors considered include among the properties of a fulfilled or authentic identity the possession of an integrated image of the self, the absence of fears of disintegration or other forms of anxiety, a perception of permanence and self-sameness throughout change, and a perception of differentiation from the internal objects. At the same time, these properties hardly exhaust the dimensions of the authenticity of an identity. Another set of such properties, to be examined in the next section, can be grouped under the heading of *vitality*.

Vitality

Moving on to the second dimension, the term *vitality* designates the experience of *joyful empowerment* which results from the fulfillment of one's central needs, from a sense of the congruence of one's present state with the memory of who one has been, and from the sense of progressing toward becoming who one wants to be. When considered from this general point of view, vitality appears to be the phenomenological or experiential counterpart of self-realization or authenticity. As with coherence, also with regard to vitality it is possible to isolate a number of subdimensions or aspects of a more specific character, which in a way, being virtually ignored in the philosophical and sociological literature on identity, represent, along with the properties grouped under *maturity*, the most distinctive contribution of psychoanalytic theory to our understanding of what it means for an individual identity to attain authenticity. Under one aspect, the dimension of vitality has to do with the immediate and joyful experience of the self as *worthy of love and esteem*. The opposite of vitality in this case is a sense of *indignity* or *shame* associated with our self-representation.

Vitality as a sense of the loveworthiness of the self is a dimension of authenticity addressed not only, as we would expect, by authors who decidedly adopt a relational perspective (for example, Fairbairn, Winnicott and Kohut), but also by those who try to combine a significant element of such perspective with the classical drive model of psychic life. In fact, some of the most interesting remarks on this subdimension can be found in the work of Melanie Klein, Edith Jacobson, Margaret Mahler and Otto Kernberg.

For Klein a defective differentiation of good and bad object bears important consequences also with regard to the subdimension of self-confidence and the sense of one's dignity. The individuals who do not trust their own judgment often are also not sure about the goodness of their object and feel insecure with regard to their own good feelings.[38] In another context Melanie Klein mentions the "devaluation of the self" as a defense against envy, a defense typically adopted by tendentially depressed people in lieu of the more common devaluation of the object.[39] Furthermore, the dimension of vitality is also connected with the theme of reparation, understood as a non-manic compensation for aggressiveness, namely as a "profound urge to make sacrifices, in order to help and put right loved people whom in phantasy have been harmed or destroyed" (Klein 1975: 311). A successful reparation results indirectly in the restoration of a feeling of *plenitude* and *reconciliation*. In this sense, the work of reparation, similar to the catharsis of the forgiven sinner, resembles the work of mourning: both operate in the service of the reappropriation of vitality on the part of the ego.

For Jacobson, non-distorted object relations, accompanied by optimal frustrations, favor the vitality of an identity, understood as a stable self-confidence and sense of one's worth.[40] In her essay on post-adolescent identity Jacobson brings together these two aspects of vitality. She points out that distorted object relations, which have undermined the formation of stable identifications and the development of the superego during childhood, are likely to give rise, during adolescence, to problems of identity both in the sense of depersonalization and in the area of self-confidence. In fact, when primitive narcissistic conflicts reemerge during adolescence, they tend to be associated with a constant lack of self-esteem, which in turn manifests itself again in terms of *shame* and *feelings of inferiority*.[41]

Mahler connects the perception of the self as worthy of love and esteem with the process of separation-individuation and in particular with the delicate phase of *practicing*. In this phase any severe failure on the mother's part to fully accept the child's complex response to the exhilaration of managing to walk is likely to result in a lack of self-esteem and a heightened narcissistic vulnerability.[42]

Partly following Jacobson's account, Kernberg links the lack of a cohesive identity with vitality in a causal nexus. The individual with a pathological fusion of images of the self, of the ideal self and of the ideal object also has, typically, an extremely volatile self-esteem. This creates in the individual a heightened narcissistic vulnerability and generates, in response, a propensity to withdraw from social contact. The identity of the narcissistically disturbed individual shows then the typical combination of feelings of inferiority and "overde-pendence on external admiration and acclaim," and is characterized by "chronic feelings of boredom and emptiness" and by a "chronic uncertainty and dissatis-faction with life." The presence of these traits leads the person to a compensatory search for "brilliance, wealth, power, and beauty" (Kernberg 1976: 331) – a search doomed to failure in the long run despite temporary successes, in that the admiration supposed to compensatorily strengthen and enliven the self undergoes a sudden devaluation as soon as it is received.

Finally, Sullivan connects this subdimension of vitality with the satisfaction of the need to express one's abilities, from infantile play to the creativity or aesthetic receptivity of the adult.[43] To a successful and uninhibited expression of these abilities corresponds, according to Sullivan, a perception of the self linked with joy and with heightened self-esteem.

Traces of this subdimension of vitality, however, can be found even on the inhospitable terrain of Freudian metapsychology. As early as 1896, in his "Further remarks on the neuropsychoses of defence," Freud points out that in obsessional neuroses the primary symptom which the patient forms against an originary self-accusation is a total lack of self-confidence,[44] while the primary affect generated by the self-accusation is *shame*. Also in his "Draft K" and in subsequent works, up to his 1917 discussion of melancholia, Freud continues to include shame among the affects associated with self-deprecatory feelings.

From a second perspective, vitality can be understood as a *capacity for enjoy-ment* and for *taking interest in life*. Its opposite is an attitude of apathy and withdrawal. Interesting remarks on this subdimension can be found again in Freud and also in Sullivan and Klein.

In the "Drafts," vitality as a capacity to enjoy and take interest in life is related by Freud to the phenomena of mourning and melancholia. One of the components of melancholia is the loss of all interest in sexuality and some-times in food: anorexia is considered by Freud a case of melancholia in individuals whose sexuality has not yet fully developed. This loss of interest in sex and food, however, is conceived by Freud as a symptom of a broader loss of interest in life, a sort of letting oneself live. The relation of melancholia to this aspect of vitality becomes clearer as the meaning of the term "melan-cholia" gradually shifts within Freud's work. While in 1895 melancholia was defined as a "mourning over loss of libido" (Freud 1895a: 201), in 1917 he characterizes it as a "profoundly painful dejection," an "abrogation of interest in the external world," a "loss of the capacity to love," an "inhibition of all activity" and, finally, he associates it with an "extraordinary fall in self-esteem" linked with an "impoverishment of the ego on a grand scale" (Freud 1917b: 457).

The same elements, except the fall in self-esteem and the impoverishment of the ego, define mourning. A crucial difference, however, separates mourning and melancholia. Mourning is in the service of life in that it performs the func-tion of detaching the libido from the lost object through the evocation and temporary overcathexis of all the memories and expectations linked with the lost object. When this work of detachment and separation is accomplished the ego "becomes free and uninhibited again" (Freud 1917b: 457), ready to orient its interest toward the external world again, to cathect new objects and undertake new activities. The work of mourning consists, from the perspective outlined here, of favoring the individual's reappropriation of his or her own vitality after the loss of the object. As a pathological condition in which the lost object has remained unconscious, instead, melancholia exhibits a number of traits that fall under the heading of a lack of vitality as lack of self-esteem: (1) a self-diminishing of the ego (here used as an equivalent of the self); (2) the moral condemnation of one's ego; (3) the sense of its unworthiness and of the unworthiness of everything associated with it. However, this attitude, strangely enough, does not generate the sense of shame and withdrawal which could be expected, but rather leads the melancholic to an "insistent talking about himself" associated with a sort of "pleasure in the consequent exposure of himself" (Freud 1917b: 458). Typically, melancholia issues in a kind of manic pseudovitality which Freud views as its flip side. Once the libido is detached from the object onto which it was directed, melancholia tends to turn into maniacal forms of "joy, triumph, exultation." This phenomenon takes place because at that point "the whole amount of anti-cathexis which the painful suffering of melancholia drew from the ego and 'bound' has become available" (Freud 1917b: 463). As when a long and toilsome battle is finally won or when an intensive effort is rendered superfluous by the fortuitous attainment of its goal, so when the libido is detached from its object a tremendous quantity of psychic energy is released and made available, and this release of energy results in a joyous and light-hearted mood, in a boundless self-confidence and in a propensity to undertake new endeavors. Here we find a surprising anticipation, within Freud's work, of Kohut's basic idea of an oscillation between the actual emptiness and inertia of the self and the activation of compensatory grandiose fantasies accompanied by a narcissistic pseudovitality.

The notion of vitality as the opposite of apathy plays an important role in Sullivan's view of the optimal development of the self. Vitality as such ultimately means for Sullivan maximization of psychic dynamism. From a genetic point of view vitality as *active interest in life* and a *capacity to enjoy it* has its roots in the relationship with a non-anxious mother – namely, a relationship in which the terrifying experience of total anxiety, destined to be internalized as the not-me, is reduced to a minimum and the experience of increasing anxiety, less devastating but nonetheless negative, does not confer preponderance to needs for security within the personality. If, instead, the first object relations have been heavily marked by experiences of increasing anxiety and of terror, a kind of disturbance will follow, which Sullivan characterizes as "apathy" with reference to the instinctual plane and as "somnolent detachment" with reference to the object-relation plane. Apathy is for Sullivan a psychic dynamism which enables the child to protect him- or herself against the dreadful experience of combined lack of maternal empathy, anxiety and terror. Apathy protects the child's psychic integrity at the cost of his or her vitality through the temporary attenuation of the child's primary needs, for example hunger and thirst. However, the child who faces a state of intense and prolonged anxiety induced by the relation to the mother usually responds not simply with apathy but with what Sullivan calls "somnolent detachment," a kind of emotional "pulling the plug" on the environment responsible for the state of terror.[45]

Melanie Klein brings out the relation of vitality (understood as "capacity of enjoyment") to envy.[46] Noteworthy here is Klein's tendency to associate enjoyment and libido or, better said, enjoyment and love – otherwise her reference to gratitude could not be explained – as well as her neglect of the relation of enjoyment to self-realization. Furthermore, in the case of the "overadapted child," discussed in *The Psychoanalysis of Children* (1959), a disturbed relation to play and the imagination is argued to reflect a general lack of vitality. Underneath the appearance of a "good and clever" child often lies an internal lack of vitality, understood as a lack of genuine interest and curiosity, as an inhibited approach to play which confines the child to "games with no imaginative content," and as a "repression of imaginative life" which is part of a larger renunciation of life – the price to be paid for the containment of one's anxiety and feelings of guilt.[47] This aspect of vitality, which in the child is connected with play, in the adult is related to the capacity of truly "enjoying," in a less instinctual and more existential sense, one's own interests and successes.

Closely related to the readiness to enjoy life is a third sense in which the theme of vitality appears in psychoanalytic theory, especially in Mahler's and Jacobson's work. Vitality becomes synonymous with an *effervescent mood*, a sanguine euphoria which can be contrasted with depression and a sense of depletion. Mahler points to a general mood of "low-keyness" which results from separation anxiety and from an excessively prolonged absence of the mother.[48] Interesting considerations on the opposition of euphoria and depression can also be found in Jacobson's *Depression* (1971) and in Kernberg's *Internal World and External Reality* (1985).

A fourth aspect of the vitality of an identity – emphasized by many authors – has to do with a sense of *undoubtful self-presence* and with the unproblematic, immediately self-evident quality of being who one is and doing what one is doing. The phenomenological correlate of the lack of this aspect of vitality is best reflected in the words of Helen Deutsch's patient who says "Everything seems unreal to me" (Deutsch 1942: 301). The subdimension of immediate and undoubtful self-presence is present mainly in Sullivan and Fairbairn. For Sullivan the sense of unrealness is caused by the prevailing of what he calls *needs for security*, satisfiable only through unconscious but unavoidable "operations," such as acting "as if" and dissimulating, over what he calls *needs for satisfaction*, concrete and satisfiable in a direct and conscious way. The repeated recourse to operations aimed at satisfying needs for security leads the individual to a sort of rigidity and emotional impassiveness from which follows a sense of detachment from reality, a sense of the self being quite "not there" (Sullivan 1953: 346–7).

The subdimension of vitality as undoubtful self-presence is implicitly presupposed also in Fairbairn's discussion of schizoid states and personalities. The schizoid individual remains entangled in the following double bind: on the one hand his or her failure to cathect the object leads to the loss of the object, but on the other hand, because the libido possesses a destructive quality for the schizoid personality, also the successful object-cathexis results in the ultimate loss of the object.[49] The insoluble quality of this dilemma generates a sense of impotence and futility which characterizes, as the opposite of vitality, the identity of a schizoid individual and is felicitously described by that patient of Fairbairn's who says: "I can't say anything. I have nothing to say. I'm empty. There's nothing of me. . . . I feel quite useless. . . . I don't feel anything. . . . I can't express myself; I feel futile" (Fairbairn 1986: 51). What we hear from this patient is but an extreme form of a self-perception which in milder forms is quite widespread. In fact, in his essay "Schizoid factors in the personality" Fairbairn denies that any person, even the most normal, might be entirely free from ego-splitting: "The basic position in the psyche is invariably a schizoid position" (Fairbairn 1986: 8). The reason for this universality of the schizoid position lies, according to Fairbairn, in the fact that the splitting of the ego in turn derives from the internalization of bad objects[50] and that such internalization, caused by the unavoidable frustrations to be experienced in any object relation, is completely involuntary. A complete absence of splitting, whose phenomenological counterpart would be a crackless integration of the ego and a perfect vitality, could only exist in the case, extremely improbable though in principle not impossible, of an individual who has never undergone any frustration.[51]

Finally, related to the vigor and immediacy of one's self-feeling is a fifth and fundamental aspect of vitality: namely, the perception of one's self as *genuine* and *spontaneous*. The opposite of vitality, in this case, is a feeling of emptiness, meaninglessness and futility often accompanied by an experience of the self as not simply "absent" but also false, "phony." Winnicott and Kohut are the two authors who more insistently have emphasized this specific dimension of a fulfilled or authentic identity.

In his 1960 essay "Ego distortion in terms of true and false self" Winnicott compares the sense of strength and vitality linked with the self-perception of the true self with the sense of futility and unreality linked with the self-perception of the false self. The true self emerges spontaneously as a way of being experienced by the individual within a relationship with a holding environment. The true self is spontaneity of gesture and the perception of this spontaneity as expressive of the self; it is related to the primary process and has an active and not reactive nature: its inherent vitality originates in these qualities. Instead, when the mother's capacity for mirroring is inadequate – for example, because she is incapable of first creating and then sustaining her child's illusion of omnipotence, or because she insists on imposing her own gestures as the sole gestures endowed with meaning, or because she lets the illusion of omnipotence break down in a traumatic way – a *false self* arises, which is assigned the function of hiding and protecting the true self, and of managing the individual's transactions with the external world on an overadaptive basis.[52] The false self, modeled via imitation after the expectations first of the mother and then of the other significant figures, experiences even its own drives and affects as coming *from without* – namely, as demands imposed by the environment – and consequently views its own actions as mere responses to external stimuli and thus as inauthentic.

The possible relations between true and false self range from the pathological extreme of a false self which *completely conceals* the true self to the absolutely normal use of a superficial false self, which is in charge of *polite* social conduct and of procuring the person "the place in society which can never be attained or maintained by the true self alone" (Winnicott 1960: 143). At the various intervals on the scale we find, moving from the more pathological to the closer to normality, personalities in which the false self defends the true self as a potential future identity and allows it a secret life, personalities in which the false self "has as its main concern a search for conditions which will make it possible for the true self to come into his own" (Winnicott 1960: 142–3), and personalities in which the false self is built upon archaic identifications. Interesting is the fact that for Winnicott the line between the pathological and the normal by no means coincides with the presence or absence of a false self. Optimal is for Winnicott a personality which exists and manifests itself mostly as a true self but is also able, if necessary, to comply with the environment through a false self without giving this compliance any meaning other than that of a temporary compromise. When the existence of the self is jeopardized, the normal person immediately breaks the compromise and pierces through the veil of the false self. The line between pathological and normal thus has to do for Winnicott with the easiness or difficulty (up to the extreme of impossibility) with which control over one's conduct can be shifted back to the true self once the false self is in charge.

An important characteristic of the true self and of the feeling of vitality and spontaneity linked with it is its potential for an exponential growth. In other words, the more undisturbed the development of the true self, the more the child grows able to work through without damage the interruptions in the continuity of "true self living" which are required by the environment, and to assimilate experiences of temporary interaction on the basis of a false self without undermining the possibility of a subsequent return to the spontaneity of the true self.[53] Winnicott shares with Fairbairn and Kohut the idea that the process of consolidation of the self does not need to be stimulated from without, but from the outside can only be blocked, delayed or distorted if the person undergoes negative experiences of traumatic proportion. Interesting also is the way in which Winnicott reinterprets the concept of "ego strength," spelled out by Freud in terms of self-reflection, from the standpoint of vitality. The dimension of vitality comes to acquire, through its connection with the reformulated notion of "ego strength," a new facet, constituted by the feeling of "existing in one's own right."

In *Playing and Reality* (1971), Winnicott enriches the dimension of vitality with new connotations that originate in a parallel with creativity and play. Purely fantastic play, then interactive games, and finally that most elaborate form of play constituted by culture, art and religion all originate in that intermediate space between the self and the external world called by Winnicott "the space of transitional phenomena."[54] These phenomena share with culture and play the property of being located neither inside nor outside, of being neither pure hallucinations nor actual perceptions. Rather, they occupy a space and a status in between the two worlds. They are situations, activities and symbolic complexes in which, as in magic or in that reality *sui generis* created by the work of art, the contact with, and the transformation of, the external world take place in the service of fantasy. The boundary between the special worlds of art, religion and culture on one hand and pure hallucination on the other is conceived by Winnicott in developmental and intersubjective terms. Art and delusion have common roots, but their difference with respect to hallucinations lies in their social, shared, communal as opposed to private, idiosyncratic nature.

> There is a no-man's land between the subjective and what it is objectively perceived that is natural to infancy. . . . The infant is not challenged at first, does not have to decide, can be allowed to claim of something that is borderline, that it is at one and the same time self-created and perceived or accepted from the world. . . . Someone claiming indulgence in this respect at a later age is called mad. In religion and in the arts, we see the claim socialized so that the individual is not called mad and can enjoy, in the exercise of religion or the practice and appreciation of the arts, the rest that human beings need from absolute and never-failing discrimination between fact and fantasy.
>
> (Winnicott 1988: 107)

According to Winnicott, only in play is the individual in a position to be *creative* in the sense of being able to act with spontaneity, to engage his or her entire personality and to realize his or her true self. This is not to say that other activities, for instance politics, scientific research, managerial action, sport or medical practice do not allow for the expression of creativity. Rather, in these activities, for Winnicott, creativity is possible insofar as one is able to transfer within them, at least partially, that way of relating to the world which is typical of play.

Play stands, according to Winnicott, in a complex relationship with the self and with the drives. Play is not to be understood as a domain of action within which the individual can search for his or her true self in the sense of trying to understand who he or she is. To the contrary, the self must already exist in order for play to be possible.[55] Furthermore, the pleasure brought by play has nothing to do with pleasure in an instinctual sense. Rather, it is linked with the expression of the true self. In fact, the breaking in of the drives within a playful activity immediately interrupts the "play situation" and instates, in its lieu, a "serious" activity of an erotic or aggressive nature.[56] From this perspective the exercise of creativity, which Winnicott separates from artistic activity and considers from the standpoint not of its end result but of the ongoing process of self-expression, is strictly linked with the dimension of vitality. In Winnicott's words:

> It is creative apperception more than anything else that makes the individual feel that life is worth living. Contrasted with this is a relationship to external reality which is one of compliance, the world and its details being recognized only as something to be fitted in with or demanding adaptation. Compliance carries with it a sense of futility for the individual and is associated with the idea that nothing matters and that life is not worth living.
>
> (Winnicott 1971: 76)

Together with coherence, vitality as spontaneity and genuineness of the self is a crucial dimension of the fulfillment of an identity for Kohut.[57] In general, the perception of the self as genuine is considered by Kohut not only another product of the empathic mirroring and successful idealization which form the basis of the *coherence* of the self, but also a function of a specific capability of the self – namely, its capacity to reconcile the search for pleasure and the striving for its own realization. Harmony between these two aspects of psychic life is at the basis of the individual's feeling of being living a satisfactory life, whereas conflict between them leads to a feeling of stagnation and meaninglessness. As Kohut points out, harmony and conflict between the pleasure-seeking and the fulfillment-seeking aspects of the person depend not on quantitative factors, such as the proportional distribution and strength of the two areas, but rather on the *way* in which they are related. On one hand the possible primacy of the fulfillment-seeking tendencies over the pleasure-seeking drives need not lead to intrapsychic conflict,

> if the pleasure-seeking sector subordinates itself smoothly to the supraordinated goals of the self; no conflict, in other words, arises under these conditions if the individual is able to enjoy the exercise of his special talents and of his workaday skills in the service of the nuclear ambitions and ideals of the self. The predominance, on the other hand, of the pleasure seeking tendencies does not lead to conflict if the self can subordinate itself, i.e., if the self is able to relinquish its

insistence on the expression of its basic design and is satisfied with the limited supraordinated function of lending a sense of wholeness and continuity to the area of pleasures and skills, of lending a sense of purposive unity to man of love and work.

(Kohut 1978: 760)

Kohut does not say much about the cases in which the two components enter a conflictual relation. While the history of art, of literature and of science abounds with cases of individuals who have succeeded in combining a life of fulfillment-oriented and creative achievement with instinctual frustration, it remains unclear how it could be possible, from Kohut's perspective, for someone to give up the search for the realization of the nuclear core of his or her self without thereby dooming him- or herself to an endless depression and ultimately to a self-disintegration best exemplified by Ivan Illyitch, Tolstoy's character who ends his life in despair upon realizing that he has wasted his life in pursuing those things which he actually has managed to attain. In another passage, however, Kohut allows for the possibility that an individual might renounce self-realization while nonetheless continuing to perceive his or her self with joy and pride, if only the person is able to alienate a part of his or her autonomy to a collective or an ideal aim which becomes the object of total identification. "This kind of psychological balance," adds Kohut, "might well be of great importance in the totalitarian societies of our time and could become the healthy norm in the mass societies of the future" (Kohut 1978: 760). In other words, the link between vitality and self-realization can be severed if one is prepared to abdicate one's *autonomy*. This leads us to a third dimension of the fulfillment of an identity: *depth*.

Depth

In its most general sense the dimension of *depth* designates a person's capacity to have access to his or her own psychic dynamisms and to reflect such awareness in the construction of his or her identity. From this perspective, the depth of an individual identity is located somewhere on a continuum delimited by two extremes that are equally non-human. At one extreme we find the *absolute shallowness* of an identity which contains no reference whatsoever to its constitutive mechanisms – for example, the spatio-temporal identities of the animals belonging to the more developed species. At the other end of the spectrum we find the *absolute transparency* of an identity which has access to, and incorporates in a reflective way, *all* its constitutive psychic processes – for example, the identity of such philosophical creatures as Kant's "pure rational beings," Hegel's Spirit at the stage of Absolute Knowledge, or Nozick's "self-choosers."

Within depth, just as within coherence and vitality, different subdimensions can be discerned. In the first place, it is possible to conceive the depth of an identity in purely cognitive terms, as *self-knowledge* or *self-reflection*. This aspect of the fulfillment of an identity has traditionally exerted the greatest influence within Western culture, from Plato to Freud. Only in our century have we begun to see it under a more skeptical light and to understand it as just *one* element of self-fulfillment. From the standpoint of self-reflectiveness, for an individual to have depth means to be as aware as possible of the nature and force of his or her motivations. To be shallow, instead, means to ignore one's own inner dynamics and to be unwittingly "acted upon" by them. Should we reductively equate authenticity with this specific understanding of *depth*, our conception would then be vulnerable to Sartre's charge of internal inconsistency.[58]

In its pure form, a view of the depth of an identity as self-knowledge or self-reflectiveness can be found only in Freud's early writings. "To make the unconscious conscious" is the famous formulation with which Freud, in *The Interpretation of Dreams*, tries to capture not only the therapeutic aim of psychoanalysis but also an implicit view of psychic "normality."[59] Even within the framework of *The Interpretation of Dreams*, however, self-reflectiveness is never understood by Freud as the psychological counterpart of an absolute self-transparency of the subject. A complete transparency of the self remains impossible for Freud.[60] His view of ontogenetic and philogenetic development does not allow for such a possibility. According to Freud, in fact, initially – at the origins both of the species and of the individual – the psyche in its entirety is constituted by the unconscious. The preconscious arises only subsequently. Thus there must exist a set of psychic events and states which precede the topographical differentiation of the psyche and cannot – as the later states and events – be worked through via the use of associations. Only the subset of the unconscious constituted by repressed contents can, through a difficult and toilsome exploration, be brought back to light and made accessible to consciousness. Thus "to make the unconscious conscious" means, within a metapsychological framework according to which the prime movers of the psyche are conceived as *wishes*, to become aware of the unconscious wishes which influence our conscious motivations. It also means to become aware of the way in which unconscious wishes, by entering complex combinations with more superficial materials capable of "carrying" them, gain access to the dream stage or give rise to parapraxes, symptoms and the like. To make the unconscious conscious ultimately means, as Freud put it a few years later, "to enable the patient to obtain a conscious grasp of his unconscious desires" (Freud 1909: 120).

The expression "to be acted upon," as opposed to "to act," leads us to the second facet of depth – an aspect which is sometimes difficult to sharply distinguish from the first. This second aspect has to do with a *practical* plane and with the realm of action rather than with a cognitive axis. The important distinction is here between *autonomy*, understood in a broad sense as the independence of the will from external influences, and *heteronomy* understood as the condition of being the instrument of someone else's will. Depth in the sense of *autonomy* is the subdimension best captured by Freud's revised formulation of his therapeutic ideal. With the rise of the structural model the older formula "to make the unconscious conscious" becomes "Where id was, ego shall be."[61] An indication of the completion of the transition from the notion of fulfillment as self-reflection to a view of fulfillment centered on autonomy is offered by the occurrence of new metaphors. In his *New Introductory Lectures* Freud describes the realm of the repressed as an "inner enemy territory" (Freud 1933: 57) which the ego must conquer, and characterizes the therapeutic aim of psychoanalysis as "to strengthen the ego, to make it more independent of the Super-ego, to broaden its perceptive field and improve its organization, so that it can annex new territories of the id." Therapy is ultimately a matter of "land-reclamation as, for instance, the reclamation of the Zuidersee" (Freud 1933: 80). Unlike the Zuidersee, however, the id cannot be reclaimed in its entirety. If it could be drained completely, furthermore, this would put an end to all vitality.[62] The issue is addressed by Freud on the basis of another metaphor, in which the pair horse/rider stands for the pair id/ego.[63] It is unclear whether for Freud an ideal psychic state can be imagined in which the rider can lead the id without ever being led or if, instead, the "not precisely ideal situation" in which the rider only leads the horse in the direction where the horse has decided to go anyway is an inevitable corollary to the human condition. Later, Freud ironically observed that in this respect we are all "Sunday riders" or "dilettantes."

The subdimension of autonomy plays a significant role also in Melanie Klein's theorizing. For example, she suggests that a relation not merely censorious but also cooperative between ego and superego must be present within the individual who attains a normal post-adolescent balance. The cooperative dimension of the relation allows the person to develop internal and self-imposed standards. On the other hand, the failure to reach such relative independence from the standards of one's internalized objects is viewed by Klein as a "characteriologic failure" which dooms one to remain for the rest of one's life in a state of subservience to the external environment.[64]

Finally, to possess depth means to be *relatively self-sufficient*, as opposed to being pathologically dependent on someone else's resources. In this sense depth manifests itself as a *capacity to be alone* – namely, as the ability to suspend *only temporarily* one's relations to the self-objects, a suspension that leaves the relation intact and raises no claim to an overcoming of the need for mirroring and idealization.

In an essay on the subject Winnicott suggests that the capacity to be alone emerges from the experience "of being alone, as a small child, *in the presence of the mother*" (Winnicott 1958) – an experience which presupposes the existence of a dependable mother – a mother whose reliability enables the child to be and at the same time to enjoy being alone for a limited period of time. This relation is the forerunner of a *mature dependency*, to put it with Fairbairn, or of a *relative independence* from others, in which the capacity to enjoy "being alone" rests on the capacity to trust the continuity of the mirroring provided by the other person.[65]

In a sense, the entire history of the psychoanalytic tradition can be seen as a gradual taking-distance from the cognitivistic ideal of knowing as much as possible of the unconscious. Even Freud, as we have seen, expressed the ideal in such terms only in *The Interpretation of Dreams* and soon replaced it with a more differentiated vision, articulated in the formula "Where id was, ego shall be." In *Civilization and its Discontents* we find a more radical relativization of the moment of self-reflection within the dimension of depth. While on one hand the ego's propensity to detach itself, through knowledge, reflection and rationality, from the immediacy of the id is considered an adaptive asset, on the other hand Freud describes such detachment as a severance from the true sources of psychic life and thus somehow as an impoverishment. Later, the theorists of the object-relation school, and especially Heinz Kohut, by focusing on the relation of the self to its constituents, would relativize the relevance of depth for self-fulfillment even more. During the last years of his life Freud's implicit view of the fulfillment of an identity and of the role of depth underwent another change of emphasis, again in the direction of a further downplaying of autonomy and self-reflection. In *Analysis Terminable and Interminable* (1937) a new relation of fulfillment to depth and coherence begins to emerge. Freud suggests that the permanent and definitive neutralization of an instinctual urge cannot be equated with its complete disappearance. Such disappearance would be "in general impossible" and *not at all desirable* (Freud 1937: 225). Instead, expressions such as "permanent elimination" and "complete mastery on the part of the ego" are to be understood as simply referring to a sort of "binding" of the drive, whereby the drive "is brought completely into the harmony of the ego, becomes accessible to all the influences of the other trends in the ego and no longer seeks to go its independent way to satisfaction" (Freud 1937: 225). Psychoanalytic cure is no longer conceived as a matter of totally eliminating the past repressions. Neither can it be likened to the yearly clean-out of an attic, when all the contents of the attic are displayed in the living-room in order to choose what, after dusting or mending, is still worth keeping and what is to be thrown away. The "strengthening of the ego" has come to mean, in this new context, an *ex post facto* rectification of the older repressions.[66] What at the beginning was posited as the aim *par excellence* of psychoanalysis – the "bringing to light what is hidden in the id" – is now considered only "half" of the analytic task by Freud. The *other* half has to do with the analysis of the ego's mechanisms of defense, which "recur in the treatment as *resistances* against recovery" (Freud 1937: 224–5). But *knowing* these resistances is no longer enough. The analytic process does not come to an end with the awareness of resistances and of the episodes of repression of which they are the repetition, but must proceed one step further and replace the defenses with equally reliable but egosyntonic mechanisms. In sum, the later Freud embraces a more complex view of the person and of identity – a view in which the primacy of autonomy replaces the ideal of self-knowledge and is counterbalanced by a holistic and integrative perspective that brings the dimension of coherence to centerstage.

Half a century later, a significantly different conception of the role of depth within the fulfillment of identity can be seen at work in Kohut's "psychology of the self." Kohut discusses several clinical cases in which it appears counterproductive to push analysis beyond a certain point in the attempt to throw light on the archaic traumata of the patient.[67] More generally, when confronted with the compensatory and defensive structures built by the patient in order to remedy the empathic failures of early self-objects and attain fulfillment, the analyst guided by the "psychology of the self" must strive to firm of the patient's self by stimulating a resumption – favored by the analysts' ability for mirroring, more than by their ability for interpretation – of the process of transmuting internalization. The unraveling of the most archaic roots of the patient's disturbance, instead, is seen by Kohut as an attempt of no therapeutic relevance and potentially harmful. From a broader theoretical standpoint Kohut takes distance from Freud's faith in the intrinsic desirability of self-reflection and in the impossibility of "excessive" self-knowledge, as well as from Freud's ideal of acquiring the capacity to "accept the truth, reject the illusions" (Freud 1933: Lecture 35). Kohut considers such stances an expression of the Enlightenment prejudices characteristic of the early psychoanalytic movement and of its scientist faith in the possibility of an objective knowledge of the psyche. Despite his polemical tone, it must be noted that Kohut too cannot but implicitly assign an important role to the dimension of depth. The individual who knows more about the nuclear program of his or her own self, or at least about the pole of ambitions within that program, is more likely to succeed in attaining self-realization. Finally, in Kohut's work another facet of depth is present which represents an important variation on the theme of autonomy – a subdimension which I will call "sovereignty" and to which I will return after discussing the dimension of maturity.

Maturity

Finally, a fulfilled identity possesses to some extent a quality of *maturity* understood, in general, as the ability and willingness to come to terms with the facticity of the natural and social world, as well as of the internal world, without thereby compromising one's coherence and vitality – without becoming another. The dimension of maturity also includes a number of specific aspects. First, maturity can be understood as the capacity to distinguish between one's own representations, projections or wishes, and reality "as it is" or, better said, as it appears to those who interact with us and to unconcerned third parties. From this standpoint the difference between maturity and immaturity can be conceived as the opposition between a *rigorous application of reality-testing* and *indulgence in wishful thinking*. A special emphasis on this subdimension can be found in the work of Freud, Klein, Jacobson and Kernberg, whereas dissonant variations are present in Winnicott. Freud's distinction of primary and secondary processes represents an extremely dichotomous way to conceptualize this idea of maturity, but conveys the essential point. As early as in his "Project for a scientific psychology" Freud addresses the distinction between primary and secondary processes and develops a sketchy idea of "reality-testing" (Freud 1895b: 324–7). In *The Interpretation of Dreams*, he illustrates the importance of the role of the secondary process with reference to the evolution of the individual and of the species. Initially the psychic apparatus is a reflex apparatus so designed "that any sensory excitation impinging on it could be promptly discharged along a motor path" (Freud 1900: 565). While this discharge cannot in and of itself assuage the internal need, which continues to make itself felt, a perceivable change occurs when a *gratifying* experience, fortuitously obtained, temporarily interrupts the stimulus. The mnemic image of the perception which led to satisfaction (for example, the image of food), argues Freud, "remains associated thenceforward with the memory trace of the excitation produced by the need." Consequently, every time the need arises "a psychical impulse will at once emerge which will seek to re-cathect the mnemic image of the perception and to reevoke the perception itself, that is to say, to re-establish the situation of the original satisfaction" (Freud 1900: 565–6). This psychic impulse is a wish. But if the re-evoked perception rests on hallucination rather than on a modification of the external world, gratification cannot last in the long run and the original need reemerges unchanged. One must then assume, argues Freud, that a "bitter experience of life must have changed this primitive thought-activity into a more expedient secondary one" (Freud 1900: 566), in which a second psychic system, namely the ego, seeks to satisfy desires and needs *indirectly*, by modifying reality through the use of motility in the service of predetermined goals. The dream, however, with its hallucinatory mode of satisfaction, continues to exist as an evolutionary remnant of the most primitive mode of functioning, much as "primitive weapons, the bows and arrows, that have been abandoned by adult men, turn up once more in the nursery" (Freud 1900: 567).

Also for Melanie Klein the ability to tell reality from wishes is an important subdimension of the fulfillment of an identity. It takes, however, a somewhat different coloring. The ability to form realistic images of our objects means, from her perspective, to be able to form images that reflect both the good and the bad aspects of the object. This capacity develops in three stages. First the child projects outside phantastic, and usually aggressive, objects which are generated internally. These phantasies are accompanied by a sense of omnipotence and leave almost no room for reality-testing. Subsequently the projective images of internal objects become fused with the properties of real objects as they are perceived by the child. The presence and the loving qualities of such real objects in turn contribute to mitigate the terrifying character of the phantastic objects. Finally, the ego tries to reconcile the two sets of objects in stable images of new internal objects, more realistic and integrated.[68]

Also for Jacobson, a realistic perception of others and the capacity to relate to them in a projection-free way are fundamental aspects of the fulfillment of an identity. Their rise depends on the attainment of (1) the capacity to conceive the future, (2) the capacity to isolate single characteristics, physical and psychic, of one's love objects, (3) the capacity to grasp similarities and differences between objects, and (4) the capacity to distinguish between self and objects. From her perspective, the achievement of maturity consists in the substitution of the desire to be *like* the loved objects for the more archaic desire to remain *part* of them or to *incorporate* them into one's self.[69]

For Kernberg this subdimension of maturity is connected with the dimension of coherence and, more specifically, of demarcation: the failure to realistically perceive self and others depends, according to Kernberg, on the pathological fusion of images of the ideal self, the ideal object and the real self – a confusion caused by the inadequacy of maternal empathy or by an exceptionally strong aggressive drive. This fusion leads, among other things, to a devaluation and destruction of the internalized object images. This does not mean that the individual has no internal images of the object – "it would probably be impossible to live under such conditions" – but that "the remnants of the internalized object representations acquire the characteristics of real, but rather lifeless, shadowy people" (Kernberg 1976: 233). These images of other people appear almost like caricatures,

> and the patient has great difficulty integrating the perception of others into a significant whole; therefore, he has no or very little capacity for empathy or for realistic judgment of others in depth, and his behavior is regulated by immediate perceptions rather than by an ongoing, consistent, internalized model of others, which ordinarily would be available to the self.
>
> (Kernberg 1976: 138)

As anticipated above, there are some dissonant voices. Winnicott is one of these. In *Playing and Reality* (1971), he adds a cultural and aesthetic facet to the dimension of maturity, often conceived solely in instrumental or adaptive terms. According to Winnicott, it is in playing rather than in the context of instrumental activities that "the individual child or adult is able to be creative and to use the whole personality" (Winnicott 1971: 63). In the special reality created by the presumption of magical omnipotence typical of the child, by play and by the work of art emerges the positive valence of the experience of *illusion*. The originality of Winnicott's thought consists in his reconciling, or at least somehow connecting, two things that the culture of the Enlightenment, to which Freud's work is heir, sought to separate by an unbridgeable cleavage: human maturity and the capacity to create and enjoy illusion. Winnicott's uneasiness with the adaptive orientation of the "party of maturity" emerges from a passage of *Playing and Reality* in which he contrasts maturity and vitality. Writes Winnicott:

People may be leading satisfactory lives and may do work that is even of exceptional value and yet may be schizoid or schizophrenic. They may be ill in a psychiatric sense because of a weak reality sense. To balance this one would have to state that there are others who are so firmly anchored in objectively perceived reality that they are ill in the opposite direction of being out of touch with the subjective world and with the creative approach to fact.[70]

(Winnicott 1971: 78)

In a second sense, the maturity of an identity includes the capacity to maintain a certain congruence between our ideal self and the actual potentials of our real self. From this perspective, the opposition of maturity and immaturity comes down to the opposition between a *narcissistic grandiosity*, either of an exhibitionistic or of an idealizing nature, and the *perspicuity* or *lucidity* of a person who, under the guidance of experience and reflection, is able to realign the ideal self with the reality of his or her needs and capacities. The notion of "coming to terms" with internal reality, however, must not be confused with conformity. It is not with one's *social opportunities* that the choice of who one wants to be must be commensurate, but rather with one's own *internal configuration* of needs and abilities. In fact, many fulfilling human lives have been lived in opposition to normative orders which limited the person's social opportunity to be who he or she, internally, wanted to be and could have been.

On this dimension of authenticity, understood as a taming of the quasi-natural propensity toward feelings of omnipotence, interesting reflections can be found in Freud's "On narcissism: an introduction" (1914) as well as in *Totem and Taboo* (1913). The "primitive mind" is naturally inclined toward *megalomania*, maintains Freud. It is characterized by an "overestimation of the power of wishes and mental acts," by its belief in the "omnipotence of thoughts" and by its faith in "the thaumaturgic virtue of words" (Freud 1914: 75). This feeling of omnipotence, continues Freud in some of his more positivistic passages, today lives on only in the way in which young children and neurotics relate to the external world. But then within the same paragraph Freud observes quite ironically that something of this omnipotence still survives in the modern mind, in the form of a faith in the capacity of the human mind to grasp the laws of reality.[71]

This aspect of maturity understood as realism in conceiving one's ideals and as a capacity to emotionally accept one's limitations is echoed by almost all the authors considered. For example, it is echoed in Sullivan's account of the "security operations" enacted by individuals who create grandiose images of the self or "wish-fulfilling fantasies" for the purpose of controlling their own anxiety,[72] in Jacobson's theory of the transition from the archaic desire to merge with the object to the wish to be like it (a transition in which one has to give up precisely an archaic sense of omnipotence), in Mahler's view of the separation–individuation process,[73] and in Kernberg's theory of narcissistic disturbances as stemming from the pathological fusion of real self, ideal self and ideal object.[74] Finally, we find in Kohut a notion of maturity as the gradual relinquishing of the grandiose fantasies of the exhibitionistic self and the gradual "relativization" of one's ideals, which means not to devalue such ideals but to abandon the pretense of their absolute perfection and, furthermore, to relativize *all* claims to perfection. In a mature individual, grandiose exhibitionism and the search for absolute perfection give way to a "healthy self-affirmation" and a "healthy admiration" for one's idealized self-objects. From the standpoint of pathology, instead, traumatic frustrations in the phase of consolidation of the self lead to a quest for fusion with omnipotent figures or for the compensatory attainment of symbols of their power.[75]

A third aspect of maturity, emphasized mainly by Freud and Edith Jacobson, concerns the opposition of *flexibility* and *rigidity*. There are many ways of pursuing one's ends and of trying to fulfill one's self. A mature individual takes this variety into account, knows how to select alternative ways of coming to terms with the world, can readily grasp the equivalence of alternative routes to his ends, and is prepared to backtrack when the chosen path proves to be a dead end. The complex of abilities summed up under the heading of *flexibility*, however, must not be confused with the unprincipled directionlessness of a weak identity. The contrary of flexibility is represented by the *rigidity* with which the obsessive neurotic individual follows his or her rituals and depends on them for giving sense to his or her conduct, or by the rigidity with which normal but immature individuals cannot distance themselves from what was previously planned. Lack of maturity in this particular sense is exemplified, for Freud, by the rigidity which characterizes the obsessional neurotic's dependency, for the satisfaction of certain needs and instinctual aims, on the fastidious repetition of rituals that cannot be infringed but at the cost of intense psychic suffering.[76] Edith Jacobson gives flexibility a moral turn. For her rigidity is connected with obsessive traits and with the lack of autonomy from parental models, while flexibility stands for a capacity to reconcile the demands of culture with the drives.[77]

From another perspective, maturity can be viewed as the capacity to tolerate *emotional ambivalence* in a broad sense. An immature identity, from this standpoint, is an identity characterized by a kind of *psychic Manichaeism*, i.e. incapable of perceiving nuances and of emotionally coming to terms with the simultaneous presence of positive and negative, good and bad aspects in the objects that come within its field.

Freud understands this constituent of maturity, present in a strong ego to a greater extent than in a neurotic one, as the capacity to tolerate "the direction toward the same person of contrary – affectionate and hostile – feelings" (Freud 1917a: 428) while continuing to operate under the influence of ambivalence so defined without regressing from the viewpoint of the attained libidinal stage or of the structuredness of the ego.[78]

For Melanie Klein maturity means, from this standpoint, the capacity to tolerate not only ambivalence, but also anxiety, and rests, from a developmental point of view, on the ego's capacity to reconcile the threats originating in the superego with the libidinal and aggressive drives. She illustrates the point with reference to the analytic process. One of the most difficult and painful turning points of any analysis is when the patient is required to accept interpretations concerning his or her feelings of hate or envy *vis-à-vis* the good object. If the material is worked through appropriately, however, the person acquires more confidence in his or her capacity to *repair*, and becomes less afraid of his or her envy and aggressiveness as well as less afraid of being overwhelmed by the split off, destructive aspects of the self. This increased confidence, in turn, contributes to accrue the person's maturity, understood as a "greater tolerance towards one's own limitations," as the improvement of one's object relations and as a "clearer perception of internal and external reality" (Klein 1957: 232).

Jacobson understands the capacity to accept ambivalence primarily as the capacity to accept the similarities and differences between self and others without regressive reactions. For the psychotic, instead, "likeness and difference are equally frightening, because likeness threatens to destroy the self and difference the object" (Jacobson 1964: 69).

Finally, it is possible to identify a subdimension of maturity – spelled out mainly by Kohut – which could be called an *ironic acceptance of one's finitude*. The dimension of maturity has an ambiguous place in Kohut's conception of the well-being of an identity. On the one hand, as in Winnicott, maturity is somewhat downplayed relative to vitality and coherence. In fact, Kohut in various passages defends the thesis that a moderate immaturity, understood as an underdeveloped capacity to come to terms with the world, is often compensated for by the creative results that it may generate. On the other hand, maturity receives an unprecedented emphasis under the heading of *wisdom*. Maturity for Kohut is ultimately wisdom, and wisdom is spelled out as the acceptance of the limits of one's physical, intellectual and emotional powers, as a sense of humor and irony and, like in Kernberg, as the acceptance of one's finitude.[79] More specifically, wisdom entails an acceptance of the "transiency" of all human things and enterprises which does not result in the devaluation of that which is lost. In this sense, maturity is different from sarcasm and cynicism – which both are attempts to minimize the significance of one's limitations through a "sour grapes" attitude.[80] The wisdom of the mature personality, continues Kohut, has a quality of lightness that distinguishes it from any tone of pompous seriousness or "unrelieved solemnity": "The truly wise are able in the end to transform the humor of their years of maturity into a sense of proportion, a touch of irony toward the achievements of individual existence, including even their own wisdom" (Kohut 1978: 109).

Kohut's view of maturity as wisdom contains also a contribution to the understanding of the dimension of depth – a contribution anticipated above but left thus far unaddressed. The dimension of depth, given by Freud a cognitive coloring at first and then understood as relative autonomy of the ego from the id, acquires in Kohut the new meaning of an ideal of the *sovereignty* of the ego *in*, rather than *over*, the self. To have sovereignty means, from this vantage point, to *govern wisely* the internal realm – a relation which includes not only knowledge of drive-related and self-related needs, but also the capacity to fully represent, in the *political* sense of the term "representation," psychic constituencies made of ambitions, desires and needs. The sovereignty of the ego is not the same as self-control in that it does not rest on the repression of the unreconciled aspects of the self. Sovereignty is, rather, characterized by the ego's effort to mediate and reconcile the dissonant parts of our psychic being. Kohut's ideal of sovereignty points to the possibility of a non-repressively integrated subjectivity, a "non violent unity of the self," a "fully embodied integration of the ego and the drives" or, in another vocabulary, to an authentic relation of the self to itself. In this sense it also offers us an insight into the psychodynamic basis for our cultural appreciation of the ability to bring diversity to (non-coercive) unity – the appreciation of the artist's ability to bring a multiplicity of motifs, materials, styles and motivations into the unity of a work of art, as well as the ability of those who can fuse a multiplicity of interests, dispositions, projects and affects into the unity of a single life-course.

Concluding remarks

By way of concluding this reconstruction of the constitutive dimensions of fulfilled or authentic subjectivity implicit in psychoanalytic theory, let me briefly comment on the status of these four dimensions. We should not ask them to give us something which they clearly cannot provide. Coherence, vitality, depth and maturity are not to be understood as *criteria* which define in a strict sense the good for a concrete identity. They lack the determinacy that we associate with the notion of a criterion and cannot be ranked. There is no way of saying whether it is *generally* better to lose something on the dimension of depth in order to gain on that of coherence, or to lose some coherence in order to gain vitality. It depends on the concrete case. Another reason against understanding these four dimensions as criteria for human fulfillment is that while it make sense to reconstruct our intuitions concerning the good for an individual identity *in general*, it makes no sense to assess the fulfillment of a *concrete* identity on the basis of a checklist of criteria to which it ought to correspond. For that would mean to reduce such assessment to the model of determinant judgment.

On the other hand, these dimensions are not *values* either. For values have an intrinsic motivational force which the evaluative dimensions of identity lack. To uphold a certain value, for instance liberty or equality, means also to want that certain things should be the case or to prefer certain states of affairs over others, but from the fact that an individual has a coherent self or a mature identity nothing directly can be inferred as to his or her will. Furthermore, while values are often part of our reasons for acting in a certain way, we hardly ever justify our course of action on the basis of its enhancing our coherence or maturity. We say, rather, that we chose it because we *are* mature or coherent, but not for the sake of maturity or coherence.

These dimensions then fall somewhere in between the strict cogency of criteria and the contingency of value orientations. They are best understood as *guidelines* rooted in certain shared intuitions, which as such *orient* our reflective judgment concerning the good for an identity – where to orient must be understood along the lines specified in my reconstruction of Kant's view of validity in reflective judgment – without being able to dictate to us what the best choice is.

6

THE FULFILLMENT OF COLLECTIVE IDENTITIES

The four dimensions of the authenticity or fulfillment of an individual identity can be useful, *mutatis mutandis,* also in order to reconstruct our intuitions concerning the realization of *collective* identities. When we evaluate the fulfillment or authenticity of a collective identity, we use concepts and address questions that are somehow related, though of course they are couched in a different vocabulary, to the intuitions about the good which I have tried to reconstruct from within the vocabulary of psychoanalytic theory in the previous chapter. However, before discussing the relevance of the notions of *coherence, vitality, depth* and *maturity* for the case of collective identities, a number of features that characterize any superindividual identity should be briefly highlighted.

The nature of collective identities

Collective identities cannot be conceived as mere aggregates of individual identities. They possess specific properties not reducible to the sum total of the psychological processes which take place in the individuals who compose them. The struggle of sociology to be recognized as an autonomous social science testifies to this fact. The impossibility of psychological reductionism does not mean, however, that we cannot gain access to what it means for collective identities to attain fulfillment by building on what it means for individual identities to undergo such experience. Collective identities, just like individual identities, are basically *representations* or symbolic constructs. Distinctive of these representations, when they are shared within a group, is the special property of allowing individuals to use the pronoun "we" in a strong sense. Unlike those cases when the pronoun "we" is used in order to denote an accidental grouping of people, or in order to deny that the set of people within which the speaker is included forms a group at all, whenever one uses the pronoun "we" in a strong sense to refer to a number of people as a group of which one is also part, one also associates with it an understanding that each person included in the group is someone "like" the speaker. The existence of a collective identity is what allows one to think of another person as "someone like oneself." It then becomes possible to

108

speak of as many *types* of collective identity as there are distinct standpoints from which one person can be similar to another.

When I share a *cultural* collective identity I consider the other person mainly as someone who possesses beliefs and values similar to mine. "He is someone like me" means, in this case, that the person views the world from the same perspective as I do and shares similar views also concerning what makes a life fulfilling, a person worthy, an action just, an end worth pursuing. To be part of a common *social* identity means to view the other as a participant in the same division of labor, as located somewhere in the same social stratification, and as someone who shares with us certain codes of status and certain *interests*. To share a collective *political* identity means to recognize that the other person is subject to the same system of obligations, obeys the same authorities and considers legitimate the same pattern of communal will-formation. To share an enemy – which Carl Schmitt has considered the center of any political identity – is an ingredient, from this perspective, of any political *alliance*, and as such is often the first step in the formation of a political identity, but is neither a necessary nor a sufficient condition for the existence of a collective political identity. Many allies do not share the same political identity in our sense and, on the other hand, collective identities exist which can be stabilized even in the absence of an external enemy. In the case of *psychological* identities, a collective identity binds its members together not so much through shared orientations, shared interests or shared obligations, as through the common dynamism of face-to-face interaction, through participation in the same process of leader selection, tension management, etc. Typical instances of psychological collective identities are *family* identities. Obviously we can talk of many other types of collective identities, such as *historical* identities, *generational* identities, *gender* identities and so on, depending on the distinct nature of the perspective from which we can perceive similarity and difference.

It is virtually impossible to overestimate the artificial quality of these distinctions. In all concrete cases of identity formation, identity change or identity collapse that we might examine, we are bound to find a web of interrelations between these different types of collective identities. The common beliefs and values at the basis of certain cultural identities, for example, are often rooted in a common position within the social stratification – this, if anything, is the positive legacy of Marx's social theory. At other times these common beliefs and values are rooted in common formative experiences (such as, for instance, the experiences of war, migration, epidemics, economic crises etc.) which are shared on a generational basis, as Inglehart's studies on the diffusion of postmaterialist culture in Western society suggest.[1] Conversely, sometimes social actors perceive certain *interests* as common because they interpret the situation in the light of shared values. Furthermore, being subject to the same system of obligations contributes to create a commonality of interest.

Thus only at an analytical level is it possible to keep these different types of collective identities, and relations of recognition underlying them, separate. In fact, only *groups* exist. And groups find their cohesion around different combinations of psychological, social, cultural and political factors. Certain groups, such as families, friendship networks and very small communities, for example, coalesce mainly around shared psychological-affective dynamics, though their members eventually come to share also, to a different extent, ideas, values, interests and obligations. Other groups, such as professional associations, unions and cartels, are integrated mainly through shared interests, though their members usually end up, with varying degrees of probability, sharing also cultural and political orientations. Finally, groups like scientific schools, artistic movements, academic faculties and editorial boards primarily coalesce around cultural orientations, though eventually social interests and political affinities also play a role in their integration.

Before moving on to consider the dimensions of collective authenticity which purportedly capture our intuitions on the matter, it should furthermore be noted that it is also possible to distinguish several perspectives from which we can look at cultural, social, political, psychological, historical, generational and gender identities. More particularly, it seems worth distinguishing a *cultural*, a *sociological*, a *political* and a *psychological* perspective.

When we consider a cultural, social, psychological or other type of collective identity from a *cultural* perspective, the minimal components that we attribute to it are: (1) the possession, on the part of the participants in the identity, of some kind of common memory or tradition, usually in the form of documents, narrated history and revered texts (be they mythological, religious, philosophical or scientific); (2) a configuration of needs linked with the reproduction of the identity, in this case the internal requisites of the reproduction of cultural forms (shared language, shared interpretive perspective, method of transmission); and (3) a projection of a future desired state of the collective identity (usually in the form of the accomplishment of some normative-aesthetic mandate which lies at the core of the group and is seen as constituting its *raison d'être*). This projected image need not necessarily be objectivated in some cultural product, but is a construct necessarily presupposed by the participants, where the word "necessarily" means that it is self-contradictory to maintain that a certain collective identity exists and yet it embeds no such futurized and idealized image of itself.

When we consider a collective identity of whatever nature from a *sociological* perspective we attribute to it at least: (1) a representation of the origins, history and boundaries of the group; (2) a set of requirements for the reproduction of the division of labor, of social stratification and the integration of interests; (3) an anticipatory representation of the future desired state of the group, from the standpoint of its boundaries, inner stratification and interest structure. Notice that the first component in this case differs from the first component attributed to a collective identity considered from a cultural perspective in that no assumption is made that the participants *identify with* or otherwise highly prize what they share in common: someone can share nothing in common – in the sense of values and perhaps even beliefs – with a professional association and yet understand quite clearly how it came into being, who belongs to it and so on. With regard to the second component, the integrative aspect is essential to any sociological perspective on identity. For normally collective identities do not collapse or give way to new ones any time a conflict of interest arises among the participants. On the contrary they do possess mechanisms for integrating diverging interests and preventing them from degenerating into conflict.

If we consider a collective identity from a *political* perspective, we attribute to it as constituents at least: (1) a representation of the origins, the history and the present boundaries of the group; (2) a set of requirements linked with the reproduction of the legitimation of authority and of the process of collective will-formation; and (3) an anticipatory representation of the future desired state of the group, from the standpoint of its boundaries, authority structure and location in a network of inter-group political relations (a network which includes friends and foes, dominant and dominated groups etc.). The first component is similar to the homologous component in a sociological identity, except for the fact that at the core of the representation is the distribution of power and authority, and the obligations thereto attached, within the group as well as the record of inter-group, as opposed to intra-group, strife. Evidence for the salience of the second component comes from the fact that two common ways to attack the cohesion of a political collective identity are (1) by way of undermining the legitimacy of its authority system and (2) through undermining the social identity underlying it, by way of causing interests to diverge.

When we consider a collective identity from a *psychological* perspective, we presuppose that it consists of: (1) a set of sedimented memories of past interaction, as well as a representation of the boundaries of the group; (2) a set of needs linked with the psychological structure of the group; and (3) an anticipatory image of a future desired state of the group from the standpoint of its interactional modality and internal differentiation processes. It may not be immediately self-evident what the *psychological* needs of a collective identity could amount to, especially if one is, as I am, unwilling to assume that a collective identity is a sort of individual mind writ large. These needs are to be conceived as related to the interactive infrastructure of the group self-representation: typical examples are the needs for a balanced and smooth feedback between the leaders' individual needs for narcissistic gratification and the capabilities and organization of the group, or the need for morale-boosting in relation to the leaders' ability to provide it, or the needs that related to the coordination of the in-group processes of coalition formation.

Finally, two basic differences should be mentioned, which seem to suggest a negative answer to the question: Can the dimensions of *coherence*, *vitality*, *depth* and *maturity* jointly capture also our intuitions about the fulfillment of a collective identity? First, while in the case of individual identities alienation and fulfillment possess a specific emotional correlate – in the form of joy or despair – in the case of collective identities this experiential or phenomenological

111

correlate of self-realization seems at best very indirect and tenuous. Groups "feel" only in a metaphorical way, through the web of influences that they exert on their individual members. Furthermore, when the coherence or vitality of a collective identity is threatened, the threat is not automatically transferred to the individual identities that are part of the collective identity. The experiences of coherence and vitality are undergone by a collective identity only in a mediated way, through the self-reflection of its members and in third-person appraisals on its state. Consequently, the four dimensions of fulfillment assume slightly different meanings when applied to the evaluation of an individual or a collective identity. Let me point out some of the differences.

For both individual and collective identities to be coherent means to have the chronological sequence of their states susceptible of being expressed in the form of a narrative. But the *demarcation* aspect of coherence is realized differently in the two cases. The biological link of the mind to one and only one body makes the demarcation of an individual identity problematical only "from within" – namely, with respect to the internal representations of other identities. In the case of a group, the demarcation of identity may become problematical also "from without" – namely, from the standpoint of an external observer. Collective identities with a low degree of coherence are characterized by a great indeterminacy as to the boundaries of the group also in the sense that it becomes difficult to say who belongs and who does not.

A second difference between the ways in which the dimensions of authenticity apply to individual and collective identities is that while the cohesion of an individual identity is a product of certain integrative functions of the ego (verbal and cognitive competencies, memory etc.) in the case of collective identities cohesion is mainly a function of the consistency of its constitutive belief systems, norms, values and of the life-world in which it is immersed. Despite these obvious differences, I believe it makes sense to reconstruct our intuitions concerning the fulfillment of collective identities against the background of the four dimensions highlighted before, and in the rest of this chapter I will proceed to do so. Of course, such reconstruction will draw on a vocabulary other than that of psychoanalytic theory. In the case of collective identity, the most fine-grained and differentiated vocabulary available for capturing our intuitions concerning its flourishing is doubtlessly provided by the tradition of classical and contemporary sociological theory. Once again, the distance which separates the approaches and perspectives associated with the names of Durkheim, Marx, Simmel, Weber and Parsons corroborates the significance of their converging on what appears to be a common set of similar, albeit differently emphasized, dimensions.

Coherence

Let me start with the case of *coherence*. Also in the case of collective identities, coherence – a dimension ultimately related to the possibility of unifying the plurality of vicissitudes undergone by a given identity into a narrative – can be understood as a complex dimension including at least the aspects of *cohesion*, *continuity* and *demarcation*. Within coherence, the subdimension of *cohesion* is certainly the single aspect of the fulfillment of a collective identity on which the sociological tradition has most insights to offer. Durkheim, for example, develops a fully fledged theory of cohesion.[2] He distinguishes between different *modalities* of cohesion (mechanical and organic solidarity) and investigates the different relations between individual and collective identity within each modality. In the context of this discussion, he is the first social theorist who links the notion of "cohesive force" with empirical indicators. As far as mechanical solidarity is concerned, the indicators of the force of cohesion include "the relation between the volume of the common conscience and that of the individual conscience," "the average intensity of the states of the collective conscience" and "the greater or lesser determination of these same states" (Durkheim 1964: 152). In the case of organic solidarity, instead, certain specific variations in the suicide rate, discussed by Durkheim under the headings of "egoistic suicide" and "anomic suicide," can be considered empirical indicators of two differently originating kinds of insufficient cohesive force.[3] Furthermore, Durkheim develops a phenomenology, centered on the notion of anomie, of the pathological forms of social cohesion – the so-called "abnormal forms of the division of labor" (Durkheim 1964: 353–95) – and, finally, offers some important insights into the relation of social cohesion to justice and to the sense of the sacred.[4]

Weber's reflections, instead, point in a different direction. Weber understands the cohesion of collective identities primarily as a function of the *consistency* of their symbolic ingredients – such as beliefs, norms, values. Weber's theory of the rationalization of religious cultures is based on the assumption that cohesion – understood as the explication of value premises for the purpose of rendering these premises consistent with one another – is crucial to *any* culture and is a fundamental motive underlying every creative endeavor. In fact, the process of cultural rationalization is fueled, according to Weber, by the need to overcome the contradictions and tensions which exist within the web of representations of which every identity consists. A totally monolithic cultural identity, devoid of any tension or contradiction, would be thoroughly impermeable to rationalization. On the other hand, an identity which posited internal tension or self-contradictoriness as a positive value would not be open to rationalization either. Thus Weber's theory of rationalization presupposes two postulates both related to the dimension of coherence broadly understood. The first postulate concerns the inevitability of cultural tensions and contradictions. The second posits the existence of a quasi-natural drive, typical of group life and individual life alike, toward the overcoming of cultural tensions and their reconciliation in the guise of a new and more complete coherence of the cultural form. Such enhanced coherence of a cultural identity, in turn, is understood by Weber mainly as an accrued *logical consistency*, measured in terms of the absence of logical and semantical contradictions in the central area of the identity – a condition that serves as a regulative idea and is obviously not intended as a concretely attainable state.[5]

Weber's thesis concerning the superior potential for rationalization embedded in the Puritan ethos with respect to the potential for rationalization typical of medieval or Counterreformation Catholicism rests on the argument that Puritanism embedded a better solution to the cultural tensions arising from the clash of the traditional "ethos of brotherliness" with the motivations presupposed by economic and political relations on their way to modernization – better in so far as it eliminated or at least allayed more of such tensions. Alongside this specific superiority in dealing with the cultural tensions of an incipient modernization, Puritanism for Weber was superior to all other ethical strands of early modernity also in a respect that is actually linked with the dimension of depth. Namely, it embedded a superior potential for engendering a rational conduct of life and for the rationalization of social action in more domains.

Finally, Simmel sheds light on other facets of the subdimension of cohesion. Simmel's main contribution to the understanding of this dimension of the fulfillment of a collective identity consists in his conception of conflict. Simmel does not consider intra-group conflict as the opposite of cohesion, but rather as one of the forms that the cohesion of a collective may take. Conflict, writes Simmel, "is itself a form of sociation" (Simmel 1955: 13). The contribution of conflict to cohesion is twofold. First, a certain pattern of internal conflict may be typical or characteristic of a group or, in the terminology used here, may be constitutive of its collective identity. Marriage is a good case in point. A conflict-ridden marriage, to the extent that it lasts, is by no means "less" of a marriage then a marriage which manifests lower levels of conflict. Rather, conflict – or, better, *a specific conflict* – becomes a distinctive aspect which makes a marriage that particular marriage.[6] Second, while normally conflict opposes groups to one another, it also brings closer together those who are on the same side – a theme developed also by Durkheim, when he observes that egoistic suicide tends to be less frequent in all those contexts when conflict becomes pervasive in society, in the form of war, revolution, civil unrest and the like.[7] Interestingly, Simmel underscores that such "coming closer together" on the part of the members of a group when the group is involved in conflict with another group has its roots in an analogous dynamics typical of individual identities – namely, in the individual's tendency, when entering conflict, to "pull himself together" or to concentrate all of his or her energies in one point "so that they can be employed at any moment in any required direction" (Simmel 1955: 87).

It would be misleading to think that the subdimension of *cohesion* is addressed only in the works of Durkheim, Weber and Simmel. Many other authors converge on this point. Auguste Comte, for example, being quite skeptical about the integrative effects of the dramatic increase in the division of labor that occurred during the Industrial Revolution, and actually fearing, like Burke, that an accrued fragmentation of society would result from the consequences of the individualistic ideology of the Enlightenment, insisted on the dimension of "social consensus" as a countervailing factor. Such a dimension, in turn, rests on what Comte calls a "social morality," understood as a normative dimension that generates a cohesion-bolstering consensus which is focused on mythical and religious cosmologies in primitive and ancient societies, on metaphysical world-views in premodern and early modern societies and on a scientific attitude toward the world in the industrial societies of the mid nineteenth century. Aside from his assumptions on human nature and the "laws" of society, Comte must be credited for having shifted the focus of the sociological discussion about modern society from the issue of the advantages and disadvantages of an increased division of labor (central in the opposite stances of Smith and Rousseau) to the issue of its potential dangers to social cohesion, for having investigated the possible countermeasures against the most serious among these dangers and for having highlighted the role of value-consensus in this respect.

A quite similar motif can be found, a century later, in Parsons's view of the social system.[8] In the *Working Papers on the Theory of Action* and in the later essay "General theory in sociology" the central category of *functional imperative* for the maintenance and reproduction of a social system is articulated with reference to the so-called AGIL scheme. Among the four functional imperatives that every system must satisfy in order to survive we find also two categories that are directly, though not exclusively, related to the dimension of cohesion. First, the imperative of "integration" ("I"), mainly attended to by the sphere of law, of moral norms and by the judicial institutions, requires that all the activities of, and interaction between, the parts of the system be coordinated. Second, the imperative of "pattern maintenance" ("L"), attended to by the cultural subsystem and by socializing agencies, is charged with the task of securing and disseminating the cultural resources – primarily *values* – that are required for purposes of "internal tension management" (Parsons 1965: 7) and thus for avoiding the anomic drifting apart of the individual and superindividual components of a collectivity. In his later volumes *Societies. Evolutionary and Comparative Perspectives* (1966) and *The System of Modern Societies* (1971), Parsons attributes the crucial function of securing social cohesion to a new component located ideally at the core of the social system and called *societal community*. The societal community inherent in every modern society contributes to the cohesion of the larger society through defining the modes and boundaries of the often conflicting loyalties owed by members and subunits to one another and to society as a whole.[9] In order to be cohesive, a society, argues Parsons, "must constitute a societal *community* that has an adequate level of integration or solidarity and a distinctive membership status.... This community must be the 'bearer' of a cultural system sufficiently generalized and integrated to legitimize the normative order" (Parsons 1966: 17).

We find in Parsons two important points of convergence with Weber. First, the cohesion resulting from a successful discharging of the integration function is in the last analysis related to the capacity of the cultural system to provide the members of a collectivity with *consistent* patterns of motivation. Conflict is understood once again as the opposite of cohesion and is always linked, as in Weber's theory of cultural rationalization, with the internal tension of the cultural system and, more specifically, with the tensions arising between general values and specific norms. Parsons's view of cohesion, however, converges with Weber's also in a second sense. No social system can be completely integrated or cohesive and the functional imperative of integration can never be fully satisfied. For "no one system of value-orientation with perfect consistency in its patterns can be fully institutionalized in a concrete society" (Parsons and Shils 1962: 231). Tensions and inconsistencies, especially "between role expectations and performances of roles," will never disappear from social life. Interesting in this connection are Parsons's considerations on the converse theme – the impossibility of a total fragmentation of social cohesion. As he puts it:

> There is never likely to be a completely disintegrated society. . . . Even societies ridden with *anomie* (for example, extreme class conflict to the point of civil war) still possess within themselves considerable zones of solidarity. No society ever "disintegrates completely." . . . Complete disintegration is a limiting case toward which social systems might sometimes move, especially in certain sectors of the structure, but they never arrive there. A particular social system might, of course, lose its identity, or it might be transformed into one which is drastically different and can become absorbed into another social system. It might split into several social systems where the main cleavages follow territorial lines. But dissolution into the "state of nature" is impossible.
>
> (Parsons and Shils 1962: 204)

The aspect of *continuity*, within the dimension of coherence, is addressed under a variety of headings and from a number of different perspectives in the sociological tradition. One of these headings and perspectives is constituted by the Durkheimian notion of *collective conscience*, understood as "the totality of beliefs and sentiments common to average citizens of the same society" (Durkheim 1964: 79). Durkheim's *collective conscience* is "independent of the particular conditions in which individuals are placed; they pass on and it remains." The collective conscience, furthermore, "does not change with each generation, but, on the contrary, it connects successive generations with one another" (Durkheim 1964: 80).[10] One of the modern heirs to Durkheim's "collective consciousness" is once again the "L" component in Parsons's AGIL scheme, whose functions, along with the tension-management one mentioned above, include also that of providing a collectivity with a sense of continuity, by way of ensuring that the members of the collectivity develop roughly the same appropriate motivations, needs and capacities over the generations (see Parsons 1965: 7).

116

The aspect of *demarcation* within the complex dimension of coherence is discussed by Durkheim from three distinct perspectives. In a first sense, demarcation appears to be synonymous with a *need for differentiation* which Durkheim views as the product of the increasing *density* of any human group. Such need for differentiation manifests itself as the conscious urge to distinguish the group from all other groups and to overcome a sort of malaise – a kind of stifling of potentialities – which Durkheim associates with an excessive undifferentiated extension of any identity.[11] Durkheim presupposes here that an excessively extended identity becomes an insufficiently individuated identity, a blurry identity, an identity too little demarcated with respect to its own members. As the language of the mass media, in adapting to large and varied audiences, must lose something in richness of nuances and become less and less the expression of one recognizable community, so the broad variance of those who are admitted as members of a communal identity inevitably contributes to blur the boundary which separates the inside and the outside of the collective identity.

From a second perspective, Durkheim conceives of demarcation as the attainment and stabilization of an optimal level of differentiation between individual and collective identities. Too much distance or the tolerance of an excessive degree of diversity between the contents of the individual and the group identity result in a high risk of a centrifugal falling apart from the collective identity, due to its inability to "bind" the individual members with enough centripetal pull in order for them to keep considering themselves as belonging in the collective. Such is the thesis expounded by Durkheim in his reflections on egoistic and anomic suicide.[12] On the other hand, an excessive flattening of the individual identity onto that of the collective identity within which it is inscribed – as it characteristically happens in groups integrated through mechanical solidarity – results in a symmetrically specular risk of collapse through implosion. An excess of centripetal force leads the individual to merge completely with the group life and thus causes the group to lose the enlivening benefit of the two-way relation of influence between individuated individual and collective identity. The group collapses due to the complete breakdown of exchange between the inside and the outside. Such is the gist of Durkheim's view of altruistic and fatalistic suicide.[13]

On the dimension of demarcation a significant convergence can be found in George Herbert Mead and Georg Simmel. From different standpoints both develop the same insight into the relation between the quantitative size of a collectivity and the individuation of its members. Because the self comes into being, according to Mead, only as a reflection of an interactive process, and more specifically by learning to perceive itself through the refraction it produces in the eyes of a significant other, the individuation of such a self increases in the same proportion as does the breadth of the community with respect to which the self learns to situate itself (Mead 1974: 265). From our own perspective, the more individuation grows, the sharper the demarcation between the individual identity and the communal identity from which it arises. In his essay "Die

Ausdehnung der Gruppe und die Ausbildung der Individualität" (in Simmel 1890) Simmel also argues that a direct and positive proportion exists between the extension of a social group and the degree of individuation which its members have the opportunity to develop. The narrower the group, the stronger and more constraining are the boundaries within which it succeeds in confining individuals. On the other hand, the larger the group, the more numerous the chances for its members to adopt lifestyles, beliefs, attitudes and value-orientations that deviate from those prevailing in the group. Thus also for Simmel, no less than for Mead, the sharpness of the dividing line between the identity of a group and the identity of its members is a function of the size of the group. In the essay "The Web of Group-affiliations" (in Simmel 1955) Simmel explores another facet of demarcation: the sharpness of the inward demarcation of the group identity from the identities of its members is seen as a function of the multiplicity of simultaneous group-affiliations in which an individual is allowed to be involved (see Simmel 1955: 150–4).

Vitality

In the case of collective identities, the dimension of *vitality* takes on the meaning, in the first place, of a joyful, spontaneous and earnest participation on the part of the majority of the members in those rituals which bear a crucial significance for the stabilization of the identity. Generally, a low degree of vitality translates in the fact that the members of the group perform the rituals constitutive of their group's identity exactly in that manner which we call "ritualistic" (i.e. instrumentally, insincerely and "tongue in cheek"). The dimension of vitality also receives a different specification when different types of collective identities are concerned. To lose in vitality means, for a *cultural* collective identity, that its members only externally and cynically orient themselves to its core values – like Goffman's social actors, they merely pay lip-service to such values. For a *social* identity a loss in vitality consists in the unenthusiastic attitude with which the integration of diverging interests is attended, in the resigned passivity with which members participate in the division of labor and in their skeptical taking distance from the main symbols of status and the social stratification that they presuppose. For a *political* identity low vitality means, among other things, the fact that its members fulfill their obligations mainly out of the fear of external sanctions.

In his *Elementary Forms of the Religious Life*, Durkheim points out the nexus of ritual and identity-maintenance. However, while Durkheim emphasized mainly the relevance of rituals for the *cohesion* of a community, for our purposes it is important to emphasize that the *vitality* of a collective identity is related to the *way* in which participation in rituals takes place. The integrative force of the sacred is not given once and for all. It must be continuously revived and renewed, lest it undergoes erosion and fades away. When a group is in a state of communion, its cohesiveness stimulates and enhances the vitality of the cultural identities of the individuals who are members of it. Herefrom draw their power those rites, especially the positive ones, which bring the believers to convene and to renew their adherence to the central themes of their communal identity. Without rites an identity has no means to revivify itself, and is doomed to extinction. But what distinguishes a rite which carries the potential for such revivification from one which fails to bring about any such effect? The difference lies in the different potential that rituals have to elicit fervor, "effervescence" and the spontaneous participation of the individual members of a group.[14] A collective identity has lost its vitality, understood here as the power to revivify itself, if its traditional rites can stimulate only a formalistic, hypocritical or merely instrumental kind of participation in the members of the identity. Something of the kind, argues Durkheim, has already happened to the rituals of our Western tradition which have survived the onset of modernization.[15]

Furthermore, it is possible to find in Durkheim also a notion of the vitality of a collective identity which parallels the meaning of vitality as the perception of the worthiness of the self for an individual identity. The collective identity of a group, in fact, can be humiliated or exalted by certain symbolic acts performed by the group's members. The individual member needs to perceive the collective identity in which he or she participates as worthy of his or her respect and love. This esteem of the collective identity is enhanced whenever the sense of the sacred is strong in the community and, on the other hand, is diminished or radically falls whenever the community enters a situation of endemic anomie, i.e. a situation of endemic fluctuation of the social meanings linked with the distributive arrangements, the social stratification and the idea of justice.

Finally, the propensity of a group to defend the core of its identity from offenses and deviant conduct through penal means highlights another aspect of the vitality of a collective identity – an aspect homologous to the sense of immediate self-presence and immediate certainty as to who one is which characterizes, at least in part, the vitality of an individual identity. The punitive response, institutionalized in penal law, with which a collective identity confronts any violation of the normative order is thus, for Durkheim, an indicator of its own degree of self-certainty. A poorly cohesive, insecure, enfeebled, anomically fluctuating or decaying collective identity does not react with the same degree of determination. An identity which hesitates to punish its offenders lacks in the self-certainty aspect of vitality.[16]

Also for Weber the vitality of a collective identity constitutes an important dimension of its fulfillment. Weber's notion of vitality, however, is much less differentiated than Durkheim's: it designates a quality of *readiness to accept change* – change in the direction of disenchantment and rationalization in the first place – which may characterize a collective identity. The opposite of vitality is, in this case, the *traditionalism* of collective identities which oppose change merely out of their own inertia and symbolic viscosity. Examples of this conception of vitality can be found in Weber's discussion of the constraints imposed by cultural traditionalism on the development of piece-rates,[17] or in his discussion of the "impulse to make money" and the attitude toward innovation that it stimulates.

A highly positive, indeed enthusiastic, appraisal of this specific aspect of vitality is present also in Marx's account of the specificity of the bourgeoisie as a ruling class. Among all the ruling classes that have existed, the bourgeois class is unique in grounding its rule on constant change rather than on a sheer conservation of past arrangements:

> Constant revolutionizing of production, uninterrupted disturbance of all social relations, everlasting uncertainty and agitation, distinguish the bourgeois epoch from all earlier times. All fixed, fast-frozen relationships, with their train of venerable ideas and opinions, are swept away, all new-formed ones become obsolete before they can ossify. All that is solid melts into air, all that is holy is profaned, and men at last are forced to face with sober senses the real conditions of their lives and their relations with their fellow men.
>
> (Marx and Engels 1978: 475)

The extraordinary vitality of such a ruling class lies in its *anti-traditional dynamism* which, more than for its historical results, is considered by Marx with admiration for the process, the energy it radiates and the moment of true liberation and enhancement of all human potentials that it entails.[18]

Finally, yet a different coloring is acquired by the dimension of vitality in the thought of Tocqueville. In *Democracy in America* we can find an implicit notion of vitality as the property of a public, and more precisely as a readiness to mobilize and participate in political deliberation, the opposite of which is constituted by the *apathy* that a certain culture of privatism and the ensuing "soft despotism" jointly contribute to produce in the citizenry. The culture of privatism, in turn fueled by the equality of conditions typical of a democratic society, induces the citizens to withdraw from participation and to entrust the government with all their affairs. Their elected government soon comes to acquire an "immense, protective" power – a power that is "absolute, thoughtful of detail, orderly, provident, and gentle" – and "covers the whole of social life with a network of petty, complicated rules that are both minute and uniform" and in the end "hinders, restrains, enervates, stifles and stultifies" all initiatives and communal projects. At the end of this process the once active public of citizens is reduced to a "flock of timid and hardworking animals with its government as its shepherd" (Tocqueville 1969: 692). This apathetic public regains a semblance of vitality only at election times, keeps it long enough to choose its masters and then falls back into its state of dependence.[19]

Depth

The *depth* of a collective identity bears a closer resemblance than coherence and vitality, in all its constituents, to the correspondent dimension of the fulfillment of an individual identity. It designates the awareness, on the part of the members of a group, of the central requisites for the maintenance and reproduction of their shared identity. Again, Marx is among the authors who have most to say about this dimension. His notions of "ideology" and "commodity fetishism" are too well-known to need any elucidation. Problematic as his assumption of a self-representation entirely free of ideological distortions might be, the negative ideal of reducing the distorting influence of interest over the representations of social reality and over the formation of a collectivity's self-representation has continued to exert an unceasing appeal well beyond the boundaries of the Marxist tradition. The same holds for the intimation to make use of descriptive languages that do not obscure the dimension of agency inherent in the phenomena depicted by them. Both of these moments of Marx's legacy are part of our intuitions about what fulfillment means for a collective identity in the sense that, much as it is the case with Freud's guiding ideals of "making the unconscious conscious" and "having the ego govern the id," and despite the distance that separates our sensibility from Marx's and Freud's faith in the possibility of objective knowledge, the very idea of a human collectivity that pursues its own fulfillment and yet does not attend to these notions appears somewhat contradictory to us.

Interesting considerations on the dimension of depth can be found also in Durkheim and in Weber. According to Durkheim, the evolution of the collective conscience, paralleling in this respect the evolution of the notion of divinity, takes place along the axis of an increasing abstractness and generality of content,[20] but a second aspect of the depth of a collective identity, which results from this evolution of the collective conscience, is the increasing level of self-reflexivity required of the individual in order to apply more abstract and general prohibitions and precepts to the given contexts of action. Third, in a number of passages on the subject of "social representations," Durkheim mentions the becoming more and more reflexive of society as a whole. In fact, by the term "social representations" he understands certain states of the collective conscience which "convey the way in which the group conceives itself in its relation to objects which affect it."[21] Elsewhere such self-reflexivity is explicitly presented by Durkheim as the foundation of the superiority of one kind of social order or one collective identity over another. For example, at the end of a lengthy (and datedly ethnocentric) passage in which he praises the wisdom of those believers who refuse to jettison their faith even in the face of their inability to provide rational grounds for all details of dogma and ritual – for they would be unconsciously aware that the aim of religion is not to explain things but to integrate the community – Durkheim characterizes such "favorable prejudice" or "urge to believe," which allows the believer to overlook the non sequiturs and the contradictions in his own faith, as the true basis of the authority that religion commands both among the Australian natives and the European peoples. The superiority of the latter, however, would reside – continues Durkheim – in the fact that the Western believer is more aware of the psychological processes underlying his or her religiosity. He or she knows that in the end "it is faith that saves" (Durkheim 1967: 403). Durkheim's most interesting considerations on the theme of depth, however, have a critical tone and point to the risks linked with an excess of self-reflectiveness. Those considerations can be found in some passages on the aetiology of the different types of suicide, where echoes of the Nietzschean theme of self-reflection as detachment from, and negation of, the life-process can be heard. If our consciousness, writes Durkheim,

> individualizes beyond a certain point, if it separates itself too radically from other beings, men or things, it finds itself unable to communicate with the very sources of its normal nourishment and no longer has anything to which it can apply itself. . . . To think, it is said, is to abstain from action; in the same degree, therefore, it is to abstain from living.[22]

> (Durkheim 1951: 279–80)

In his theory of cultural rationalization Weber too emphasizes the dimension of depth as one of the main constituents of the fulfillment of a collective identity. Depth is conceived also by Weber mainly as self-reflectiveness, but other meanings are present as well. As for Durkheim, a higher level of self-reflectiveness represents the specific element which renders a more rationalized culture "superior" to a less rationalized one. In his essays on the sociology of religion Weber often suggests that a given ethical system or religious culture as a whole is to be considered superior to another. When he claims that a religious ethic of norms embeds a more rational response to the dilemmas of human existence than a magical ethics, or when he claims that an ethic of conviction, such as the Puritan ethos, constitutes an advance over the ethic of medieval Catholicism, Weber usually supports these theses with reference to specific judgments on the cultural forms at issue, but says very little about the criteria that guide these judgments. Such implicit criteria, if spelled out, amount to a restatement of the relevance of self-reflectiveness among the dimensions of the fulfillment of a collective identity. They include, in fact, the range of actors bound by the moral judgments or prescriptions generated within a given religious ethic (a particular set of actors, such as the members of the clan or tribe, or larger groups, up to the entire human species), the kind of justification considered acceptable for the normative claims implicit in it, the complexity of the object of ethical evaluation (ranging from single acts to the conduct of an entire life-course) and different levels of minimal cognitive ability presupposed by the various types of ethics (ranging from the mere ability to tell *is* from *ought*, to the principled autonomy required by the Puritan ethos and to the flexible autonomy guided by judgment which is presupposed by an ethic of responsibility).[23]

Particularly relevant is the second among these criteria. When considered in its light, the evolution of religious ethics takes the appearance of the acquisition of ever-increasing levels of *reflexivity*. While within the least rationalized ethical views, and obviously within the social groups integrated through them, only single acts and subsequently classes of actions are assessed in light of the community's norms, for the groups integrated through a modern, principled kind of ethical culture as the one ushered in by Puritanism it becomes possible to gain access to a further level of reflexivity, regarded by Weber as one of the distinctive aspects of a fully fledged cultural rationalization: namely, it becomes possible – though by no means always feasible in practice – for a group to consider its own ethical norms, and not simply the actions performed, in the critical light of second-order and more general *principles*.

The dimension of depth becomes more specific, finally, in Habermas's discussion of the requisites for the reproduction of *social* identities. The social identity of a collectivity acquires depth, according to Habermas, insofar as it embeds an awareness of three main types of requisites: requisites linked with the reproduction of the *symbolic* aspects of the collective identity (shared beliefs and norms), requisites linked with the *integration* of the group (reflective thematization of the procedures used for regulating conflict), and requisites linked with the *socialization* of the new generations (relativization of the communal practices of child-rearing and education).[24] The relevance attributed by Habermas to the dimension of depth, understood as awareness of these requisites, is suggested by the crucial valence that he assigns to such processes as the transition from a conventional to a postconventional morality, from a conventional role-identity to ego-identity, from a conventional to a "rational" pattern of societal integration.

Maturity

Finally, also, the dimension of *maturity* can be applied to collective identities. It is possible to distinguish cases in which a basic congruency exists between the self-image on one hand and the cultural, social or political reality of the group on the other, from the case of groups which indulge in a narcissistically grandiose image of themselves. Furthermore, it is possible to distinguish groups that are flexible and realistic in their strategies from groups which adopt defensive strategies that are rigid and unrealistic,[25] groups that are more capable than others of an ironic self-distance from groups which appear pervaded by a "deadly earnestness," and ideologically oriented groups from pragmatically oriented groups. Again, in the work of classical social theorists many interesting reflections on this theme can be found.

The dimension of maturity, for example, is implicitly presupposed by Weber's notion of the process of rationalization. The rationalization of culture, in fact, leads not simply to the development of a more consistent and self-reflective collective identity, but also to a more *mature* cultural identity – that is, to a collective identity more *disenchanted* and, as such, more capable of resisting the illusion of its own magical omnipotence. Nowhere does this aspect of the process of rationalization come into focus more than in Weber's account of the transition from a magical ethics to an ethics of norms.[26] The transition from Catholicism to Protestantism, with the abandonment of the practice of confession and more generally of the sacramental way to salvation, represents another crucial step in the distancing of our culture from the mentality of the "enchanted garden."[27] Further contributions to the understanding of the relation of rationalization to maturity can be found if we consider other processes investigated by Weber under the heading of the rationalization of action and of broader societal rationalization. In these contexts, as Habermas has pointed out, Weber's concept of rationalization comes to acquire a meaning different from the elimination of cultural tensions. For example, if we consider that ultimate stage of ethical rationalization constituted in Weber's eye by an *ethic of responsibility*, and try to envisage the collective identity of a group whose members mainly orient themselves to such an ethics, then the term rationalization would appear to designate, among other things, the sense of an increased commensurateness of the means to the chosen ends, the sense of a greater attention paid to the foreseeable consequences of one's action, the sense of a capacity to mediate reasons of principle (intentions and values) and pragmatic reasons of utility in shaping one's conduct, the sense of an ability – somehow related to the tolerance of ambivalence that we associate with the maturity of an individual identity – to accept the relativization of one's values and principles, the sense of a radicalized and rigorous application of reality-testing as opposed to indulging in the illusory omnipotence of magical thinking. Finally, the rationalization of action in light of the ethic of responsibility acquires in Weber also the sense of an ability to accept the inevitable limitations of one's projects. For example, maturity for a scientist means to accept the inevitability of specialization in the context of a scientific community and to give up the pursuit of "visions."[28]

Echoes of this notion of maturity can be found also in the notion of "societal rationalization" presupposed by Weber's characterization of Western rationalism in his "Author's Introduction" to the whole body of his studies on the sociology of religion, often and misleadingly utilized as an introduction to edited versions of *The Protestant Ethic*, after Parsons's usage.[29] In this text, for a rationalized society to be more *mature* means not only being more disenchanted, but also being more capable of institutionalizing a larger number of patterns of purposive-rational conduct, of replacing the exceptionality of charisma with administrative routine and legal forms of domination, and of developing further the spheres of law and science – again, two spheres in which the stronger is the emphasis on reality-testing and the aversion from projective mythologies and fantasies of omnipotence. A new aspect of the relevance of Puritanism for the rationalization of the Western ethos is here highlighted by Weber – an aspect connected with the potential, inherent in Puritanism, for inducing in its followers that supreme form of commensuration of the means to the ends which consists of the unification of all the local, context-bound action into a "rational way of life." This "rational way of life," once again, attributes a crucial role to reality-testing, encourages the "examined life" and orients the individual toward a thorough self-control directed against the inordinate pursuit of pleasures not for the sake of following a tradition but for the sake of bringing the plurality of one's experiences under the orderliness of an original life-project. Maturity becomes here synonymous with *moderation* or *restraint*.

The aspect of *flexibility* within the maturity of a collective identity is touched upon also by Simmel and Durkheim. In his essay on "Conflict" Simmel points out that groups can be characterized also through their qualities of *resilience* or *rigidity*.[30] A similar point is made by Durkheim. The superiority of the organic form of solidarity over mechanical solidarity ultimately rests on the greater *flexibility* of the political and social arrangements typical of a society integrated through organic solidarity in relation to the *rigidity* of the institutions typical of societies integrated through mechanical solidarity. The notion of maturity as flexibility is also presupposed by Durkheim in his discussion of "fatalistic suicide" – a kind of suicide induced by the excessive rigidity of a collective identity. This notion does not receive as much theoretical attention as the notions of egoistic, altruistic and anomic suicide. Yet, one is led to believe that such category would have been assigned a more than just cursory mention had Durkheim been able to envisage the totalitarian societies of our century, with their multitudes of dissenters, exiles, refugees and "boat-people" who willingly risk their lives in order to flee the oppressive rigidity of a form of life.

Finally, every society is bound to form an ideal image of itself as it would like to be – an image which usually is cast in religious terms. "A society," writes Durkheim, "can neither create itself nor recreate itself without at the same time creating an ideal." Such creation of an ideal image "is not a sort of work of supererogation for it [the society], by which it would complete itself, being already formed; it is the act by which it is periodically made and remade" (Durkheim 1967: 470). As in the case of the individual identity, such an ideal can be realistically commensurate with the society at issue or it may largely be made of projective material which, again, belies fantasies of grandeur and omnipotence on a collective scale.

Concluding remarks

The discussion of how the components of the notion of fulfillment for the case of an individual identity apply to the case of collective identities could be continued and the comparisons made more detailed. I will leave that for a future investigation and would like for the time being to go back to the broader coordinates within which this understanding of normative validity, centered around the notions of authenticity and judgment, is comprised. The notion of the good has for a long time been treated as a residual category within contemporary moral philosophy, as something which at some point it is necessary to mention but which remains outside the scope of philosophical reflection proper.[31] The roots of this predicament are to be found in the contingencies of the rationalization of Western ethics *after* the rise of the new, fully modern, moral tensions opened by the affirmation of the Protestant ethic. As a result of the direction taken by modern ethics we have today on the one hand a differentiated vocabulary for discussing questions of justice, and on the other hand a rather underdeveloped and undifferentiated moral language for discussing questions concerning the good. Correcting this imbalance is the first step toward a postmetaphysical ethics capable of sidestepping, if not healing, the modern split – which all liberals uncritically take for granted – between ethics that revolve around justice but have little to say about the good (for instance, all deontological ethics from Kant to Habermas) and ethical views that address the question of the good, mainly under the heading of "being oneself" or authenticity (Rousseau, Kierkegaard, Nietzsche, Jaspers), but have little to say about justice.[32] Recently the picture has begun to change. On the one hand a number of contemporary authors have begun to address again the question of the good, mainly under the heading of an ethic of virtue.[33] On the other hand we begin to see attempts to bridge the gap between the deontological neo-Kantian ethics of the right and the teleological neo-Aristotelian ethics of the good via a formal notion of the good.[34] It is to the development of this new area that the present volume is aimed, seeking to contribute by way of suggesting one possible way of enriching our vocabulary about the good. Yet, the reconstruction of the "postmodern eudaimonia" attempted here cannot and should not be expected to do the job that Archimedean points, such as the categorical imperative, "reason in history," "the greatest happiness for the greatest number", were supposed to do before the Linguistic Turn.

All that can be done, and that I hope to have moved some steps toward doing, is to isolate enough aspects of a "common vocabulary," sufficiently differentiated and yet accessible from a vast number of historically situated vocabularies, through which to articulate our intuitions regarding which combination of coherence, vitality, depth and maturity constitutes the best approximation of the good that a concrete identity can attain. The Eskimos are known to have four different words to refer to snow. If the good as self-fulfillment is to be taken as central for our culture as snow is within their life-context, then it is perhaps not a bad idea for us too to be able to distinguish at least four aspects of the good.

7

AUTHENTICITY, THE TEXT AND THE WORK OF ART

A notion of validity based on authenticity can be claimed not only to match our intuitions concerning the fulfillment of individual and collective identities, but in a derivative way can also capture our understanding of the interpretation of symbolic objects, such as texts and works of art. Needless to say, in the case of such objects – as well as of other types of symbolic entities which cannot be discussed here, such as disciplines, practices, organizations, traditions, institutions, styles and so on – we can speak of "fulfillment" only in a highly metaphorical sense. Yet we do constantly exchange judgments concerning the fact that such objects appear to be or to fail to be internally coherent and capable of forcefully projecting complex structures of meaning or, in the case of symbolic objects bound up with the temporal dimension in the way disciplines, practices and organizations are, judgments on their "flourishing" or their entering stagnation and decadence. In this chapter I will address the relevance of the four dimensions outlined above for the purpose of reconstructing our intuitions concerning what it means for texts and works of art to "succeed" or to be "well-formed" and what it means for our interpretations of them to be correct.

It is not my intent to offer methodological recipes but, rather, to offer an authenticity-based account of what we mean by *validity* in the realm of text-interpretation and art criticism. Nor will I attempt to design rules of thumb for best approximating valid interpretations, in the way followed by Hirsch in his seminal book *Validity in Interpretation* (1967). For Hirsch took for granted two things that are in fact quite problematical. First, he assumed that the meaning of a text coincides with the meaning that its author intended to convey and, second, he conceived of what he called the "validation of interpretation" on the basis of the model of determinant judgment.

Rather, I will be concerned with the following questions: What do we mean when we say that an interpretation of a text is better than another? What do we mean when we say that a work of art is "well-formed"?

The "author's intention" approach

One of the traditionally most renowned and influential answers to the first question rests on the idea that the superiority of an interpretation with respect to another is connected with its ability to capture more faithfully the intention of the author of the text. Hermeneutics in its original meaning is identified with a kind of restorative endeavor, namely the attempt to bring out the author's original intention which the contingencies of time, distance, decay of the supporting media, or deliberate correction have obscured. The two chief examples of a hermeneutic practice understood along these lines are theological hermeneutics – e.g. the Reformers' defense of their interpretation of the Scriptures against what they held to be the Counterreformation's misunderstanding thereof – and the secular humanists' effort to rescue classical literature. The first articulate formulation of this view of textual meaning is offered by Schleiermacher's theory of empathic understanding, soon followed by Dilthey's theory of historical consciousness.[1] I will not be further concerned here with the archaeology of hermeneutics, except for the purpose of recalling that to understand a text means, from this Romantic and later historicist perspective, to empathically place oneself within the mind of the author in order to reconstruct the creative act which gave origin to the text.[2] In other words, alongside the creative genius there exists a homologous interpretive genius, capable of acts of "divination," which amount to the empathic assimilation of the self into the other. The interpretive genius gains access to the meaning of the text better than the author – a formulation, comments Gadamer, which contains the whole problem of hermeneutics. It involves making conscious many aspects of the production of the text that were unconscious for the author. The corollary of this position is that the creator of a text is not necessarily its best interpreter.[3]

More than as a piece of intellectual archaeology, Romantic theories of interpretation continue to exert a powerful influence on us through many strands of thought which in one way or another inherit and transform for their own purposes its basic point: namely, twentieth-century linguistics, mainstream analytic philosophy of language, the theory of text or discourse analysis and legal positivism, just to mention a few. If we exclude some views of meaning, such as the once-fashionable extensional theories of meaning, according to which to understand the meaning of a sentence involves understanding the conditions under which the sentence would be true,[4] the entire field of the study of language with few exceptions (for example, the ethnomethodologically oriented studies on conversation and the ethnography of speaking)[5] takes for granted that to understand the meaning of a sentence or text means to understand what the speaker meant by it. Let me mention two examples. One is the theory of speech acts developed by Austin and Searle, the other is Van Dijk's discourse analysis. For Searle we understand utterances by identifying the different acts – locutionary, illocutionary and perlocutionary – that are performed through them.[6] Complex utterances, such as texts and conversations, are viewed as mere aggregates of elementary acts, bound together through the orderliness of sequencing-rules, social conventions and the like.[7] For Van Dijk, to understand the meaning of a text means to be able to give a summary of it, i.e. to identify the most relevant and higher order information from within the chain of local sentences that compose it.[8] Although Van Dijk does not address the point explicitly, the correctness of the summary is understood as a correct matching of the intentions underlying the production of the text. In this direction points his remark that the production and the "processing" of a text are two sides of the same coin, namely the expansion of a macrostructural kernel into a series of surface sentences or its reconstruction therefrom.[9]

Instead of questioning the reductionism inherent in the conflation of textual meaning and author's intention, the traditions of contemporary linguistics and philosophy of language seek to replace the empathic reconstruction of such intention with the certainty of a methodology based on rules. Searle's polemics against Grice's theory of meaning illustrates the point. In lieu of Grice's unqualified grasp of the intention of the speaker Searle insists that essential to the correct grasping of meaning is the fact that we perform this step through the intersubjective cogency of conventional rules of meaning.[10] More generally, the whole of post-Chomskyan linguistics (for example generative semantics, the theory of meaning postulates, the study of presuppositions, the theory of implicatures and the like) can be seen as the attempt to reconstruct the shared basis of conventions which enables native speakers of English to map linguistic forms onto the intentions of the speaker. The guiding ideal, again, is that of bringing the reconstruction of how we go from perceived utterances to their meaning within the framework of determinant judgment.

It could be objected at this point that it is unfair to criticize contemporary language studies for being the unwitting heir to the reductionism of the Romantic theory of meaning. After all, language studies – it could be argued – cannot at some point but be concerned with explaining *communication*, and communication necessarily involves, among other things, the reciprocal understanding of the participants' intentions. Even less fair would be to accuse the qualitative-sociology practitioners of reductionism if they view textual meaning merely as a function of the speaker's intention. What else could they be interested in, when they examine the transcript of an interview, other than what the respondent means?

Things are more complicated than they appear at first sight, however. First, the analysis of data collected through qualitative methods, including the transcripts of orally collected life-stories, is not the only context within which a question of appropriateness of interpretations emerges for an interpretive sociology. Research carried out within the framework of interpretive sociology must also come to terms with the interpretation of action, of sets of shared norms and written doctrine, of cultural expectations and evaluative stances, and in all these cases the idea of reducing the meaning of texts to the author's intention seems much less applicable, in fact not even sensible. However, this view of meaning is unsound also in the case of the interpretation of life-stories. For one of the implications of living in a complex society, where the existence of a plurality of cultural orientations and value-stances is a permanent feature, is that we can never be sure that the *prima facie* transparency of the meaning of a text really means that we have understood it fully. We must, especially if our interpretation is guided by a research interest, always probe our understanding beyond the superficial appearance of agreement. We can never take for granted that we and the respondent use certain salient terms, loaded with evaluative overtones, precisely in the same way. To put this point with Gadamer, we understand all the texts that we come in contact with, including those that we use as data in qualitative research, "on the basis of expectations of meaning which are drawn from our anterior relation to the subject" (Gadamer 1975: 262). And in complex societies we can never count on a "preestablished harmony" of the perspectives with which a researcher and a respondent relate to the same set of questions – especially if these questions concern or even just touch upon the area of what Charles Taylor has called "strong evaluations."[11]

Furthermore, as Gadamer has shown, we cannot even begin to interpret a text unless we provisionally take for granted that the text has a unity and coherence of its own. The same is true of respondents' texts. If we take seriously this presupposition underlying every act of interpretation then we must pay more attention to *what is said in, as opposed to what is meant by, the text* than the author's intention perspective would have us do. Even though by definition they are interested in what people *think* rather than in texts as such, and actually precisely for this reason, social researchers gain access to people's attitudes and opinions only through an interpretation of what is actually *said* – some of the time unintentionally – in texts, protocols and transcripts.

Finally, the author's intention view of textual meaning proves inconsistent with the assumptions embedded in the methodological self-understanding of qualitative social science in yet another sense. It is part of this self-understanding, as articulated for instance by Blumer, that whatever the object of his or her inquiry, the researcher doesn't want to frame the respondents' answers into pre-molded boxes, but on the contrary has to strive to preserve as far as possible the original symbolic texture of the answer.[12] For a number of methodological positions inspired by the work of Blumer, Garfinkel and Cicourel, the point of a qualitative-research approach is to leave more space, relative to other approaches, to the possibility of an ongoing revision, in the light of what respondents say, of the framework within which the research question was formulated in the first place. Then understanding the meaning of a text *a fortiori* seems linked not only with simply getting at the respondent's intentions but also with grasping the way in which his or her meaning impinges on our framework. Understanding and interpretation then necessarily entail a partial and selective suspension of our theoretical, if not cultural, prejudices, and consequently the opening up of the possibility of self-correction.

Interpretation as "fusion of horizons"

Gadamer's view of interpretation in terms of what he calls *fusion of horizons* suggests itself as one of the most promising alternatives to the reductionism of the author's intention approach. Without claiming to do justice to the complexity of Gadamer's account of the interpretive process, let me briefly recall three points made by him.[13]

The first point is the ontological turn that, following Heidegger, he gives to his account of interpretation. The second is the self-reflexivity that is implicit in the notion of the fusion of horizons, and the third is the specification of the fusion of horizons in terms of a logic of question and answer.

Gadamer views the hermeneutic circle not as an epistemological or methodological problem but as an ontological condition that is typical of humans as beings who are always already implicated in processes of understanding, who live by understanding:

> the process that Heidegger describes is that every revision of the fore-project is capable of protecting before itself a new project of meaning, that rival projects can emerge side by side until it becomes clearer what the unity of meaning is, that interpretations begin with fore conceptions that are replaced by more suitable ones. This constant process of new projection is the movement of understanding and interpretation.
>
> (Gadamer 1975: 236)

The soundness or objectivity of interpretation is here thought of as confirmed "by the things themselves," namely as "the confirmation of a fore-meaning in its being worked out." Conversely, "the only thing that characterizes the arbitrariness of inappropriate fore-meanings is that they come to nothing in the working-out." This "coming to nothing" manifests itself in the experience "of being pulled up short by the text." Either the text "does not yield any meaning or its meaning is not compatible with what we had expected" (Gadamer 1975: 237). The key to maximizing the chances of interpreting correctly a text is then not the attempt to empathically grasp what its author had in mind, but "the conscious assimilation of one's own fore-meanings and prejudices" (Gadamer 1975: 238).

This self-reflective dimension of interpretation – here I come to the second point – can be best captured in terms of the notion of a *fusion of horizons*. According to the author's intention theory of interpretation, the act of interpretation naturally finds its *terminus ad quem* in the exhaustive apprehension of the intentions of the author: "the circular movement of understanding runs backwards and forwards along the text and *disappears* when it is perfectly understood" (Gadamer 1975: 261, emphasis added). Following Heidegger, instead, Gadamer conceives the understanding of the text as a process "permanently determined by the anticipatory movement of fore-understanding": thus "the circle of the whole and the part is not dissolved in perfect understanding but, on the contrary is *most fully realised*" (Gadamer 1975: 261). Our own fore-meanings and prejudices are best understood as a *horizon* – a term that has a crucial importance. In fact, for Gadamer this pre-given set of "prejudices" should not be understood as a finite set of assumptions, in the same guise as Artificial Intelligence seeks to list in propositional form the "background knowledge" that is necessary in order for a computer to draw commonsense inferences. This would be a naive and misleading way of conceiving culture. For cultures are never collections of discrete cognitive and normative items but symbolic complexes that function and make sense holistically. As Gadamer puts it:

> The historical movement of human life consists in the fact that it is never utterly bound to any one standpoint, and hence can never have a truly closed horizon. The horizon is, rather, something into which we move and that moves with us. Horizons change for a person who is moving. Thus the horizon of the past, out of which all human life lives and which exists in the form of tradition, is always in motion. It is not historical consciousness that first sets the surrounding horizon in motion. But in it this motion becomes aware of itself.
>
> (Gadamer 1975: 271)

Thus the interpretation of a text, either from the past or from a different culture, "does not entail passing into alien worlds unconnected in any way with our own" but means to enlarge our own horizon by making it move "from within, and beyond the frontiers of the present" (Gadamer 1975: 271). A valid interpretation, from Gadamer's perspective, results in the constitution of a single horizon which contains the unsolvable differences of perspectives between us and the text. Thus when interpreting a text we are not required to disregard our concrete situation in order to imagine ourselves into another concrete situation. Rather, what we are required to do is, over and beyond reconstructing the cultural horizon of which the text is an expression, "to bring ourselves," with our questions and perspectives, into the other horizon. In so doing, we bring the two horizons, ours and that implicit in the text, to a fusion. To speak of forming one horizon, however, is somewhat inaccurate. For the hermeneutic task consists "in not covering up this tension by attempting a naive assimilation but consciously bringing it out" (Gadamer 1975: 273). In this dialectic of a strangeness that is not to be totally abolished and a familiarity that cannot be taken for granted lies the domain of understanding.

Finally, the best way to conceive the fusion of horizons without falling prey to the Romantic notion of empathy is to formulate the notion of understanding in terms of a *logic of question and answer*. Gadamer accepts Collingwood's thesis that we can understand a text only when we have understood the question to which it is an answer, but for Gadamer "the question that we are concerned to reconstruct has to do not with the mental experience of the author, but simply with the meaning of the text itself" (Gadamer 1975: 335). Collingwood is wrong, argues Gadamer, "when he finds it methodologically unsound to differentiate between the question to which the text is imagined to be an answer and the question to which it really is an answer" (Gadamer 1975: 335). Here the concept of horizon finds its best explication. To understand the question to which the text is an answer means to gain access to the horizon of meaning within which that question makes sense and can be raised. But at the same time the text asks a question of us, as its recipients.

> The voice that speaks to us from the past – be it text, word, trace – itself poses a question and places our meaning in openness. In order to answer this question, we, of whom the question is asked, must ourselves begin to ask questions.
>
> (Gadamer 1975: 337)

Thus the reconstruction of the question to which the meaning of a text is to be understood as an answer, passes into our own questioning. For the text must be understood "as an answer to a real question" (Gadamer 1975: 337), where "real" means "relevant for us." If we are not able to recover this *actualité* or contemporary relevance of a text we have not understood it at all. Thus the fusion is truly achieved only when we reframe the original question to which the text is an answer into a question that makes sense *for us*. Only at that point have we brought together the horizon within which the original question was raised and our own. Vice versa, we can also say that we learn to seek the equivalent of our contemporary questions within the horizon that is inherent in the text.

Interpretation as "making the most" of a text

A number of questions, unanswered within Gadamer's perspective, call in my opinion for a further development of his framework, but before discussing how the authenticity approach could be helpful in this respect, let me briefly recall another important competitor of the author's intention approach, the view of interpretation developed by Ronald Dworkin in his hermeneutic theory of law. Dworkin is not a philosopher of language or a theorist of text but a philosopher of law. At the center of his interest in *Rights Taken Seriously* and *Law's Empire* is, among other things, the process of adjudication, its inner dynamics and what validity means within it. What does it mean to say that one sentence or opinion of the Supreme Court is more right or just than another when different interpretations of the law are in conflict? Dworkin rejects both the legal positivist view, popular among conservative jurists, according to which the just sentence is the one that keeps closer to what the existing statutes and past court decisions prescribe, and the pragmatic view, popular with leftist lawyers and the Critical Legal Studies movement, that the right sentence is the one which promotes more progressive policy objectives. Interesting for our purposes is

Dworkin's argument against legal positivism. On the one hand he rejects the very distinction between "what the law prescribes" and "what the law ought to prescribe" as misleading. For the identification of what is to be included in the law is subject to interpretation in the first place. Judges confronted with a statute must still construe what the printed words mean and what their implications for the matter at hand are. On the other hand, Dworkin considers even more problematic the view according to which the normative content or meaning of a statute can be equated with the legislator's intention in conceiving the statute. His critique unfolds in three steps.

First, Dworkin points to the difficulty of determining who precisely is to count among the authors of a statute. Should we take into account the intentions of every member of the parliament that enacted it, including the intentions of those who voted against it but were defeated? Should only the intentions of those who approved it be taken into account? This latter solution is inconsistent with our notion that a statute is an expression of the will of the parliament or Congress as a whole, as determined by majority rule. More problems arise as soon as we try to determine which and whose intentions count most toward defining the meaning of the statute. Should only official speeches, as reported in the Congressional Record, count? Couldn't the intentions of those who didn't speak, but were the target of lobbying, have played a larger role? And then, should a legislator's intentions as expressed in a speech before an empty parliament count more toward defining the meaning of the statute than his or her responses in an interview broadcasted on the evening news and watched by millions of people?[14]

Second, Dworkin points out that even in the event that an agreement could be reached concerning who the real authors of the statute are and which kind of intentions should be attributed a more important role, a further difficulty emerges: their intentions in voting the statute may be very different and even conflicting. Should we then take the intentions shared by the greater number as the ones that define the meaning of the statute, or should we construe a kind of "average" intention that "comes closest to those of most legislators, though identical to none of them." (Dworkin 1986: 320).

Third, even if an agreement could be found also on this issue we would still have to decide which kind of documents could be taken as reliable indicators for the legislators' intentions. Once again, should official speeches as recorded on the Congressional Record be privileged as reliable indicators? What about the members of parliament or congress who wished that a certain goal be reflected in the statute but had no power to have a clause or amendment to that effect approved? They may have voted for the final version of the statute, though their intention was that the statute should be read as implying certain things that they did not have the power to make explicit in the text of the statute. Shouldn't those intentions count as well?[15]

The alternative suggested by Dworkin in order to avoid the difficulties of the legislator's intention approach to the meaning of law is close in certain respects to Gadamer's view. It relies on reflective judgment and it is a view of adjudication as guided by *integrity*. According to Dworkin, for all texts, including literary ones, the best interpretation is the one that "makes the object or practice being interpreted the best it can be" (Dworkin 1986: 77), a formulation close to Gadamer's ideas of the presumption of completeness and of the strengthening of the text's point. In legal matters, the best sentence when conflicting interpretations of the law exist is the one, accordingly, that *makes the most* of the existing legal tradition, understood not only as a collection of statutes, but also as a tradition of academic jurisprudence, as a series of relevant court decisions, all interpreted against the background of the history of the community of which the legal tradition is an expression. Thus in every just sentence a judgment is implicit regarding the best identity for the community in whose name the sentence is pronounced. This judgment obviously includes a reconstructive moment in which one takes into account the past history, legal and political, of the community, but it includes also a projectual moment. In the end Dworkin puts forward a claim that Gadamer in different words could subscribe to as well: the judge who writes a sentence on an important and controversial constitutional case is like someone who inherits a half-finished novel and decides to add an extra chapter. He or she must take into account the whole context created by the substantive, narrative and stylistic features of the existent manuscript and make the new chapter somehow fit them, without being thereby prevented from introducing innovative features, for example a new turning point in the plot. The best new chapter, among the attempts put forth hypothetically by different writers, is then the one which combines a maximum of originality and innovativeness with making the most of the extant narrative texture that defines the context.[16]

In this view we find a reformulation, from within a different vocabulary, of Gadamer's point that understanding always involves the calling into question of one's presuppositions and the establishing of some kind of relevance of the text for us, namely doing justice to the horizon of the text but bringing that meaning into a horizon that includes our own as well. Gadamer would also agree on the fact that the kind of judgment involved in this operation is reflective. Gadamer, as we know, would contest the possibility of sharply distinguishing our horizon and the horizon of a text from the past as self-enclosed wholes. So would Dworkin. No flat distinction can be drawn

> between the stage at which a chain novelist interprets the text he has been given and the stage at which he adds his own chapter, guided by the interpretation he has settled on. When he begins to write he might discover in what he has written a different, perhaps radically different, interpretation. Or he might find it impossible to write in the tone or scheme he first took up, and that will lead him to reconsider other interpretations he first rejected. In either case he returns to the text to reconsider the lines it makes eligible.
>
> (Dworkin 1986: 232)

The text as a symbolic identity

Both Gadamer's and Dworkin's conceptions of what it means for an interpretation to be better than another are formulated at a very high level of generality. Even though it would be inconsistent for an authenticity view of validity to suggest *criteria* of interpretive validity, we could try to bring the reconstruction of our intuitions concerning the validity of interpretations to a stage of greater differentiation.

Building on Gadamer and Dworkin, our initial question – What do we mean when we say that an interpretation is better than another? – can be reformulated as a set of more specific questions: What does it mean to best bring horizons to a fusion? What does it mean to "make the most of a text"? What does the ability, on the part of an interpreter, to bring out the completeness of the text amount to?

The authenticity approach to questions of validity can help us answer these questions in two steps. The first step consists in an illustration of the thesis that a text can be considered as a symbolic whole with a kind of identity *sui generis*. Persons have unique identities in the sense that their psychic constitution is so organized that certain features cannot be changed without thereby undermining the possibility for us to recognize the person as the same person. Identities can be well-formed or deficient in different ways: for example, we can speak of identities that have different degrees of coherence, of continuity, of demarcation, of vitality, of self-reflectiveness, of maturity and so on. In a metaphorical sense, texts and other symbolic complexes which I cannot consider here – for example, disciplines – have identities too, which can be more or less well-formed and to which our interpretations can do more or less justice.

That texts can be well-formed to various degrees will come as no surprise to anyone. A sequence of sentences does not *per se* count as a text, as discourse analysis and text-linguistics very well remind us. Native speakers of a language and members of a culture recognize as acceptable texts only those sequences of sentences which satisfy certain requirements, including a certain internal coherence, recurring and interweaving references to the same set of actors, objects and actions, thematic progression, and above all a well recognizable pragmatic "point" by reference to which we can understand the functions of the single parts of the text as well as the relevance of the utterance of the text *qua* social action. Less obvious is the idea that the step from reading the sentences of a text to grasping the meaning of the text can no more be brought under the scope of methods or, more generally, determinant judgment, than the attribution of a certain kind of personality to someone can be strictly deduced, on the basis of a method, from the observation of his or her external conduct. Thus the answer to the question *under which conditions are two texts the same?* cannot be that two texts are the same text when all the surface sentences are the same. For changing one sentence obviously does not give me the right to publish under my name the entire text of *Remembrance of Things Past*. Nor would the omission of a chapter do, perhaps not even a skillful paraphrasis of the whole text. On the other hand, in the text of a diplomatic agreement or in two drafts of the same statute even the change of one word within one sentence, let alone the omission of an entire clause, would be a legitimate basis for denying that the old and the new text are the same. In sum, the impossibility of providing a priori and external criteria for the self-sameness of texts supports the idea that we understand texts as symbolic wholes with an identity of their own.

As it is the case with individual or collective identities, also the *symbolic identities* characteristic of texts have built-in *evaluative dimensions* on the basis of which we appraise their integrity, fulfillment or realization – where the meaning of these notions is metaphorically derivative from the meaning of the equivalent expressions that we apply to the case of individual identities. In our case these dimensions orient our judgment as to what we accept as a well-formed text. Let me briefly review them.

First, for a sequence of sentences to constitute a text it must possess a certain degree of *coherence*. Also when conceived as a property of symbolic identities coherence is a complex notion, which includes at least two subdimensions. It includes a subdimension of *cohesion*, which can be understood as *consistency* and also as the property of possessing a core of meaning that encompasses the entire surface of the text – what Van Dijk has called a *macrostructure*. Another facet of the coherence of a text is its internal *continuity*, which we can understand in terms of the progression of a story, if we are dealing with a narrative, or as the thematic progression of an argument, if we are dealing with a non-narrative text. It is the subdimension of continuity that produces the sense that the single sentences do lead somewhere after all. The ordered graduality, as opposed to erraticness or abruptness, of the transition from local structures of meaning to the overall meaning, which falls under the heading of continuity and more generally of *coherence*, must be distinguished from a second dimension of the symbolic identity of a text, which falls under the heading of what we might call, if you allow me the parallel with individual identity, the *inner vitality* of a text or perhaps the *vividness* of the "point" that unifies the whole text.

For literary texts the dimension of *vividness* versus banality or boringness assumes a special relevance or even, according to some aesthetic traditions, ultimately sums up their intrinsic value. However, also in the case of the ordinary, communicative texts, it is possible to distinguish between texts that do manage to convey a point after all but do so in a clumsy, unappealingly intricate or orderly banal way, and texts in which the symbolic material is organized in a strikingly imaginative, colorful and appealing way, namely texts that convey their central point in a *vivid* way. It is interesting to notice that the dimension of vividness bears a different relation to the well-formedness of a text than the dimension of coherence. In fact, while in a sequence of sentences with no identifiable core meaning or no thematic progression we simply fail to recognize a text, a boring or banal text is a text nonetheless. Despite this different status –

its not being a *condicio sine qua non* – the dimension of vividness plays, as we will see, an important role in the evaluation of interpretations.

Third, every well-formed text possesses somehow a dimension of *depth*, understood as a kind of built-in self-reflectiveness. There are texts that embed a questioning of their own presuppositions or that self-referentially address their own internal structure – i.e. contain references to the relation between their sentences or larger portions of meaning – to an extent larger than other texts. Depth, understood as the self-referential addressing of the text's own structure of meaning, can go from a virtual zero degree to the total self-referentiality of certain short stories by Borges. Most texts fall somewhere in between. Depth, like vividness, is not a *necessary* condition for textuality. A text with no depth can still be a text, but depth, like vividness, is nonetheless a distinctive feature of its identity, an ingredient that helps us identify a given text and tell it apart from others.

Finally, well-formed texts possess a property of *commensurateness* that can be compared, *mutatis mutandis*, with the maturity of an individual or collective identity. In general, the maturity of an individual, as we have seen in Chapter 5, can be conceived as the capacity to come to terms with the facticity of the world in the pursuit of one's projects without thereby losing the uniqueness of one's identity. One of the facets of this dimension – namely, the subdimension which concerns the commensuration of our ideal self to the potentialities of the real self – retains a special relevance also in the case of *symbolic* identities. In fact, one feature of a good text is a certain commensuration of the means deployed within it by the author – be they argumentative means, empirical evidence or stylistic features – to the pragmatic object of the text *qua* social action or better *qua* macro-speech act. A more specific aspect of the commensurateness of a text has to do with the alignment of the question *explicitly* addressed by the text – if such a question finds a realization at the level of the surface structure of the text – and the *real* question to which the text constitutes an answer. How often do we read research reports where the questions addressed in the introduction suddenly undergo a drastic reduction in scope when it comes to the presentation of the findings?

To sum up, it belongs to our notion of a well-formed text – of the *textuality* of a text – that the sequence of its sentences is organized around a *coherent* focus, does not contain internal contradictions (*cohesion*), exhibits a thematic progression (*continuity*), brings out with *vividness* the overarching meaning that unifies the whole surface sequence, possesses a modicum of *depth*, in the sense of embedding references to the way the parts–whole relation is constituted, and considered as a structured sequence of speech acts is *commensurate* to the pragmatic goal underlying the text.

Interpretation as judgment on the fulfillment of a symbolic identity

The second step toward a reconstruction of our notion of validity in interpretation along authenticity lines can now be taken. While all interpretations can be understood as reflective judgments that enable us to identify the well-formedness or *textuality* of a text – where textuality is understood in terms of the four dimensions mentioned above – when we assess the validity or adequacy of a specific interpretation of a text we are concerned with the adequacy of that first-order judgment. Such assessment is based on a second-order reflective judgment that takes the appropriateness of an interpretive judgment on the textuality of a text as its object. When we try to assess the extent to which an interpretation makes the most of a text or brings our horizon and that of the text to an optimal fusion, we are basically in the same position as a psychoanalytic supervisor who evaluates the appropriateness of his supervisee's diagnosis concerning the identity of a patient, or in the position of someone who evaluates critically the adequacy of judgments given by art critics on works of art.

A theory of validity in interpretation of the kind discussed here entails one further step in reflexivity. It is a reconstruction of what we generally do when we perform these second-order reflective judgments on the adequacy of specific first-order interpretations.

When we are confronted with competing interpretations of the same text we check for how they can go wrong in the process of understanding. And this is when the new level of differentiation introduced by referring to the coherence, vividness, depth and commensurateness of a text, and to their respective sub-dimensions, can be useful. These dimensions can generate new questions, more than provide criteria or methods. In lieu of simply wondering whether the interpretation under scrutiny has failed to do justice to the meaning of the text or, conversely, has read into it meanings that were not really there, the identity approach can help us differentiate the very notion of the going wrong of an interpretation. In Gadamer's approach the conceptualization of what it means for an interpretation to go wrong takes on phenomenological overtones: he mentions the experience of the coming to nothing of certain fore-meanings or of being pulled up short by the text. The authenticity approach to interpretation can render such conceptualization more specific. Instead of simply speaking of meanings that were in the text and the interpretation failed to reflect, or of projected meanings which were not in the text, it allows us to raise further questions: Has the interpretation done justice to the coherence of the text, and more specifically to the internal consistency of its local structures of meaning and to the development of its thematic progression? Has the interpretation grasped the vividness of the central meaning of the text? Has the interpretation done justice to the self-referential depth of the text, to its implicit or explicit self-questioning, distancing from, and hedging of, its own presuppositions? Has the interpretation brought to light the congruency of the argumentative, narrative or stylistic means deployed by the author with the overall pragmatic goal that inheres in the text?

Furthermore, according to Gadamer, an interpretation can be inadequate in the sense that it fails to bring our own horizon and that of the text to a fusion, or brings about this "fusion" in a less complete way than another interpretation. Again, the authenticity approach allows us to spell out further what this means. The process called by Gadamer "fusion of horizons" can be seen as the *ad hoc* formation, within a specific interpretive context, for a certain pragmatic purpose and within certain situational constraints, of one common symbolic identity out the interpreter's cultural identity and the cultural horizon underlying the text. This account rules out a crypto-quantitative view of the fusion of horizons, as though it were a matter of bringing two areas to overlap as far as possible. If that were the case, verbal twisting and the deliberate use of ambiguous expressions could produce more fusion of horizons than other means. Instead, the authenticity approach allows us to submit the fusion of horizons brought about by an interpretation to further scrutiny by treating it as a *symbolic identity of its own*. The new symbolic identity resulting from such fusion can in turn be evaluated in terms of its *coherence* (i.e. the consistency and the smoothness with which its different components are integrated), its *vividness* (i.e. the crisp, self-evident and dynamic, as opposed to inelegant or clumsy, quality of the two-way translation of the central questions), its *depth* (as built-in awareness of, and reference to, the interpretive process that brought the fusion about), or its *commensurateness* (as a considered, "reflective equilibrium"-like balancing of the constitutive elements of the two horizons, the opposite of which is a shortcircuiting, magical or wishful-thinking kind of fusion).

To conclude, the answer to our initial question – What do we mean when we say that one interpretation of a text is better than another? – cannot take the form of a list of criteria that one interpretation meets better than the other. This is not the sense in which the four dimensions of coherence, vividness, depth and commensurateness are to be interpreted. Just as it is the case with the dimensions through which we make sense of the good for individual and collective identities, they lack the determinacy of criteria and cannot be ranked. We cannot say a priori and in general whether the interpretation of a text is improved by modifications that, for example, bring about a gain on the dimension of capturing the vividness of the text but entail a loss on the dimension of grasping its coherence. In this sense the dimensions of textuality are not criteria in the "determinant judgment" sense of the word. They do not allow subsumption of the particular under a predefined universal concept. They are best understood as *guidelines* that *orient* – in the sense attributed to the notion of "oriented reflective judgment" in Chapter 3 – our first-order reflective judgments concerning the textuality of texts and our second-order reflective judgments concerning the adequacy of interpretations.

The identity of the work of art

Let us turn now to the second kind of symbolic identities that the authenticity approach to validity can help us evaluate in new terms: the work of art. What do we mean when we say that a work of art is *well-formed*? The expression "well-formed" is used here – despite its unwelcome logical connotations – in order to avoid terms which in one way or another might convey some reference to the traditional categories of the *beautiful* or the *sublime*. "Well-formedness," understood as an equivalent of the German substantive "*Gelungenheit*" (*success-fulness*), is designed to be neutral with respect to the connotations conveyed by both extremes of that aesthetic dichotomy. The "beautiful" conveys an intrinsi-cally harmonistic, Apollonian, classicist, consolatory and ultimately conservative view of the aesthetic validity of a work of art. The notion of the "sublime", on the other hand, appears to be inextricably linked with the Romantic view of aesthetic value as the product of genius, with an equally Romantic and anti-Kantian priority of genius over taste, and with the Dionysian tendency to cherish the authentically perverse, the authentically obscene and the authentically provocative.

On one level, for a work of art to be well-formed means not so much to assuage that tension between conformity to a stylistic canon and innovation which is constitutive for all artistic practice, as to keep it vibrating in an ongoing dynamic balance. More specifically, to be well-formed means to keep that tension vibrating in ways capable of generating an *aesthetic experience*, an experience of *dépaysement*, or that kind of experience which Arthur Danto has felicitously called "the transfiguration of the commonplace" (Danto 1981). To this constitutive capacity of the well-formed work of art to make us question a habitual perspective on, and a certain way of relating to, the world refer also those who, like Heidegger, conceive of the aesthetic experience as *world-disclosure*.[17] As Kant suggested, somehow this kind of aesthetic experience is related to the potential, possessed by the work of art, for bringing all of our mental faculties into a never-ending play. The same property is emphasized by Italo Calvino when he describes the artist's capacity to induce an aesthetic experience as the capacity to "follow the lightning like track of the mental circuits that capture and establish connections between points far apart in space and time" (Calvino 1988: 47). Such experiences, captured under the comprehensive heading of the "aesthetic experience," originate in the fact that the work of art, *qua stylistic metaphor*, is capable of bringing diversity to unity without suppressing or doing violence to the particularity of the particular. In its capacity for keeping the elements of a diverse constellation in an ongoing dynamic tension the work of art enters a metaphoric relation with itself *qua* theater of the tension between stylistic conformity and innovation and also enters a metaphoric relation with such constitutive aspects of subjectivity as the tension between cohesion and fragmentation, self-congruity and dispersion.[18]

141

It is possible to speak of the work of art as constituted by a complex of tensions in two senses. First, in every work of art a tension emerges and manifests itself between the aesthetic idea that pervades it – not its "contents" but the artistic *project* underlying it, which as such is inherently an inextricable nexus of form and substance – and the materials which are designed to convey that idea. If this tension could be entirely assuaged, the work of art would fail. It would be totally flat, so to speak. As Adorno puts it, "there exist works of art in which the artist has expressed in a straightforward and plain way what he wanted to convey: the end result is but a sign of what the artist meant and is thus little more than a coded allegory" (Adorno 1975: 218). Second, in every work of art a certain tension survives between the unity of the underlying aesthetic *project* and the particular elements of meaning that resist being integrated within this unity. There can be no such thing as a "perfect" work of art. If such a work existed, notes Adorno, by virtue of its existence it would dissolve the very concept of art. Instead, only "deep" works of art exist, namely works of art which "neither conceal divergent or inconsistent aspects nor leave it alone without attempting a reconciliation" (Adorno 1975: 319), which is just another way of saying works of art which are never *entirely* but always *to various degrees* "well-formed."

If we assume that each work of art, just as each human life, succeeds or fails *in its own way* and that we cannot measure success or failure as distance from an externally defined *telos*, what sort of properties do we look for when we try to assess an artistic object? One of the assumptions implicit in the authenticity approach is that our judgments on the well-formedness of works of art share many features in common with our judgments on the fulfillment or authenticity of an individual identity. Aside from the traditional eighteenth-century understanding of the artistic and the psychological domains as two aspects of the aesthetic sphere, this thesis will represent no surprise to whoever is inclined to favorably consider Dewey's idea of a deep continuity between art and the human experience (see Dewey 1980). Both in Dewey's theory of action and experience and in Winnicott's notion of "creative living" we find an approach in terms of which the functioning of the artistic side of the aesthetic – for example, the capacity of the great works of art to set our imagination in motion and to afford us a pleasure connected with the feeling of the "furtherance of life" – is best understood in connection with our reaction to the exposure to instances of a life well lived. In the case of Dewey the explanation for this lies in a certain homology between experience and art. Both are ways for responding to alterations of rhythms, for restoring a certain kind of integration between the person and the environment. As Dewey puts it:

Experience in the degree in which it *is* experience is heightened vitality. Instead of signifying being shut up within one's own private feelings and sensations, it signifies active and alert commerce with the world; at its height it signifies complete interpenetration of self and the

world of objects and events. . . . Because experience is the fulfilment of
an organism in its struggles and achievements in a world of things, it is
art in germ. Even in its rudimentary forms, it contains the promise of
that delightful perception which is esthetic experience.

(Dewey 1980: 19)

From another vantage point the same idea is at the center of the psychoanalytic
theory of culture and creativity developed by Winnicott. Winnicott's plea for
the word "creativity" not to be reductively associated with "the successful or
acclaimed creation" runs throughout his late work. The great artist's creativity is
rooted in the same kind of human experience as the creativity of every human
being who has been allowed by a sufficiently empathic mother to develop a
relation to the world which is not based on mere compliance, but contains
elements of self-expressiveness. The creative impulse, suggests Winnicott, "is
present when *anyone* – baby, child, adolescent, adult, old man or woman – looks
in a healthy way at anything or does anything deliberately, such as making a
mess with feces or prolonging the act of crying to enjoy a musical sound"
(Winnicott 1971: 80–1). Artistic creation and creative living are distinct but
share in common the potential for inducing "the feeling that we are alive, that
we are ourselves" (Winnicott 1986: 43): once again, Kant's notion of the
furtherance of life reemerges with undiminished relevance.[19]

The basic idea of a continuity between art and everyday human experience
– which stands opposite to the intuition underlying Adorno's understanding of
aesthetics – can be fruitfully expanded in a number of directions where more
elements of convergence can be found. One of these directions is the attempt
to trace structural similarities between the work of art and the identity of an
individual. First, both in the case of the work of art and in that of an individual identity we are confronted with symbolic entities (the psychological
identity as an internal representation of the self, the identity of the work of art
as that which renders it different from all other artworks) which are *unique*
and *irreplaceable*. To the uniqueness of every individual identity corresponds an
irreplaceability of every work of art in the sense that the unique aesthetic
experience induced by exposure to it cannot be reproduced by any surrogate.
Second, both an individual identity and a work of art possess the qualities of a
totality or of a *Gestalt* whose central parts or components cannot be freely
substituted for without loss of value, and even relatively minor modifications
of the peripheral components do affect the global quality of the overall configuration. Third, both works of art and identities share a certain *imperviousness
to instrumental rationality*. Neither aesthetic value nor *eudaimonia* understood as
self-fulfillment can be means to other ends without thereby contradicting their
own primary meaning. Fourth, the work of art and the identity of a person
enter a peculiar relation with their *material substratum*. While neither of them
can be *reduced* to this sensuous, material, bodily dimension, on the other hand

our representation of them can never entirely prescind from reference to it either. As Heidegger has put it:

> Works of art are shipped like coal from the Ruhr and logs from the Black Forest. During the First World War Hölderlin's hymns were packed in the soldier's knapsack together with cleaning gear. Beethoven's quartets lie in the storerooms of the publishing house like potatoes in a cellar. All works have this thingly character. . . . Even the much-vaunted aesthetic experience cannot get around the thingly aspect of the artwork.
>
> (Heidegger 1993a: 145)

Fifth, both identities and works of art are permeated by processes of *communication*, but communication does not exhaust their meaning. In fact identities and artworks possess a quality of *openness* – a connotative openness that resists the closure of denotation, a motivational openness that resists the closure of behavior, a surplus of sense that leaves eternally unaccomplished the task of mapping the relation between central and peripheral elements. The difference lies in the fact that while the identity of a person reaches a definitive completion only when the life of the person ends, the work of art has a life of its own even after the artist has formally completed it – a symbolic life or *Wirkungsgeschichte*.[20]

To these similarities is largely due the fact that by and large the dimensions which account for our intuitions concerning the fulfillment of individual identities maintain their relevance also when we try to make sense of the dimension to which we intuitively direct our attention in the process of assessing the well-formedness of works of art. While it would be self-contradictory to think of well-formedness in terms of adequacy to anything other than a principle of authenticity as *exemplary self-congruency*, nonetheless it can legitimately be claimed that in the process of assessing a work of art we focus on a set of dimensions or aspects which, for all the diversity of emphasis embedded in various poetics and critical orientations, constantly recur as ingredients of aesthetic well-formedness.

First, when confronted with an object which *prima facie* appears to be a work of art – a painting, a book whose title and contents suggest it to be a novel, a sculpture, a movie etc. – we wonder whether the multiplicity of diverse elements that constitute it (a multiplicity of sentences and paragraphs, of chromatic effects, of brush strokes, of plastic forms) is in fact held together by a unity of intent. In fact, we could not even perceive the material object that forms the substratum of the work of art as a meaningful object if we didn't presuppose that underlying the work of art is such a unity of intent which provides it with *coherence*. Nor could we make sense of any work of art if we didn't also presuppose a certain successful *demarcation* of it from its surrounding milieu.

Individual identities have been said to possess a dimension of vitality. Just as the dimension of coherence cannot exhaust the meaning that we associate with the fulfillment or realization of an individual identity – for instance, the life of a monomaniac chess player might very well exhibit a high degree of coherence, but can hardly be taken as an example of fulfillment if the other dimensions are underrepresented – so when confronted with an object that looks like a work of art we also wonder, over and beyond whether a coherent intent has guided the artist in shaping it, what kind of inner principle or idea "enlivens," "animates," "lightens" or "brings life" to it as a symbolic object. For what makes of one of the many existing complexes of symbols this particular and indeed unique work of art is not merely the fact of being organized around an intention that somehow contains a reference to the production of an aesthetic effect, but also the presence of a kind of "spark," the kind of thing for which Kant and the Romantic aesthetics have coined the notion of "genius" – the kind of thing which makes separate spheres of our experience communicate with one another, leads us to question the obvious, opens up new possibilities for the perception of the self and the world. In a sense, a work of art that is not in some sense unsettling – in the Freudian sense of the "*unheimlich*" – is not art, but a mere ornament. As a matter of fact, doesn't a negative answer to the question whether a certain painting or musical performance or movie has deeply "impressed" us always imply a negative judgment?

Furthermore, if by *depth* we understand an individual's capacity to incorporate constitutive aspects of his or her identity into the project that is also part of that identity, then in a sense such a dimension is also relevant for our assessment of works of art. Just as in appraising the fulfillment of an individual identity we wonder whether the person knows enough about him- or herself and their real motives, so in judging the well-formedness of a work of art we always wonder to what extent the various aspects and moments of the creative process have found a reflection in that stylistic metaphor that the work of art is. Especially when we are confronted with the art of our century, the act of assessing a work of art always includes an interrogation concerning the degree to which the formative process, the carrying of the initial intention through the confrontation with the aesthetic material, has come to be somehow represented or taken into account in the final product and has thus given substance to a radicalized reflexivity which modernity has posited as an ultimate aesthetic value.

Finally, if by *maturity* we understand the capacity to come to terms with the world without losing the sense of one's direction in life and the distinctness of one's identity, then again it is not difficult to see the relevance of this dimension to the practice of aesthetic judgment. No assessment of the well-formedness of a work of art can prescind from addressing the question whether and to what extent in pursuing his or her own intention the artist has really done justice to the materials treated (be they physical or symbolic materials such as a stylistic tradition), whether and to what extent such materials have been violently molded after something which has in the end remained external, or whether on the contrary that a unique consonance has been created from which emanates that message of true respect for, and receptivity to, otherness which is part and parcel of every well-formed work of art.

Are these not the dimensions on which every masterpiece excels? Are these not the dimensions around which the contest among rival poetics takes place? One need only recall the competition between poetics which emphasize the primacy of maturity as expertise in mastering the materials (all classicist and mannerist poetics) and poetics that on the contrary emphasize the immediacy and "democratic" character of art ("Everybody can be an artist"), between poetics that emphasize the self-reflexivity of the work of art (all the poetics underlying expressionism, conceptual art, dodecaphonic music etc.) and poetics which stress the intentional and often polemic absence of self-reflexivity (all naive movements and "Ready Made" art), between Romantic or sublime-oriented poetics which emphasize vitality over technical mastery, or even the coherence of artistic intent, and realistic poetics which stress certain substantive guidelines and the unity of purpose (Lukacs's realism, for example).

Concluding remarks

Much more work than these tentative considerations is needed in order to articulate the notion of authenticity of a symbolic identity and to outline its significance for a reconstruction of our intuitions concerning the well-formedness of texts and works of art. Other symbolic objects – academic *disciplines*, scientific, intellectual and other kinds of *traditions*, as well as *complex organizations* and *institutions* – may also be said to constitute the object of evaluations that again revolve around the attribution of an identity and the assessment of its degree of fulfillment. In all of these cases we couch our evaluations in a plurality of vocabularies that can be said to draw on the four dimensions of the fulfillment of identities. The authenticity view of validity can provide a new perspective for making sense of the new approaches to managerial action in complex organizations – for example, of "postmodern" and "symbolic" approaches – and of the new "governance" approach to the functioning of institutions. It is in the domain of the study of scientific traditions and academic disciplines, however, that the most innovative results can be expected. After the revolution brought about by Kuhn's "postempiricist" philosophy of science, no one has been able to come up with a convincing reconstruction of what validity means at the level of paradigm choice or assessment – when we are confronted with the necessity of choosing between alternative paradigms that possess different distributions of theoretical advantages and disadvantages. Kuhn's discussion of the role of scientific values can be taken as the starting point for considering paradigms as the identity component of scientific disciplines and traditions, as an identity to which the adoption of one among the competing theoretical alternatives can bring a fulfillment *sui generis*, a fulfillment usually assessed in terms of the values of accuracy, coherence, scope, elegance and fruitfulness. Once again, these values appear to function as guidelines for the scientist's assessment of the validity claims of interparadigmatically contested theories in a way not too dissimilar from the way in which the dimensions of authenticity outlined above are supposed to guide our judgment about the fulfillment of other kinds of identities. This whole line of development of the authenticity approach will be the object of a future investigation.

8

RETHINKING THE PROJECT OF MODERNITY

In the preceding chapters several facets of the *authenticity-thesis* have been explored – including the relevance of authenticity to the reconstruction of our intuitions concerning the fulfillment of individual and collective identities, and the validity of interpretation. It is now time to address, in a reflexive turn, the status of the *authenticity-thesis* as elucidated thus far. The *authenticity-thesis* has been presented as embedding a critique of the early modern understanding of validity in general and, more specifically, of the generalizing model of universalism underlying it. This way of proceeding calls first of all for an elucidation of the relation of the *authenticity-thesis* and of exemplary universalism not only to contemporary culture but also to what Habermas has called the "project of modernity" – namely, the project of grounding our validity claims in the transindividually objective and yet humanly "subjective" structures of subjectivity.[1] Does the culture of authenticity still partake of the project of modernity in the sense of drawing its normativity out of a certain privileged "true" description of human subjectivity?

Furthermore, our discussion of the exemplary form of validity associated with the *authenticity-thesis* calls for a reflexive elucidation of the status of the discourse that illustrates the *authenticity-thesis*. On what basis does the implicit validity claim raised by the *authenticity-thesis* rest? These two orders of problems will be at the center of our attention in this final chapter.

Authenticity and the project of modernity

Let us go back to the image of the caravan at the ford. As we have seen in Chapter 1, *intersubjectivity* is the banner under which rally those who understand the philosophical task of the present as a *completion* of the project of modernity. According to their understanding, what is wrong about the "project of modernity" is the description of the structures of subjectivity – a description couched in an "atomistic," "methodologically individualist" or "*subjekt-philosophisch*" vocabulary that obscures the communicative and intersubjective constitution of subjectivity. An adequate grasp of such communicative nature of reason and subjectivity will allow the project to resume its course. The

148

decentered or centerless subject, instead, is the banner under which the advocates of breaking away from modernity rally. According to their view, it is not just the execution but the *project* of modernity as such that is misguided. For it takes at face value foundational discourses which are at best rationalizations of historically contingent constellations of meaning endowed with the social power to shape our representations. The alternative of bringing the project of modernity to completion versus abandoning it altogether, however, is somehow too crude and even misleading. The purpose underlying the *authenticity-thesis* is neither simply to *complete* the "project of modernity" on a line of continuity with its foundationalist premises nor to *abandon* it altogether, but rather to *radically rethink it* under new premises in order to make it finally work.

If we take the "project of modernity" as concerning the justification or grounding of normativity along immanent lines, out of subjectivity itself, or if we take it to concern the possibility of a self-grounding, as it were, of validity, then *from this specific vantage point*, the *authenticity-thesis* represents the most radicalized form that *this* project can take, and to that extent can be said to amount to a *completion* of modernity. From this perspective, in fact, it makes sense to state that while the early modern philosophers subjectivized the source of validity by relocating it from Logos to the Subject, but still conceived of "the subject" as an ideal subject or as a collective macro-subject, and thus as standing above the concrete individual just as classical Logos did, the authors who conceive of validity in the exemplary universalist terms elucidated by the *authenticity-thesis* bring the subjectivization of the foundations of validity to its ultimate resting point. While the epistemic or moral principles elaborated by early modern philosophy were, even though grounded in autonomous subjectivity, just as context-free or context-transcending as the classical notions of human nature or of a Cosmos, authors such as Rousseau, Simmel or Sartre take the subjectivization of validity to its ultimate conclusion, by understanding validity as stemming from principles rooted in *concrete identities*: "universels singuliers" (Sartre) and "individuelle Gesetze" (Simmel). From the standpoint of the *authenticity-thesis* so understood, modernity has not been modern enough up until now. It still has to become fully modern. Accordingly, the significance of the turn of contemporary culture towards authenticity and the related paradigm of reflective judgment can be described as that of further modernizing modernity or of setting the project of modernity more in tune with itself.

This narrative of a transition from a "quasi" or "pseudo" subjectivized conception of validity typical of early-modernity to the fully subjectivized notion of validity developed by the authors of the tradition of authenticity, however, cannot by itself corroborate the idea that the *authenticity-thesis* stands in a relation of mere "completion" to the project of modernity – namely, in a relation where aspects of continuity self-evidently prevail over fractures. In fact, the narrative outlined above obscures three conceptual junctures at which the exemplary universalist notion of validity embedded in the *authenticity-thesis* comes to clash with essential features of the project of modernity and thus calls for a more radical rethinking of its premises than the advocates of the "completion" thesis would be ready to admit.

First, insofar as the project of modernity presupposes an internal connection between *validity* and *demonstrability*, a dissonance with the *authenticity-thesis* arises. For the universalistic cogency implicit in reflective judgment and in exemplary universalist notions (e.g. Simmel's "individual law" or Pareyson's concept of the "law" underlying the work of art) is not susceptible of "demonstration," even in the weakest possible sense of the term – the enunciation of a thesis that "no one can reasonably reject."

Second, implicit in the *authenticity-thesis* is a rejection of the idea, underlying the nexus of validity and demonstrability, that we should on the whole be more confident about the validity of statements and norms generated by determinant judgment. In this sense, the authenticity-thesis parts ways with all versions (including the "presuppositions of communication" found in Habermas's *communicative paradigm*) of the modern notion of a neutral language of commensuration within which the testing of statements and norms generated from provincial contexts could be carried out without significant loss of meaning.

Third, the *authenticity-thesis* cannot accept an enervated view of the aesthetic as the sphere specialized in the expression of the "subjective world."[2] Without going to the opposite extreme of loading the aesthetic sphere with the burden of being the only locus where truth inhabits and can be glimpsed at through the experience induced by the work of art, the *authenticity-thesis* takes the aesthetic as a realm in which a specialized kind of cultivated self-expressiveness coexists with a potential for "world disclosure" and with a "principle of validity" – exemplary universalism – whose relevance encompasses the whole spectrum of a decentered modern Reason, including science, morality, law and politics.

These three moments of discontinuity with respect to the project of modernity make it senseless to see the *authenticity-thesis* as *merely* a completion or a radicalization of it. Rather, the *authenticity-thesis* seems to radically *redefine* the project of modernity, at least in the sense that, with reference to the above-mentioned three points, it introduces more substantial changes than the ones introduced by the communicative paradigm. In fact, the *authenticity-thesis* departs from the modern belief that what is valid can also be publicly and conclusively demonstrated to be so. It also departs from the modern idea that the distance between the locally generated meanings, norms and representations can be bridged by recourse to some neutral framework that is not itself "local" but transcends all particularity. And, finally, the *authenticity-thesis* assigns to the aesthetic sphere the special significance of constituting a path-breaking human practice which has *always* been functioning on the basis of an intrinsic and accepted pluralism of standards coupled with a normative notion of universalistic yet undemonstrable validity that falls under the heading of exemplary authenticity.

However, despite these points of divergence the *authenticity-thesis* does not amount to a *break* with the project of modernity – at least not in the sense intended by the defenders of philosophical postmodernism. Contrary to the poststructuralist, deconstructionist and postmodernist positions, in fact, the *authenticity-thesis* – on a line of *continuity* with modern thought – conceives of subjectivity as bound up more with *plenitude* than with *void* or *absence*, with *self-determination* and *purposefulness* rather than with *directionlessness*. According to the *authenticity-thesis*, the image of subjectivity that emerges from the reconstruction of our intuitions concerning the fulfillment of individual and collective identities points in that direction. But even more decidedly than such reconstruction, which the defenders of poststructuralism, deconstructionism and postmodernism might accuse of being partial and selective, such an understanding of subjectivity is corroborated, according to the *authenticity-thesis*, by the difficulties and aporias to which the rival view of subjectivity as centerless gives rise whenever we shift our attention from a philosophical anthropology shrouded in the "discourse concerning the subject" to considerations of moral and political philosophy – to all those domains where notions of imputability, responsibility, accountability necessarily hold centerstage.

Above all, the *authenticity-thesis* takes distance from poststructuralism and postmodernism in another respect: it continues to understand questions concerning validity as meaningful. This is not an obvious claim. From the Copernican revolution occasioned by the Linguistic Turn – that is, from the idea that no statement or vocabulary can claim to draw its validity from a direct access to an uninterpreted reality – a postmodernist philosopher such as Rorty has derived the conclusion that "the nature of truth" is an unprofitable topic, resembling in this respect "the nature of man" and "the nature of God" (Rorty 1989: 8).[3] One line of response to the postmodernist objection consists in pointing to the fact that while we can perhaps communicate or act without presupposing the idea of God – though Durkheim has taught us to understand the *sacred* along immanent lines, as a self-expressing idealization whose production is coextensive with social life as such – we cannot engage in the act of communicating with one another without implicitly presupposing some notion of validity. The only alternative to clarifying our implicit notion of validity is not – as Rorty claims – to live without a notion of validity but merely to live without an *understanding* of what we mean by validity. Rorty himself cannot escape this fate. Ironically – and in spite of his dislike of foundationalism, to which he cavalierly reduces all kinds of universalism, including the universalism of *phronesis*, *reflective judgment* and the *individual law* – Rorty's implicit utopia is one in which "ironism" becomes universal. Furthermore, for all his aversion to the Whiggish view of history, Rorty is in no position to deny that from his vantage point the abandonment of all inquiry into the nature of truth and rightness would somehow count as "progress." And finally, also as progress must count the increasing level of human solidarity that Rorty associates with the rise of the liberal polity.[4]

An alternative line of response to the question about the fruitfulness of discussions about validity, that the *authenticity-thesis* might follow, consists in pointing to the presence of an undeveloped theory of validity in Rorty's account of the transition from one paradigm or vocabulary to another. While questioning the usefulness of discussing validity in general, Rorty is not prepared, however, to subscribe to the conclusion that all paradigms or vocabularies are equally valid. This sets an element of ambiguity and tension within his position. He does not wish to construe cultural change of the scope of the transition from Aristotelian to Newtonian physics, from late-scholastic metaphysical thought to the Cartesian and Kantian philosophy of the subject, or from classical, virtue-based to modern, rule-based moral theory, or from classical Natural Law theories to modern contract theories as the outcome of definitive proofs or argumentation or as the result of a "subjective" decision. In his words,

> Cultural change of this magnitude does not result from applying criteria (or from "arbitrary decision") any more than individuals become theists or atheists, or shift from one spouse or circle of friends to another, as a result either of applying criteria or of *actes gratuits*.
>
> (Rorty 1989: 6)

What accounts for these transformations, then, is one's gradual growing out of the habit of describing the self, others or the natural world in certain ways and the sedimentation of a new set of tacit presuppositions which, after a while, come to constitute a new vocabulary or paradigm self-consciously adhered to. While it is clear that this view emphasizes the role of *contingency* in the shaping of vocabularies and world-views, it remains unclear, however, in what the *non-arbitrariness* of these processes would consist.[5] Some idea of what Rorty might mean by "non-arbitrariness" can be gleaned from a passage in which he seems to point to the possibility of conceiving a sort of "individual law" for an individual identity:

> Anything from the sound of a word through the color of a leaf to the feel of a piece of skin can, as Freud showed us, serve to dramatize and crystallize a human being's sense of self-identity. For any such thing could play the role in an individual life which philosophers have thought could, or at least should, be played only by things which were universal, common to us all. . . . Any seemingly random constellation of such things can set the tone of a life. Any such constellation can set up an unconditional commandment to whose service a life may be

devoted – *a commandment no less unconditional because it may be intelligible to, at most, only one person.*

(Rorty 1989: 37, emphasis added)

While the idea of an "inner constellation" could represent a promising starting point for a still undeveloped postfoundationalist notion of validity, in Rorty's case it remains limited to the realm of individual identity and even so it creates a tension with one of the basic tenets of his postmodernism which are most at risk of relapsing into a "descriptive," ontological mode: the idea of the self as a "centerless web of beliefs and desires."[6]

To sum up the argument, according to the *authenticity-thesis* subjectivity – now understood as "authentic" subjectivity – continues to exert a sort of "foundational" function *sui generis* in the context of contemporary modernity, but the function and the mode of "providing foundations" has changed. The exercise of "providing foundations" has been transformed by the Linguistic Turn from the function of providing an ultimate anchoring of our theoretical and normative views into some description of reality no longer questionable in that it must be counted as a direct, unmediated reflection of a significant portion of reality, to the more modest function of providing a "constructivist" or "reconstructive" elucidation of our intuitions. Not just the scope of "grounding" or "justifying" has undergone a transformation, however, but also its *mode*. In fact, the fall of Archimedean points brought about by the Linguistic Turn has dragged with it also the idea of "justification by subsumption" which inhered in Kant's concept of determinant judgment: it has become inconsistent for us to conceive of justification in terms other than the operation of reflective judgment. Such change in the function and the mode of justification in general bears an important consequence on the justification of the *authenticity-thesis* in particular. This leads me directly to the question concerning the validity of the authenticity approach to validity.

Radical reflexivity: metaphysical and postmetaphysical

Philosophically, we do not just live in a world marked by the "Linguistic Turn." We also live in a post-Hegelian and post-Heideggerian world – namely, in a philosophical world that has experienced the rise and the fall of Hegel's attempt to place his philosophy at the extreme limit of modernity and is still in important respects within the spell of Heidegger's antihumanist stance combined with that (mostly French) cultural phenomenon known as "critique of the subject." Thus before elucidating what it means for the *authenticity-thesis* to validate itself in a radically self-reflexive way, we need to briefly consider the illustrious precedents of this idea of justification to be found in Hegel and Heidegger.

After Fichte's initial attempt, Hegel provided the most developed and indeed all-encompassing example of a radically self-reflexive model of justification. Over and over again throughout his entire work, Hegel presents us with a spiral-like movement of reflexive thought that problematizes the horizon of modernity – the originality of subjectivity – not in order to simply restore the premodern ontological way of thinking (though of course the restoration of a newly conceived identity of subject and object, after the modern dissolution of it in the transcendental perspective, is one of Hegel's goals) or in order to bid farewell to modernity, but in order to bring the modern consciousness to its ultimate fruition via an immanent process of reflection that leads us to the frontier of modernity.

The fascination of the Hegelian model of justification lies in the radical self-referentiality that pervades such works as *The Phenomenology of Spirit* and *The Science of Logic*. In *The Phenomenology of Spirit* the justification of an "objective" standpoint – objective in a stronger sense than the Kantian transcendental necessity – proceeds on the basis of three fundamental assumptions. First, for Hegel truth is not merely a property of propositions, but it is also a property of reality. While the truth of propositions is understood in correspondence terms, for an element of reality to attain its truth means to exist in accord with its "notion" – namely to realize all the potentialities inherent in it or to become in actuality all that it could be. Second, for Hegel reality is always in the process of transforming itself: it becomes. Facts, understood as isolated states of affairs, are abstractions of the mind. The motor of this unending process of becoming is the *difference* between what potentially a given moment of reality could be – its *essence* – and what it actually is or, in other words, its *existence*. The *negativity* implicit in this difference provides a key to grasping the becoming of reality. Third, thought is understood by Hegel as part of reality and, more specifically, that part of reality which is capable of understanding itself.

On the basis of these assumptions Hegel builds an account of validity that is meant to overcome the difficulties of Kant's transcendental approach. The subject of knowledge is not conceived as standing over against the reality that it seeks to know, but as actually *part of* that reality. In such capacity as a moment of reality, the subject becomes: it evolves from a stage at which it is at great variance with its essence – namely, a stage at which its existence succeeds in expressing but a limited fraction of its possibilities – to a stage at which its existence approaches the point of being identical with its essence. Also the subject understood as "thinking process" evolves – *The Phenomenology of Spirit* is in fact a reconstruction of the inner necessity of this development of consciousness – and in the course of such development it attains a greater and greater degree of truth (truth as correspondence) in grasping its object, which happens to be the subject itself *qua* reality. Eventually, at the end of the process, the subject *qua* thinking process will be able to grasp thoroughly the fact that itself, now under the description of being a moment of reality, has attained the truth of its being, namely has fulfilled all its potentialities. It is at this point of Absolute Knowledge that the reality side (or "object" side) and the thinking side of the subject can be said to be *identical*. This is possible because on the one hand Hegel construes the notion of a full-fledged development of the subject *qua* reality as including the idea of the subject's own ability to comprehend itself fully, and on the other hand because it is part of the notion of the full-fledged development of the subject *qua* thinking that its own object – namely the subject as part of reality – has made manifest, and thus knowable, all the potentialities enshrined in its essence. In this way the gap between subject and object, thought and being, theory and practice is bridged. To attain the truth is not merely a matter of *knowing* something, it requires also a *practical* moment, because the unfolding of all potentialities of reality – a necessary condition for us to be able to understand its essential features – depends also on what the subject *does*.[7]

Eventually, then, Hegel's theory of knowledge leads to, and requires for its completion, a philosophy of history, but this is not relevant for our purposes. More relevant is the observation that at no point of the complex argument developed in *The Phenomenology of Spirit* is there any reference to principles or aspects of normativity located *outside, beyond* or *above* the process of knowing itself. In this sense, this work represents one form of reflection on the conditions of validity conducted under modern premises which is just as radical as Kant's interrogation on the transcendental conditions of knowledge without incorporating the Kantian strategy of splitting the realm of freedom and that of necessity, subject and object, reason and intellect, the knowable and the unknowable, knowledge and metaphysics – and thus without having to submit to the Kantian separation of external principles and the subject matter to which they are applied, substance and method, judgment and the thing judged.

In *The Science of Logic* the kind of radical reflexivity which is of direct relevance for the authenticity approach to validity is best evinced in the discussion of the relation between finitude and the infinite[8] and, more specifically, in the paragraph on the "Transformation of the finite into the infinite."[9] Underneath Hegel's critique of the dualistic nature of Kant's doctrine is a critique of the persisting externality of the infinite or universal. The transcendental approach to validity is antimetaphysical not in the sense of denying the validity of metaphysical propositions about absolute entities – a denial which would be tantamount to making another metaphysical statement – but in the more "modest" sense of denying the decidability of such propositions on the basis of human knowledge. For Kant human knowledge is necessarily finite. In the section of *The Science of Logic* devoted to "finitude" Hegel challenges the assumptions underlying this self-limiting nature of the transcendental paradigm. The "bad infinity" that haunts this paradigm lies in the rigid, theologically inspired and ultimately "abstract" separation of finitude and the infinite – as though finitude and the infinite partook of qualitatively different "worlds," that of the creaturely limited and that of divine perfection. Such rigid opposition then leads Kant to misconstrue both the nature of the finite and that of the infinite. On the one hand, in fact, this conception fails to recognize the moment of infinity that it attributes to the finitude of the human subject, to *Dasein*: for all of *Dasein*'s finitude, its transiency is not itself transient, but is posited as eternal, unchanging and no less boundless than infinity. On the other hand, Kant's strategy of separation does not limit itself to implicitly absolutizing the transiency of the finite: it also relativizes and finitizes the infiniteness of the infinite. For the infinite, now conceived as what lies *beyond the limits* or the *boundaries* of finitude, appears to be itself limited by the border beyond which it supposedly lies. In its failing to include the finite it appears to be not truly infinite, but only a finitude of larger size.[10]

Now, Kant is not unaware of the difficulties highlighted above, but the externalism that is causing them is not completely removed in the solution that he devises. Indeed, it would be unfair to attribute to Kant a view of the infinite as that which lies beyond the limit of the knowable – and which is consequently just as *limited* and finite as our knowledge. For Kant traces the infinite also on *this side* of the border, within the transcendental subject, in the form of the subject's need and longing to transcend the limits of its own finitude. The infinite becomes then a task, an "ought," a *Sollen* that extends its roots into the subject in the form of the categorical imperative or of the urge to confront the antinomies of reason.

Even this solution, however, ultimately fails to escape the fate of "bad infinity." For, as Hegel points out, Kant's philosophical modesty is unwittingly a false modesty: the "negative" characterization of infinity as something lying beyond the phenomenal and unknowable is a characterization that does not remain confined within the limits of knowledge but has already trespassed them – "in so far as something is determined as a limit, it has already been trespassed" (Hegel 1983: V, 145). And, conversely, the Kantian idea of a striving toward infinity – for example, in the will's orienting itself toward the categorical imperative – never seems to move even one step beyond the finite. For as soon as the abstract infinity or the *Sollen* has negated just one particular instance of the finite, immediately another one rises at the horizon. What is then negated are finite, single particulars – for example, emotions, desires, volitions and so on – but not finitude as such.[11] In the end the finite appears to be the true, unbypassable and unprescindable absolute.

Hegel's construction of an alternative relation of finitude to the infinite proceeds in an immanent way and at the same time provides one example, from within what has been called the "philosophy of the subject," of the thoroughly reflexive mode of justification that we are seeking. He notes that although the progression toward the infinite allowed by the doctrine of the two realms never really "liberates the infinite from the grip of the finite," from a different perspective in the Sisyphean negation of innumerable finite particulars the immanent presence and the power of *infinity* manifests itself.[12] The process of reciprocal evoking of finitude and the infinite presupposed by Kant's notion of "endless progress" is but the external appearance of the true mediation between finitude and infinity: namely, it designates the constant transition (*Übergang*) from finitude to infinity. The Absolute or infinity is *negativity*, namely the process whereby each finite thing undergoes its own end and yet in so doing, in its undergoing a negation of itself, fulfills the truth of its being, namely finitude, and thereby also reconciliates itself with itself.[13] Paraphrasing Giorgio Agamben's saying, "That the world does not reveal God, that is truly divine" (Agamben 1990: 65), we could say: That the finite *always* falls short of infinity, that is a true manifestation of infinity in the midst of finiteness. Not only, as Kant can readily concede, can one not conceive of the finite without at the same time presupposing the infinite, but in order to avoid the difficulties coming from conceiving of the infinite abstractly, as a bad infinity, infinity should be thought of as *immanent* in the finite, as the realization and coming to fruition of finitude's own essential finiteness. Real infinity is always *here*, in the *present*, in *actuality*. It is *bad* infinity which lies beyond the finite.[14] As Hegel once put it, "Without the world, God is not God."[15]

I have reconstructed the arguments from Hegel's *Phenomenology of Spirit* and from parts of *The Science of Logic* because they represent an extraordinary testimony of one of the greatest attempts that modern thought has made in the direction of a radically self-reflexive, immanent and exemplary mode of justification.

The lesson to be learned from Hegel is that the true "transcendental" is the process in which the making of subjectivity itself and its reflective counterpart, the narrative interpretation, come together. Validity is here grounded in an entirely immanent way. What remains questionable and not utilizable for us is the fact that Hegel understood his own philosophy as still bound up with the classical and early-modern notion of "necessity" – the necessity of the concept – and as depicting an ideal process of self-clarification, indeed of *Aufklärung,* that is not meant to receive its validity from its being exemplarily representative of the constitution of a concrete being, not even the *Geist* of Western thought. A residue of externalism, a residue of non-immanence remains in this.

For an authenticity approach to questions of validity in the age of pluralism, to think of the conditions of its own validity means, then, to draw on Hegel's lesson but to try to avoid these shortcomings. It means to justify our rescue along postmetaphysical lines of the Kantian doctrine of judgment on a radicalized Hegelian ground, as it were. The authenticity approach, as we have seen, establishes a constitutive connection between theoretical and normative validity on the one hand and the authenticity of concrete and situated identities on the other, and justifies such a constitutive connection neither with reference to objective structures of subjectivity – in this case, a sort of "drive towards self-realization" – nor with reference to unavoidable junctures of the process-bound co-implication of validity and authenticity, of finitude and infinity. In fact, to resort to forms of justification of such sort would be tantamount to claiming once again – as Hegel still does – to be able to describe the reality of things from a vantage point which stands over and beyond the partiality of language games. Rather, in order to be consistent with the Linguistic Turn, the authenticity approach must justify its own validity in a thoroughly reflexive way: namely, as the way of thinking about validity which most exemplarily fits with who we are.

The status of the discourse which states the *authenticity-thesis* is not that of a foundational discourse in the early modern sense, but in the postmetaphysical sense of outlining the one image of truth and morality in which we – we Western moderns of the end of the twentieth century and beginning of the twenty-first – can recognize the most emblematic portrait of who we are. The idea that the enlightening exemplariness of authentic subjectivity is at the center of our intuitions concerning validity cannot be validated in any other way than by its being enlighteningly exemplary of the way of thinking about validity that beings like us can develop. For every other strategy of justification would unintentionally entangle the *authenticity-thesis* in a performative contradiction. Such is the fate, for example, of the most powerful attempt, in our century, to develop a radically reflexive understanding of validity after Hegel: Heidegger's philosophy of Being.

The trajectory of Heidegger's thought – a thought that hinges on the idea that being-in-the-world, as the mode of being of *Dasein*, constitutes the "*foundation* for the primordial phenomenon of truth" (Heidegger 1962: 261) – in a way testifies to the difficulties that the project of radically reflexivizing the grounding of validity must come to terms with. In *Being and Time* the question of Being is addressed in terms of an explication of the experience of existence – where experience is not worked out in terms of the classical opposition of "existence" and "essence," an opposition that for Heidegger constitutes the equivalent of Hegel's bad infinity, but out of existence itself. Being and *Dasein* are in the same relation as infinity and finitude in Hegel's account. Part of what Hegel imputed to Kant's view of the transcendental and to modern subjectivism – a conception that turned infinity into just a larger kind of finite entity – Heidegger imputes to Western metaphysics from Plato up to Nietzsche's nihilism. The forgetfulness of the question of Being consists in neglecting the ontological difference that separates concrete beings from the Being of beings. Treating Being as an objectified being, as *timeless* substratum, is the fundamental mistake that leads the West to misunderstand Being's indissoluble link with *Dasein*: only in *Dasein* lives Being (Heidegger 1962: 255). This indissoluble link is the object of the "fundamental ontology" developed in *Being and Time* and later replaced by the "history of Being." The nature of Being, just as Hegel's immanent infinity or Hegel's Absolute, cannot be captured with a concept or a definition. It can only be hinted at and elucidated by means of working out what it means to be a being that partakes of Being: namely, what it means to be a being that is thrown in the world, is finite, is concerned about its own being, is constituted by temporality and is confronted with its own death.[16] Only humans are beings for whom the question of their own being "is an issue," and only humans can appropriate the aspects of the world into which they are thrown by *resolutely* making them their own or "*Eigen*" and attain *Eigentlichkeit*, authenticity in Heidegger's sense. Humans are beings that in trying to understand their own constitution, the Being that manifests itself in their existence, can't avoid the standpoint of choosing between authenticity and inauthenticity. An authentic appropriation of this horizon of thrownness (*Geworfenheit*) and its transformation in a project (*Entwurf*) presupposes that I avoid seeking refuge in the shared representations of the They (*Das Man*) and instead *resolutely* choose to live toward my own irreplaceable death, thereby coming to terms with my own finitude (i.e. the *nothingness* that ultimately underlies beings) and developing an attitude of *care* towards the Being of my own being. In turn, this resolution to live "authentically" brings about the experience of truth in the Greek sense of *aletheia* or "unconcealment" – the unconcealment of that Being which lives in *Dasein* without ever coinciding with any being. On one hand, Kierkegaard's existentialist notion of a personality that has "chosen itself"[17] acquires in Heidegger an *ontological* coloring under the title of *care*. On the other hand, truth has seemingly democratized and concretized itself. The Hegelian immanence of infinity in finiteness ceases to be only a philosophical concern and is understood as a concern for every human being who wishes to live authentically. Hegel's lesson is metabolized by Heidegger in his avoiding to set *Dasein*'s mortality against the infinite horizon of Being. Rather, *Dasein* is the locus of Being and *to think* means to disclose how Being inheres in beings, in the manner of a *clearing* (*Licthung*). While Being cannot be defined as beings can, nonetheless *thinking* can shed light on certain constitutive aspects of it.

In his "Introduction" to *Being and Time* Heidegger stresses that "the meaning of the Being of that being we call *Dasein* proves to be *temporality* [*Zeitlichkeit*]."[18] It is within the fundamental dimension of temporality that *Dasein* discovers the "openness of Being." Later, in Heidegger's "Letter on Humanism," the constitutive aspect of Being is conceived in different terms. The human "stands out in the openness of Being" and "Being itself, which as the throw has projected the essence of man into 'care,' is as this openness" (Heidegger 1993a: 252). In that sense Being is a *clearing* – a *Lichtung*.

Yet, here is the difficulty. The *Dasein* for whom Being is a clearing is not, at least in *Being and Time*, recognizably the *Dasein* of any historical being. Heidegger's *Dasein* has a relation to the world in which he is thrown that is "transcendental-ontological," as it were. *Dasein* constitutes the world, not in the Fichtian sense of "positing" it, but in the sense of being one of the conditions of the possibility of the existence of a world. The transcendental dimension of the relation of *Dasein* to the world and to Being, however, is purified of the cognitive aspect which played a fundamental role in Kant. It is not the possibility of knowing the world but the possibility for the world to exist that is transcendentally constituted by *Dasein*. Despite this difference, *Dasein* shares certain characteristics with the transcendental subject. It is not constituted by the world, as in the pragmatist philosophies of James and Mead, and for all of Heidegger's emphasis on the "concreteness" of his philosophy, there is no trace of material determination or of the concreteness of the body in his image of *Dasein*. In its ontological, world- and Being-constitutive capacity, *Dasein* is as disembodied as its fellow transcendental subject: it suffers no disease, has no childhood memories and formative experiences, no cultural roots, no desire, no constitutive attachments to others, no material interests, no solidarity, no mundane ends which might project a significance beyond the sphere of the "They" and affect the content of the *Entwurf* that grounds its authenticity.[19] The appropriation of death as one's own "eigenster Möglichkeit" and as the one substantive determination of authentic *Dasein* contributes to create an empty and peculiar notion of *authenticity without fulfillment*. That which differentiates my death from that of other people is not reverberated in my own attitude toward *life* – an attitude which does not appear differentiated from that of any other *Dasein*, equally and solipsistically concerned with his or her own death and with becoming a "Selbst." The contentlessness of the *Entschlossenheit* with which I embrace *care* makes the existence of the Heideggerian *Dasein* as deindividuated as that of Kant's "pure rational beings" – it has aptly been written that the existence led by authentic *Dasein* appears as uniform as a "life-long eternity locked up in the individual" (Anders 1948: 364). This lack of content appears also in subsequent stages of Heidegger's work, as for instance when, in his "Letter on Humanism," Heidegger bans all philosophical concern for the subjectivity-forming function of "values." Calling something a "value" means "robbing what is so valued of its worth" (Heidegger 1993b: 251). According to Heidegger, valuing in the modern sense, "even where it values positively," inevitably means to "subjectivize," hence to commit "the greatest blasphemy imaginable against Being" (Heidegger 1993b: 251). *Dasein* is thus further deprived of the legitimate means for constructing a reflectively authentic relation to its own life – it can only fall back on a constitutive relation to death which fails to be individuating in that it lacks the symbolic materials (values, situated projects, aspects of identity etc.) which would make each death truly "unique."

But the difficulty which makes the framework of *Being and Time* ultimately unsuitable for the kind of radical reflexivity by which a notion of exemplary as opposed to generalizing validity can be justified is the fact there is indeed little of an exemplary and reflexive nature in the way Heidegger reaches the results of his inquiry. The human being is once again *described* as an ontological being, whose very nature presses on him or her the question concerning Being,[20] just as a few years later, in "The Origin of the Work of Art," the essence of truth will be said to be that truth "establish[es] itself within beings" (Heidegger 1993a: 187). The philosophical novelty of *Being and Time* resides in Heidegger's characterization of human subjectivity and of its mode of being as bound up with *temporality*, but the implicit claim to validity of the philosophical discourse that explicates Being is still a traditional one.

Things don't change significantly, from this particular point of view, with the transition to Heidegger's later stage of thinking, when the fundamental ontology of *Dasein* gives way to the project of a "history of Being," prepared by the deconstructive revisitation of canonical authors of Western metaphysical tradition such as Plato, Aristotle, Kant, Hegel and Nietzsche. In the language of the "Letter on Humanism":

> Man is rather "thrown" from Being itself into the truth of Being, so that ek-sisting in this fashion he might guard the truth of Being, in order that beings might appear in the light of Being as the beings they are. Man does not decide whether and how beings appear, whether and how God and the gods or history and Being, come to presence and depart. The advent of beings lies in the destiny of Being. But for man it is ever a question of finding what is fitting in his essence that corresponds to such destiny; for in accord with this destiny man as ek-sisting has to guard the truth of Being. Man is the shepherd of Being.
>
> (Heidegger 1993b: 234)

The terms "authenticity" and "inauthenticity" are here severed from any "moral-existentiell" or "anthropological" dimension of meaning. Rather, Heidegger relates them to the presence or absence of an "'ecstatic' relation of the essence of man to the truth of Being" (Heidegger 1993b: 236). The "history of Being," thus, provides no more *situated* a standpoint than the "analytic of *Dasein*." To be sure, the *Kehre* from "Being and Time" to "Time and Being" is presented by Heidegger as a change of perspective which enables thinking to arrive "at the location of that dimension out of which *Being and Time* is experienced, that is to say, experienced from the fundamental experience of the oblivion of Being" (Heidegger 1993b: 231–2). Yet the history of Being is little other than the history of philosophical ways of conceiving Being, and this assumption betrays a residue of objectivism – as though Western philosophical thought were reflective of, or the vehicle for, something more "objective" than thought itself – that clashes with the project of a thorough dismissal of objectifying, "Being-forgetful" strategies of foundation.

Perhaps a more thoroughly reflexive strategy of grounding can be drawn from Heidegger's understanding of language as the "house of Being" and thus as the home of the human being's essence.[21] Again, language is not a being among others, but that which gives presence to beings while being itself absent. Language is that which lets things exist without itself existing except through their existence. This function of bringing things into the clearing, of "disclosing," is exerted primarily by *poetic* language. Poets such as Rilke and Hölderlin offer us pathways into Being by way of creating a "piety of thinking" (Heidegger 1993c) through the revivification of our own language. Rather than expressive language being parasitic on communicative language, for Heidegger it is the ordinary, communicative use of language that constitutes a derivation of the originary world-disclosing function of poetic language. A recovery of the world-disclosing power of poetic language becomes then for Heidegger the way to retrieve the forgotten Being in the midst of the technological world – a retrieval of Being not *in* but *as* language which bears a significance not just for the philosophical enterprise but for Western civilization as such. Once again, however, the peculiar contentlessness of Being makes this perspective unsuited for the purpose of self-reflexively grounding a philosophical account of validity. Heidegger's doctrine of Being is *revealed* in an allusive philosophical language, but comes from without the conscience of the beings whose experience it supposedly explicates. It is not a reconstruction of the intuitions of *Dasein*, it is an authoritative revelation that *Dasein* ignores at its own peril.

"Here we stand. We can do no other"

No less than Hegel's model of self-reflexive justification, Heidegger's recourse to the analytics of *Dasein* or to the "history of Being" appears, then, to be pervaded by residues of externalism that make it an unpromising model for making sense of the nature of the validity claim implicitly raised by the authenticity view of validity. In support of the idea that the *authenticity-thesis* cannot ultimately be vindicated by anything other than the authenticity of *our* positing it as *our* thesis concerning validity we cannot bring, consistently with our subscribing to the Linguistic Turn, any general account of the structures of subjectivity, be they the co-implication of finitude and infinity or the temporality of Being. The kind of *postmetaphysical radical reflexivity* that is truly consistent with the Linguistic Turn enjoins us, instead, to adopt a different strategy. A philosophical account of why it is authentic for us – authentic in the sense of "exemplarily congruent with who we want to be" – to adopt the *authenticity-thesis* as a reconstruction of our intuitions concerning validity ought then to appeal only to a concrete narrative about our situated identity, about our unique cultural and historical identity of Westerners on the eve of the twenty-first century. The narrative which ideally culminates with the sentence "For these reasons the authenticity view of validity is the only view that beings like us can adopt" – a narrative to which this book could be understood as a long methodological foreword – must contain reasons that are interpretations of certain historical turning points that have made us who we are and can shed light on certain future-oriented project-like elements of our identity which receive their sense from those turning points, even if only in order to subvert their direction. The status of such a narrative and of the complex of reasons that are connected with it is that of an individual philosopher's suggestion for a collective "Here we stand. We can do no other" or, in another vocabulary, an individual philosopher's interpretation of the stance that our collective "individual law" enjoins us to take concerning the nature of validity.

In what sense does such a claim have a universalistic significance? In what sense can our conception of validity possess a significance that goes beyond that of being a mere description of what we happen to believe at this point in time? In the sense that from the exemplary congruence between our stance on validity and who we are – no less than from the exemplary congruence between

Luther and his religious stance – emanates the same sense of the furtherance of life that attracts us to the great works of art of all styles and times.

The reasons mentioned in support of our "here we stand" are similar – with respect to their methodological status – to the undemonstrable yet intuitively compelling reasons that critics might give in support of their sense that a particular set of printed characters on a clothbound stack of some hundreds of pages, or a particular set of brush strokes on a canvas, constitutes a work of art. They are similar to the reasons offered by an artist in support of his or her choosing one alternative over another, or to the reasons that justices provide in order to convince each other that a certain reading of the Constitution is better than another. They are concrete, singular, context-bound reasons that cannot force us to agree as logical propositions do, but nonetheless articulate a sense of validity that ultimately rests on intuitions that we have about what Kant would call, in a language that Dewey could underwrite as well, the "furtherance of life." Like the reasons that accompany, illustrate and make intelligible to others our judgments about the well-formedness of artworks and the realization of individual identities, these formulations start concrete and finite but strike on something which is universal and not just local, on something that carries a hint of infinity, by virtue of its impinging on the ability we have – and suppose, but only suppose, that fellow human beings who articulate their visions within other language games, traditions or conceptions of the good possess as well – of judging when our life is "furthered" and when not. It is a kind of exemplary universality which cannot impose itself on us as a conqueror but attracts us as a seducer. A conqueror can crush us regardless of who we are, a seducer cannot seduce us regardless of who we are: the seducer's influence exerts itself *on* us but not *independently of* who we are.

This universality *sui generis* of reflective judgment, to which Hegel's and Heidegger's models of radically self-reflexive self-grounding ultimately fail to do justice, manifests itself in two ways. First, the more accurately the account of our identity and our reasons for adopting a certain view of validity reflect who we are, the more "others" – other cultures as well as future successors of our own culture – upon coming into contact with our authenticity view of validity will be drawn to recognize in that conception one of the most inspiring expressions of "all that is human," another peak, thus far yet unexplored, of that "mountainous crest of humanity" mentioned by Nietzsche in the second of his *Untimely Meditations*. And for this reason in their own efforts to articulate *their own* sense of validity, these "others" hopefully will want to enter into a dialogue with *ours*. Others, located in a different context, will want to enter a dialogue with our vision of validity much as an artist operating within one stylistic perspective is able to feel inspired by exemplary works couched in another style, and might then want to reconcile the two styles or import elements of the new style into his or her own.

Second, as I have tried to show in Chapter 3, our reflective judgment, especially in matters such as the different forms of validity, does not operate as a totally open field of possibilities but, rather, operates within certain *guidelines* that *orient* our appraisal of congruency or authenticity, without dictating the outcome of such appraisal in the way the criteria that guide determinant judgment do. These guidelines – intuitions about the dimensions of authenticity or fulfillment for an individual and other kinds of identities – also vary across cultures and epochs, but we can suppose that if something like "the human condition" exists, then – before a proper articulation of its meaning will historically be possible from the standpoint of an "identity of humanity" of which we can contingently only anticipate the bare outline – a vocabulary may be articulated from "here" which will somehow hit on dimensions that, perhaps combined in a different way, according to different emphases, orient reflective judgment on congruence and the furtherance of life also "there," and "there," and "there."

To conclude, the fact that the domain of application of these reasons for accepting the authenticity view of validity includes one case only – our own, *we* who "can do no other" – does not undermine its universalistic significance. For the ability of the exemplary to project a cogency outside its context of origin does not depend on subsumption, on its hitting on "the right general principle" or the "structures of subjectivity" that we all share in common, but depends, rather, on its exceptional degree of internal congruency, on its being *perfect in its own terms*. The desired transcontextual cogency of our own authenticity view of validity can only be acquired, if we want to remain true to our belief in "the fact of pluralism," through the inspiring quality of the exemplary. That is the only way in which *we* can think of validity and remain true to ourselves. At the same time, the congruence through which this view of validity acquires its significance as the best for us is due to cultural conditions and turning points that are not entirely of our own making and that, in any event, it is not entirely possible for us to undo. In this sense a dimension of necessity survives in the authenticity view. We truly "can do no other," if we want to remain true to who we are.

Paradoxically, we are driven to, and at the same time we associate a sense of necessity with, our conception of the source of validity as *uniquely singular*, precisely because that is the best way of accommodating the transcontextual relevance of validity with our convictions regarding the *genuine plurality* of values. In this embracing of extreme singularity in order to reconcile plurality and universalism also lies the best chance for the project of modernity to finally come to work.

NOTES

1 AUTHENTICITY AND VALIDITY

1 For a similar interpretation, see Heidegger (1961: 141, 195).
2 This interpretation of Taylor is indebted to Beiner (1997) and Smith (1996).
3 See Weber (1978: 25–6).
4 See Weber (1975c: 127).
5 For Kant judgment always concerns the inclusion of a particular within a universal. In the case of *determinant* judgment the universal – be it a law of physics, a principle of Reason such as the categorical imperative, or a principle of logical inference – exists prior to, and independently of, the particular which is to be subsumed under it. In the case of *reflective* judgment, instead, these conditions do not obtain. The relevant universal is identified only at the very moment when the particular is attributed to it. See Kant (*Critique of Judgment*: Paragraph 18).
6 I have argued this point in Ferrara (1993: 102–9).
7 See Bell (1976, 1980); Lasch (1979, 1984, 1991); Riesman (1950, 1963); Sennett (1978, 1990); Bloom (1987); Selznick (1992); Rieff (1973, 1975); Bellah *et al.* (1985, 1991); Berger (1979); Berger *et al.* (1973).
8 For an excellent exposition of this point see Taylor (1989, 1992). See also Taylor (1993).
9 See Weber (1975b).
10 I have commented on these two tensions in Ferrara (1993: 130–3).
11 See Habermas (1984: 333).
12 See Habermas (1990).
13 See Habermas (1993b).
14 See Habermas (1992: 128).
15 I develop this point in Ferrara (1994).
16 This is indeed the impression that one receives by reading Taylor (1989, 1992).
17 See Walzer (1990).
18 See Walzer (1990: 516).
19 On the universalistic properties of "reiterative universalism" see Walzer (1990: 527–32).
20 See Sartre (1972) and Simmel (1987).
21 On this point, see Larmore (1995).
22 See Habermas (1987) [German: p. 162].
23 See Honneth (1995a).
24 See Honneth (1995b).
25 Kant (*Critique of Judgment* 1986: 151).
26 See Kant (*Critique of Judgment* 1986: 152).

165

27 For example, see Habermas's distinction of "rational consensus" and "compromise" in Chapter IV, Section II of *Between Facts and Norms* (1992).
28 On this point see Wellmer (1991) and Seel (1985). For useful comments on Wellmer's position, see Lara (1995).

2 POSTMETAPHYSICAL *PHRONESIS*

1 See Bernstein (1983).
2 For a characterization of the essential features of paradigm choice, see Kuhn (1974: 145–9) and Kuhn (1977: 321–2, 338). For Lakatos's view of the choice between research programs see Lakatos (1970).
3 See Benhabib (1987).
4 See Seel (1985).
5 I use "conceptual scheme" as an umbrella term to designate all the specific notions that somehow are related to Wittgenstein's "language games," e.g. paradigm, episteme, life-world, tradition, culture, symbolic universe etc. See Davidson (1984).
6 The two best-known examples are Maslow's theory of needs and Scheler's "material ethics of value." See Maslow (1968) and Scheler (1980).
7 The reproduction of a collective identity can be conceived as a process similar to the reproduction of the symbolic structures of the life-world. See Habermas (1981: Vol. 2, 208–17).
8 More specifically it is one of the intellectual virtues, alongside *techne* (art or technical skill), *episteme* (scientific knowledge), *sophia* (wisdom) and *nous* (intelligence or intuition). See Aristotle (*Nichomachean Ethics*: Book VI).
9 See MacIntyre (1967: 64).
10 See Aristotle (*Nichomachean Ethics*: 1098a8–27; 1953: 76).
11 Nagel (1980: 7) concludes that Aristotle identifies *eudaimonia* with contemplation. J. L. Ackrill (1980: 28–33), on the other hand, tries to construe an alternative, inclusive view of *eudaimonia*. This view is supported also by Taylor (1986). MacIntyre (1967: 82) stresses the dominant position, but in *After Virtue* he offers a reformulation of his own and defines the good life in a formal way, as "the life spent in seeking for the good life for man" (MacIntyre 1981: 204).
12 See MacIntyre (1981: 144).
13 See Vollrath (1977: 85–8). On this point see also Aubenque (1963) and Bubner (1976).
14 See Aristotle (*Nichomachean Ethics*: I 1094a; 1953: 18–22).
15 See Höffe (1971: 191).
16 See Cortella (1987: 52).
17 See Kuhn (1960: 136) and MacIntyre (1981: 261–2).
18 See Cortella (1987: 54).
19 For a similar interpretation of Kant's political theory, see Beiner (1983: 63–71). For an interesting attempt to reconstruct a Kantian politics based on judgment, see Howard (1985: 247–70).
20 For example, this is one of the problems with the otherwise excellent discussion of judgment in Beiner (1983).
21 See Arendt (1978: 193).

3 FROM KANT TO KANT: A NORMATIVITY WITHOUT PRINCIPLES

1 See Kant (*Critique of Judgment*: Introduction; 1986: 18).
2 See Kant (*Critique of Judgment*: Paragraphs 8 and 13; 1986: 53–7; 64–5).

3 See Kant (*Critique of Judgment*: Paragraph 49; 1986: 179–80).

4 See Gadamer (1975: 53). See also Gadamer's discussion of taste and genius and of the nineteenth century's reversal of Kant's priorities, Gadamer (1975: 49–55).

5 On this point see Beiner (1983: 113–14).

6 See Beiner (1983: 51–2) and Howard (1985: 149–51).

7 For a critical appraisal of Arendt's reading of Kant on judgment, and especially of her notion of "exemplary validity," see Ferrara (1998a).

8 See Kant (*Critique of Judgment*: Paragraph 48; 1986: 172–5).

9 See Ferrara (1993: 86–91).

10 I an indebted to Rudolf Makkreel for having drawn my attention to these passages.

11 See Makkreel (1990: 155ff.).

4 REFLECTIVE AUTHENTICITY AND EXEMPLARY UNIVERSALISM

1 See Habermas (1987, 1989, 1992, 1993a, 1993b, 1994, 1995), Rawls (1971, 1993), Dworkin (1986, 1990, 1993, 1996), Ackerman (1980, 1983, 1989, 1991), Nagel (1991) and Scanlon (1982).

2 See Honneth (1995a: 265–6). See also Thiebaut (1995) and Cooke (1994, 1995).

3 See Jaspers (1955, 1957), Tillich (1952, 1962). Unfortunately, "authenticity" is also the English term commonly chosen to render Heidegger's notion of "Eigentlichkeit" (Heidegger 1962).

4 See Adorno (1973).

5 See Young (1990), Cavarero (1995), the essays collected in Benhabib and Cornell (1987), in Nicholson (1990) and Butler (1990).

6 For an account of the relation of cultural rights to the protection of collective identities see Kymlicka (1995), Margalit and Halbertal (1994), Raz (1994), Taylor (1993). On the relation of privacy to the fulfillment of identity see Schoeman (1984, 1992).

7 See Dworkin (1986: 176–275).

8 See Chapter 1, pp. 8–10.

9 On this point, see Ferrara (1998b: Ch. 2).

10 See Kateb (1989, 1992).

11 See Walzer (1987, 1994).

12 See Taylor (1992).

13 See Sartre (1966: 340ff.).

14 Kant (*Critique of Judgment* Paragraph 40; 1986: 151).

15 Kant (*Critique of Judgment* Paragraph 40; 1986: 151).

16 Also, Schiller distinguishes in a similar way two modes of beauty: "melting beauty" and "energizing beauty." On this point see Trilling (1972: 95–6).

17 See Foucault (1991: 31). For an excellent discussion of this point and, more generally, of the poststructuralist view of the relation of subjectivity to experience, see Jay (1994).

18 For a very interesting notion of "non coercive" synthesis applied to the domain of identity see Whitebook's (1995) conception of "sublimation" as bound up with the utopian possibility of a non-repressively integrated subjectivity, of a "non violent unity of the self" and of a "fully embodied integration of the ego and the drives."

19 See Schiller (1971: 107).

20 For an interesting purview of the various feminist positions see Benhabib and Cornell (1987), Nicholson (1990) and Butler (1990).

21 See Ferrara (1993: 69–109).

22 In this sense, Adorno's critique of the jargon of "Eigentlichkeit" (Adorno 1973) does not apply to the view of authenticity defended here.

23 See Larmore (1996: 86–96).
24 Simmel's point here appears to be indebted to Hegel's analysis of the consequences of rigidly opposing finitude and the infinite in the *Enzyklopädie der Philosophischen Wissenschaften* (Paragraph 95; 1983: 201).
25 See Simmel (1987: 190).
26 The relation of authenticity to difference has been explored in a very insightful way by Maeve Cooke (1995). In Section 2 of her article she reconstructs five different readings of what it means, from the standpoint of a politics of difference, to recognize the specificity of an identity.
27 See Simmel (1987: 227).
28 See Simmel (1987: 225–6).

5 POSTMODERN *EUDAIMONIA*: DIMENSIONS OF AN AUTHENTIC IDENTITY

1 See Rawls (1993: 53 note; 1995)
2 For the most recent contributions see McCarthy (1996) and Bernstein (1996), as well as Habermas (1996).
3 For a similar interpretation, see Ricoeur (1970).
4 For a more detailed discussion of this point, see Ferrara (1998b). On the eudaimonistic interest in justice see also Dworkin (1989: 503–4).
5 See Kripke (1971).
6 See Nozick (1981: 29–70).
7 See Lewis (1976). See also Williams (1973), Wiggins (1980) and Shoemaker (1963).
8 See Parfit (1984).
9 See Parsons (1968), Keniston (1960, 1968), Slater (1976), Erikson (1959, 1963).
10 See "Was macht eine Lebensform rational?", in Habermas (1991: 31–48).
11 See Kohut (1978: 471–2) and also the paragraph "The prototypical significance of the period of the formation of the self," within the essay "Thoughts on narcissism and narcissistic rage," in Kohut (1978: 623–4).
12 See Jacobson (1964), Chapter 1 ("Narcissism, masochism, and the concept of the self") and Chapter 2 ("Recent literature on identity").
13 See Freud (1900: SE, Vol. 5, 400–1, n. 3).
14 See Freud (1894: 191).
15 Freud (1926).
16 See Freud (1917a: 393–4).
17 See Freud (1917a: 454).
18 Freud (1926: 98).
19 See Freud (1938: 277).
20 In *An Outline of Psychoanalysis* Freud points out that the splitting of the ego is by no means a rare phenomenon or a phenomenon linked with fetishism, but is rather a "universal characteristic of neuroses." See Freud (1940: 204).
21 Such is the case of the schizophrenic, who feels "split in bits." See Klein (1957: 233).
22 See (Klein 1955: 313).
23 See Klein (1957: 1–24). I owe this point to Joel Whitebook.
24 See Mahler (1968: 50).
25 See the paragraph on "Evidences of dissociation" in Sullivan (1953: 316–22).
26 See Kohut (1977: 185–6).
27 See Kohut (1984: 194–5).
28 See Fairbairn (1986: 111–12).

29 See Fairbairn's essays "Endopsychic structure considered in terms of object-relation-ships" and "A synopsis of the development of the author's views regarding the structure of personality," both in Fairbairn (1986: 82–132 and 162–79).

30 See Greenberg and Mitchell (1983: 164–6).

31 See Kernberg (1985: 13). On coherence understood as demarcation see also the essay "Boundaries and structures in love relations" (Kernberg 1985: 277–305).

32 On dependency on external objects for a sense of continuity, see the case of Mr. B., in Kohut (1971: 126–30).

33 See Jacobson (1964: 56–8). The importance of optimal frustrations appears all the greater in that Jacobson postulates a kind of anti-individuating tendency, which runs opposite to the quasi-instinctual tendency toward individuation underlying Mahler's theory. On this point see Mahler (1968: Ch. 3). Also, see Kohut (1978: 446–7).

34 See Jacobson (1964: 63).

35 I owe this point to Joel Whitebook, personal letter of 5 May 1997.

36 See Mahler *et al.* (1975: 9 and 206).

37 See Mahler (1968: 82–4 it).

38 See Klein (1957 [1975b]: 187).

39 See Klein (1957 [1975b]: 218).

40 See Jacobson (1964: Ch. 4).

41 See Jacobson (1964: Ch. 12).

42 See Mahler (1968: Ch. 7).

43 See Sullivan (1964: 211).

44 See Freud (1896: 168–74 and 184).

45 See Sullivan (1953: 56–7).

46 See Klein (1957: 187).

47 Klein (1959: 151–2). See also McDougall's notion of the "normopath" in McDougall (1980).

48 See the chapter entitled "The epigenesis of separation anxiety, basic mood and prim-itive identity," in Mahler *et al.* (1975: 210–19).

49 See Fairbairn (1986: 51).

50 On the notion of bad object and the dynamics of internalization, see the essay "The repression and the return of bad objects" in Faibairn (1986: 59–81).

51 See Fairbairn (1986: 8).

52 See Winnicott (1960: 142–3).

53 See Winnicott (1960: 149).

54 Winnicott (1953: 1–30). See also Winnicott (1986: 36–7).

55 See Winnicott (1971: 64).

56 See Winnicott (1971: 45).

57 See Kohut (1977: 171–219) and Kohut (1978: 760ff.).

58 See Chapter 4, p. 59–60 above.

59 See Freud (1900: 578).

60 See Freud (1900: 580–1).

61 See Freud (1933: 57). For one of the earliest passages in which Freud explicitly takes distance from the "intellectualist bias" of his earlier view, see Freud (1913a: 141).

62 I owe this point to Joel Whitebook, personal letter of 5 May 1997. On the ambiguous character of the Zuidersee metaphor see Whitebook (1995: 117–18). Whitebook points out that as early as in *Inhibitions, Symptoms and Anxiety* Freud conceives of the new relation that the ego must establish with the previously repressed material not as a relation of "mastery" but as one of "free intercourse," and that the Zuidersee metaphor risks misleading the reader into thinking of that rela-tion as a mere "power grab" (Whitebook 1995: 118).

63 See Freud (1933: 77).

64 See Klein (1959: 260). A similar point is made in Jacobson (1964: 213–16).

65 See also Winnicott (1971: 163).

66 See Freud (1937: 227).

67 See Kohut (1977: 199–219) and Kohut (1984: 208).

68 See Klein (1959: 217 and 247–9).

69 See Jacobson (1964: 49).

70 For a notion of coming to terms with the world that does not fall prey to instrumental reductionism, see Loewald (1988: 22). I owe this point to Joel Whitebook.

71 See Freud (1913b: 88).

72 See Sullivan (1953: 348–50).

73 For example, maturity is understood by Mahler also as the capacity to renounce, during the transition from the subphase of practicing to that of rapprochment, the illusion of sharing the magical powers of the mother, i.e. to renounce omnipotence. See Mahler (1968: Ch. 1).

74 See Kernberg (1976: 265).

75 See Kohut (1977: 171–2).

76 See Freud (1917a: 257–69).

77 See Jacobson (1964: 199–200).

78 See Freud (1909: 112–13).

79 See Kohut (1978: 458). Also for Kernberg, maturity as acceptance of one's limitations is represented by the acceptance of one's existence as something which had to go that way and by the acceptance of one's death "as a final statement of 'mission accomplished'" (Kernberg 1985: 129).

80 See Kohut (1978: 458–60).

6 THE FULFILLMENT OF COLLECTIVE IDENTITIES

1 See Inglehart (1990, 1997).

2 See Durkheim (1964: 70–132).

3 See Durkheim (1951: 152–70 and 241–76).

4 The division of labor, in fact, ceases to produce its integrative effects, according to Durkheim, if its concrete, institutionalized form violates the requirements of justice. See Durkheim (1964: 375–9) and (1951: 250–1). On the relation of the feeling of the sacred to the cohesion of a collective identity, see Durkheim (1967: 257–8).

5 See Weber (1975a) and (1978: 576–610).

6 See Simmel (1955: 17–18).

7 See Durkheim (1951: 203–8).

8 See Parsons (1951) and Parsons, Bales and Shils (1953).

9 See Parsons (1971: 11–13).

10 On continuity, see also Durkheim (1967: 242–3).

11 See Durkheim (1964: 256–63).

12 See Durkheim (1951: 209–10 and 254–7).

13 See Durkheim (1951: 217–40 and 276).

14 See Durkheim (1967: 428).

15 See Durkheim (1967: 475).

16 See Durkheim (1964: 99–100).

17 See Weber (1958: 59–60).

18 For an excellent commentary on this point, see Berman (1982: 90–8).

19 See Tocqueville (1969: 693).

20 See Durkheim (1964: 287–9).

21 See Durkheim (1966: xlix).

22 It would be a mistake to think of these reflections as of marginal relevance in Durkheim's thought. The systematic connection between egoistic suicide and defective cohesiveness rests on the postulation of an intermediate element between the two: excessive individuation understood as an excess of self-reflectiveness. See Durkheim (1951: 281–2).

23 See Schluchter (1981: 39–48).

24 See Habermas (1981: Vol. 2, 212–18).

25 Drawing on Anna Freud's inventory of defense mechanisms, Neil Smelser has developed an interesting typology of collective defense mechanisms. See Smelser (1988).

26 See Weber (1978: 422–51).

27 See Weber (1958: 104–5).

28 See Weber (1975b).

29 See Weber (1958: 13–31).

30 See Simmel (1955: 93).

31 On this point, see Anscombe (1958), Von Wright (1963) and Schneewind (1990). A notable exception, within analytic philosophy, is Nozick (1989).

32 I have developed this argument in Ferrara (1993), where Rousseau is shown to be an exception in a way.

33 Nussbaum (1986, 1992, 1993, 1995, 1996), Foot (1978), Annas (1993).

34 Honneth (1995b).

7 AUTHENTICITY, THE TEXT AND THE WORK OF ART

1 See Schleiermacher (1977) and Dilthey (1970, 1976).

2 See Schleiermacher (1977).

3 For critical commentaries on Gadamer's own interpretation of Schleiermacher and Dilthey, see Warnke (1987: 10–15) and Makkreel (1975: 414–15).

4 From a variety of angles and embedded in a variety of arguments aimed at different purposes this basic thesis is shared, among others, by Frege (1960), Russell (1905), Carnap (1955) and Tarski (1944).

5 See for example Sacks (1995), Gumperz and Hymes (1972), Hymes (1972), Bauman and Sherzer (1974).

6 See Searle (1969).

7 See Searle (1980: 24–5).

8 See Van Dijk (1980, 1984).

9 See Van Dijk (1977: 158–9).

10 See Searle (1972: 143–6).

11 See Taylor (1985: 24–6).

12 See Blumer (1969: 1–60).

13 For an enlightening, contrastive analysis of Gadamer's and Hirsch's conceptions of interpretation, see Warnke (1987: 42–56).

14 See Dworkin (1986: 318).

15 See Dworkin (1986: 322).

16 See Dworkin (1986: 228–32).

17 See Heidegger (1993a). For an interesting discussion of the different meanings of "world-disclosure," see Duvenage (1999: Ch. 7).

18 On this point see Whitebook's reconstruction of Adorno's ideal of non-repressive unity or "non violent togetherness," in Whitebook (1995: 152–5).

19 The relation of artistic creativity to ordinary psychological processes is explored by Winnicott also with reference to the individual's effort to negotiate a satisfactory *modus vivendi* between his or her true and false selves. Along these lines Winnicott distinguishes two basic types of artists. See Winnicott (1988: 109–10).

20 On all these similarities, see Koppe (1990a, 1990b).

8 RETHINKING THE PROJECT OF MODERNITY

1 See Habermas (1987) and Passerin d'Entrèves and Benhabib (1996).
2 On this point, see Duvenage (1999).
3 A somewhat different attitude can be found in Lyotard (1984) and in Vattimo (1991).
4 See Rorty (1989: 192).
5 For an interesting discussion of the ambiguity inherent in Rorty's stance on relativism, see Menke-Eggers (1989).
6 For a critical appraisal of Rorty's notion of the self and of validity, see Ferrara (1990), Smith (1996: 109–13).
7 For useful commentaries on *The Phenomenology of Spirit*, see the classical Hyppolite (1946) and Kojève (1969), and also Heidegger (1950), Marcuse (1960) and Taylor (1975).
8 See Hegel (1983: V, 125–73).
9 Hegel (1983: V, 148–9).
10 See Hegel (1983: VIII, 201). For enlightening commentaries on this point see Taylor (1975: 233–44), Cortella (1995: 37–56).
11 See Hegel (1983: V, 155).
12 I follow Taylor's usage of "infinity" for designating Hegel's own notion of the immanent, non-separate infinite. See Taylor (1975: 241).
13 See Hegel (1983: V, 148).
14 See Hegel (1983: V, 164).
15 See Hegel, *Begriff der Religion*, quoted in Taylor (1975: 100).
16 One of the most suggestive renditions of what Being is has been offered by Rorty, when he says "Being is what *final* vocabularies are about" (Rorty 1991: 37). Just as in geometry there is no independent way of characterizing "space" without resorting to either Euclidean or Riemannian or some other kind of geometric conception, in the same way we cannot say what Being is independently of trying to articulate its essence within a Platonic, a Kantian, a Hegelian or a Heideggerian framework. Rorty, however, draws from this premise a conclusion that holds only if we take for granted the traditional conception of truth as correspondence. He accuses Heidegger of recoiling from the conclusion that "no understanding of Being is more or less an understanding of Being, more or less true" (Rorty 1991: 39) – a warranted conclusion, in Rorty's view, which Heidegger would contradict every time he uses the phrase "forgetfulness of Being" in order to negatively characterize Western metaphysics. Rorty's objection ceases to be relevant if we understand validity (in this case, truth) in terms of authenticity. While Being as such would then be what our diverse final vocabularies are *about*, the truth of our conception of Being lies in its being truly the conception that beings like us can authentically entertain. Also from a philological point of view, however, Rorty's objection appears to be based on a disputable reading of Heidegger. As we shall see below, there is more substantive texture to Heidegger's understanding of Being than Rorty is prepared to admit.
17 See Kierkegaard (1959: II, 181).
18 Heidegger (1979: 17).
19 Commentators such as Adorno, Habermas and Günther Anders have often insisted on the emptiness of the *Entschlossenheit* in favor of an authentic being towards death: see Adorno (1973: 92ff.), Habermas (1987: Ch. 6), Anders (1948). See also, from a different perspective, Dreyfus (1991) and Taminiaux (1991).
20 On this point, see Habermas (1987: Ch. 6).
21 See Heidegger (1993b: 236–7).

REFERENCES

Ackerman, B. (1980) *Social Justice in the Liberal State*, New Haven: Yale University Press.
—— (1983) "What is neutral about neutrality?," *Ethics*, 93 (2).
—— (1989) "Why dialogue?," *The Journal of Philosophy*, 86 (1).
—— (1991) *We the People*, Vol. 1, *Foundations*, Cambridge: Harvard University Press.
Ackrill, J.L. (1980) "Aristotle on *eudaimonia*," in A.O. Rorty (ed.), *Essays on Aristotle's Ethics*, Berkeley: University of California Press.
Adorno, T.W. (1973) *The Jargon of Authenticity*, (1964), Evanston: Northwestern University Press.
—— (1975) *Teoria estetica*, Turin: Einaudi.
Agamben, G. (1990) *La comunità che viene*, Turin: Einaudi.
Anders, G. (1948) "On the pseudo-concreteness of Heidegger's philosophy," *Philosophy and Phenomenological Research*, 8: 337–71.
Annas, J. (1993) *The Morality of Happiness*, Oxford: Oxford University Press.
Anscombe, E. (1958) "Modern moral philosophy," *Philosophy*, 33: 1–19.
Arendt, H. (1978) *The Life of the Mind*, San Diego: Harcourt Brace & Co.
—— (1982) *Lectures on Kant's Political Philosophy*, edited and with an interpretive essay by R. Beiner, Chicago: The University of Chicago Press.
Aristotle (1953) *The Nicomachean Ethics*, translated by J.A.K. Thomson, Harmondsworth: Penguin.
Aubenque, P. (1963) *La prudence chez Aristote*, Paris: PUF.
Bauman, R. and Sherzer, J. (eds.) (1974) *Explorations in the Ethnography of Speaking*, London: Cambridge University Press.
Beiner, R. (1983) *Political Judgment*, Chicago: The University of Chicago Press.
—— (1997) "Hermeneutical generosity and social criticism," in *Liberalism, Modernity and the Task of Social Criticism*, Toronto: University of Toronto Press.
Bell, D. (1976) *The Cultural Contradictions of Capitalism*, New York: Basic Books.
—— (1980) *The Winding Passage*, Cambridge: ABT.
Bellah, R. *et al.* (1985) *Habits of the Heart. Individualism and Commitment in American Life*, Berkeley: University of California Press.
—— (1991) *The Good Society*, New York: Knopf.
Benhabib, S. (1987) "Judgment and the moral foundations of politics in Arendt's thought," *Graduate Faculty Philosophy Journal*, MIT.
Benhabib, S. and Cornell, D. (eds.) (1987) *Feminism as Critique*, Minneapolis: University of Minnesota Press.

Berger, P. (1979) "Towards a Critique of Modernity," in *Facing up to Modernity*, Harmondsworth: Penguin.

Berger, P., Berger, B. and Kellner, H. (1973) *The Homeless Mind. Modernization and Consciousness*, New York: Random House.

Berman, M. (1982) *All That Is Solid Melts Into Air. The Experience of Modernity*, New York: Simon & Schuster.

Bernstein, R. (1983) *Beyond Objectivism and Relativism: Science, Hermeneutics, and Praxis*, Oxford: Blackwell.

—— (1996) "The retrieval of the democratic ethos," *Cardozo Law Review*, 17: 1127–46.

Bloom, A. (1987) *The Closing of the American Mind*, New York: Simon & Schuster.

Blumer, H. (1969) *Symbolic Interactionism. Perspective and Method*, Englewood Cliffs: Prentice-Hall.

Bubner, R. (1976) *Handlung, Sprache, Vernunft*, Frankfurt: Suhrkamp.

Burke, E. (1986) *Reflections on the Revolution in France*, (1790), Harmondsworth: Penguin.

Butler, J. (1990) *Gender Trouble: Feminism and the Subversion of Identity*, New York: Routledge.

Calvino, I. (1988) *Lezioni americane*, Milan: Garzanti.

Carnap, R. (1955) "Meaning and synonymy in natural languages," *Philosophical Studies*, 6 (3): 33–47.

Cavarero, A. (1995) *In Spite of Plato*, Cambridge: Polity Press.

Cooke, M. (1994) "Realizing the postconventional self," *Philosophy and Social Criticism*, 20 (1–2): 87–101.

—— (1997) "Authenticity and autonomy: Taylor, Habermas and the politics of recognition," *Political Theory*, 25(2): 258–88.

Cortella, L. (1987) *Aristotele e la razionalità della prassi*, Roma: Jouvence.

—— (1995) *Dopo il sapere assoluto. L'eredità hegeliana nell'epoca post-metafisica*, Milan: Guerini & Associati.

Danto, A. (1981) *The Transfiguration of the Commonplace*, Cambridge: Harvard University Press.

Davidson, D. (1984) "On the very idea of a conceptual schema," (1974), in *Inquiries into Truth and Interpretation*, Oxford: Clarendon Press, 183–98.

Deutsch, H. (1942) "Some forms of emotional disturbance and their relationship to schizophrenia," *Psychoanalytic Quarterly*, 11.

Dewey, J. (1980) *Art as Experience*, (1934), New York and Berkeley: Perigee Books.

Dilthey, W. (1970) *Der Aufbau der geschichtlichen Welt in den Geisteswissenschaften*, Frankfurt: Suhrkamp.

—— (1976) *Dilthey: Selected Writings*, edited by H.P. Rickman, Cambridge: Cambridge University Press.

Dreyfus, H. (1991) *Being-in-the-World: A Commentary on Heidegger's* Being and Time, Boston: MIT Press.

Durkheim, E. (1951) *Suicide*, (1896), New York: Free Press.

—— (1964) *The Social Division of Labor*, (1893), New York: Free Press.

—— (1966) *The Rules of Sociological Method*, (1895), New York: Free Press.

—— (1967) *The Elementary Forms of the Religious Life*, (1914), New York: Free Press.

Duvenage, P. (1999) *Habermas and Aesthetics. The Limits of Communicative Reason*, Cambridge: Polity Press, forthcoming.

Dworkin, R. (1977) *Taking Rights Seriously*, Cambridge: Harvard University Press.

—— (1986) *Law's Empire*, Cambridge: Harvard University Press.

—— (1989) "Liberal community," *California Law Review*, 77 (3): 479–504.

—— (1990) *Foundations of Liberal Equality*, The Tanner Lectures, Salt Lake City: University of Utah Press.

—— (1993) *Life's Dominion*, New York: Knopf.

—— (1996) *Freedom's Law. The Moral Reading of the American Constitution*, Cambridge: Harvard University Press.

Erikson, E. (1959) *Identity and the Life-Cycle*, New York: International Universities Press.

—— (1963) *Childhood and Society*, New York: Norton & Co.

Fairbairn, W.R.D. (1986) *Psychoanalytic Studies of the Personality*, London: Routledge & Kegan Paul.

Ferrara, A. (1990) "The unbearable seriousness of irony," *Philosophy and Social Criticism*, 16 (2): 81–107.

—— (1993) *Modernity and Authenticity. A Study of the Social and Ethical Thought of Jean-Jacques Rousseau*, Albany: SUNY Press.

—— (1994) "Authenticity and the project of modernity," *European Journal of Philosophy*, 2 (3): 241–73.

—— (1998a) "Judgment, identity and authenticity: a reconstruction of Hannah Arendt's interpretation of Kant," *Philosophy and Social Criticism*, 24 (2–3): 1–24.

—— (1998b) *Justice and Judgment. The Rise and the Prospect of the Judgment Model in Contemporary Political Philosophy*, London: Sage.

Foot, P. (1978) *Virtues and Vices*, Berkeley: University of California Press.

Foucault, M. (1991) "How an 'experience-book' is born," in *Remarks on Marx: Conversations with Duccio Trombadori*, New York: Semiotext.

Frege, G. (1960) "On sense and reference," (1892), in P. Geach and M. Black (eds.), *The Philosophical Writings of Gottlob Frege*, Oxford: Blackwell.

Freud, S. (1953–74) *The Standard Edition of the Complete Psychological Works of Sigmund Freud*, Vols. 1–24, translated by James Strachey, London: Hogarth Press. (All references are to this edition, hereinafter abbreviated as *SE*.)

—— (1894) "Draft E," *SE*, Vol. 1.

—— (1895a) "Draft G," *SE*, Vol. 1.

—— (1895b) "Project for a scientific psychology," *SE*, Vol. 1: 283–387.

—— (1896) "Further remarks on the neuropsychoses of defence," *SE*, Vol. 3: 159–85.

—— (1900) *The Interpretation of Dreams*, *SE*, Vols. 4–5.

—— (1909) "Analysis of a phobia in a five-year-old child," *SE*, Vol. 10: 1–149.

—— (1913a) "On beginning the treatment (further recommendations on the technique of psycho-analysis, I)," *SE*, Vol. 12: 123–43.

—— (1913b) *Totem and Taboo*, *SE*, Vol. 13: 1–162.

—— (1914) "On narcissism: an introduction," *SE*, Vol. 14: 67–102.

—— (1917a) *Introductory Lectures on Psycho-Analysis*, *SE*, Vol. 16.

—— (1917b) "Mourning and melancholia," *SE*, Vol. 14: 237–58.

—— (1926) *Inhibitions, Symptoms and Anxiety*, *SE*, Vol. 20: 75–175.

—— (1930) *Civilization and its Discontents*, *SE*, Vol. 21: 59–145.

—— (1933) *New Introductory Lectures on Psycho-Analysis*, *SE*, Vol. 22: 1–182.

—— (1937) *Analysis Terminable and Interminable*, *SE*, Vol. 23: 209–53.

—— (1938) "Splitting of the ego in the process of defence," *SE*, Vol. 23: 275–8.

—— (1940) *An Outline of Psycho-Analysis*, *SE*, Vol. 23: 139–207.

Gadamer, H.G. (1975) *Truth and Method*, (1961), New York: Continuum.

Greenberg, J.R. and Mitchell, S.A. (1983) *Object Relations in Psychoanalytic Theory*, Cambridge: Harvard University Press.

Gumperz, J. and Hymes, D. (eds.) (1972) *Directions in Socioloinguistics. The Ethnography of Communication*, New York: Holt, Rinehart & Winston.

Habermas, Jürgen (1981) *Theorie des kommunikativen Handelns*, Frankfurt: Suhrkamp, 2 Vols.

—— (1984) *The Theory of Communicative Action*, Vol. 1: *Reason and the Rationalization of Society*, translated by T. McCarthy, Boston: Beacon Press.

—— (1987) *The Philosophical Discourse of Modernity*, Cambridge: MIT Press.

—— (1989) "Volkssouveränität als Verfahren. Ein normativer Begriff von Öffentlichkeit," in Forum für Philosophie Bad Homburg (ed.), *Die Ideen von 1789*, Frankfurt: Suhrkamp, 7–36.

—— (1990) *Moral Consciousness and Communicative Action*, Cambridge: MIT Press.

—— (1991) *Erläuterungen zur Diskursethik*, Frankfurt: Suhrkamp.

—— (1992) *Faktizität und Geltung. Beiträge zur Diskurstheorie des Rechts und des demokratischen Rechtsstaats*, Frankfurt: Suhrkamp; English translation by William Rehg (1996), *Between Facts and Norms. Towards a Discourse Theory of Law and Democracy*, Cambridge: Polity Press.

—— (1993a) "Struggles for recognition in constitutional states," *European Journal of Philosophy*, 1 (2): 128–55.

—— (1993b) *Justification and Application*, Cambridge: MIT Press.

—— (1994) "Postscript to *Faktizität und Geltung*," *Philosophy and Social Criticism*, 20 (4): 135–50.

—— (1995) "Reconciliation through the public use of reason: remarks on John Rawls's *Political Liberalism*," *Journal of Philosophy*, 92 (3): 109–31.

—— (1996) "Reply to symposium participants," *Cardozo Law Review*, 17: 1477–517.

Hegel, G.W.F. (1983) *Werke in zwanzig Bänden*, Theorie Werkausgabe, Frankfurt: Suhrkamp.

Heidegger, M. (1950) "Hegels Begriff der Erfahrung," in *Holzwege*, Frankfurt: Klostermann, 105–92.

—— (1961) *Nietzsche*, Pfüllingen, 2 Vols.

—— (1962) *Being and Time*, (1927), New York: Harper & Row.

—— (1979) *Sein und Zeit*, (1927), Tübingen: Niemeyer.

—— (1993a) "The origin of the work of art," (1935), in *Basic Writings*, edited by D.F. Krell, London: Routledge, 143–212.

—— (1993b) "Letter on humanism," (1947), in *Basic Writings*, edited by D.F. Krell, London: Routledge, 217–65.

—— (1993c) "The way to language," (1959), in *Basic Writings*, edited by D.F. Krell, London: Routledge, 397–426.

Hirsch, E.D. (1967) *Validity in Interpretation*, New Haven: Yale University Press.

Höffe, O. (1971) *Praktische Philosophie. Das Modell des Aristoteles*, München-Salzburg: Pustet Verlag.

Honneth, A. (1995a) *The Fragmented World of the Social. Essays in Social and Political Philosophy*, Albany: SUNY Press.

—— (1995b) *The Struggle for Recognition. The Moral Grammar of Social Conflict*, Cambridge: Polity Press.

Howard, R. (1985) *From Marx to Kant*, Albany: SUNY Press.

Hymes, D. (1972) "Toward ethnographies of communication: the analysis of communicative events," (1964), in P.P. Giglioli (ed.), *Language and Social Context*, Harmondsworth: Penguin.

Hyppolite, J. (1946) *Genèse et structure de la "Phénoménologie de l'Esprit"*, Paris: Aubier.

Inglehart, R. (1990) *Culture Shift in Advanced Industrial Society*, Princeton: Princeton University Press.

—— (1997) *Modernization and Postmodernization: Cultural, Economic and Political Change in 43 Societies*, Princeton: Princeton University Press.

Jacobson, E. (1964) *The Self and the Object World*, New York: International Universities Press.

—— (1971) *Depression. Comparative Studies of Normal, Neurotic and Psychotic Conditions*, New York: International Universities Press.

Jaspers, K. (1955) *Reason and Existence*, translated by William Earle, New York: The Noonday Press.

—— (1957) *Man in the Modern Age*, (1931), Garden City: Doubleday Anchor.

Jay, M. (1994) "The limits of limit-experience: Bataille and Foucault," *Constellations* 2 (2).

Kant, I. (1986) *The Critique of Judgment*, (1790), translated by J.C. Meredith, Oxford: Clarendon Press.

Kateb, G. (1989) "Democratic individuality and the meaning of rights," in N. Rosenblum (ed.), *Liberalism and the Moral Life*, Cambridge: Harvard University Press, 183–206.

—— (1992) *The Inner Ocean*, Ithaca: Cornell University Press.

Keniston, K. (1960) *The Uncommitted. Alienated Youth in American Society*, New York: Harcourt, Brace & World.

—— (1968) *Young Radicals. Notes on Committed Youth*, New York: Harcourt, Brace & World.

Kernberg, O. (1976) *Borderline Conditions and Pathological Narcissism*, Northvale: Jason Aronson.

—— (1985) *Internal World and External Reality*, Northvale: Jason Aronson.

Kierkegaard, S. (1959) *Either/Or*, (1843), Garden City: Doubleday Inc.

Klein, M. (1955) "On identification," in M. Klein, P. Heimann and R.E. Money-Kyrle (eds.), *New Directions in Psycho-Analysis*, New York: Basic Books.

—— (1957) *Envy and Gratitude. A Study of Unconscious Sources*, in *The Writings of Melanie Klein*, (1975a), New York: Free Press; also in *Envy and Gratitude and Other Works 1946–1963* (1975b), New York: Delacorte Press/Seymour Lawrence.

—— (1959) *The Psychoanalysis of Children*, London: The Hogarth Press.

—— (1975) "Love, guilt, and reparation," in *The Writings of Melanie Klein*, (1975), New York: Free Press.

Kohut, H. (1971) *The Analysis of the Self*, New York: International Universities Press.

—— (1977) *The Restoration of the Self*, New York: International Universities Press.

—— (1978) *The Search for the Self. Selected Writings of Heinz Kohut: 1950–1978*, edited by P. Ornstein, New York: International Universities Press.

—— (1984) *How Does Analysis Cure?*, edited by A. Goldberg, with the collaboration of P. Stepansky, Chicago: The University of Chicago Press.

Kojève, A. (1969) *Introduction to the Reading of Hegel*, New York: Basic Books.

Koppe, F. (1990a) "Die Verklärung des Gewöhnlich. Zum Zusammenhang des kommunikativen und des transzendierenden Moments in der Kunst," paper delivered at the Conference "Ästhetische Reflexion und kommunikative Vernunft," Bad Homburg.

—— (1990b) "Das Kunstwerk als Metapher," paper delivered at the Conference "Kritik und Utopie im Werk von Herbert Marcuse," Frankfurt.

Kripke, S. (1971) "Identity and necessity," in M. Munitz (ed.), *Identity and Individuation*, New York: New York University Press.

Kuhn, H. (1960) "Der Begriff der Prohairesis," in D. Henrichet al. (eds.), *Die Gegenwart der Griechen im neueren Denken*, Tübingen: J.C.B. Mohr.

Kuhn, T. (1974) *The Structure of Scientific Revolutions*, (1962), Chicago: The University of Chicago Press.

—— (1977) *The Essential Tension*, Chicago: The University of Chicago Press.

Kymlicka, W. (1995) *Multicultural Citizenship. A Liberal Theory of Minority Rights*, Oxford: Oxford University Press.

Lakatos, I. (1970) "Falsification and the methodology of scientific research programmes," in I. Lakatos and A. Musgrave (eds.), *Criticism and the Growth of Knowledge*, Cambridge: Cambridge University Press, 91–196.

Lara, M.P. (1995) "Albrecht Wellmer: between spheres of validity," *Philosophy and Social Criticism*, 21 (2): 1–22.

Larmore, C. (1995) "Une théorie du moi, de son instabilité, et de la liberté d'esprit," in H. Grivois and J.-P. Dupuy (eds.), *Mécanismes mentaux, mécanismes sociaux*, Paris: La Découverte.

—— (1996) *The Romantic Legacy*, New York: Columbia University Press.

Lasch, C. (1979) *The Culture of Narcissism*, London: Sphere Books.

—— (1984) *The Minimal Self*, New York: Norton.

—— (1991) *The True and Only Heaven: Progress and its Critics*, New York: Norton.

Lewis, D. (1976) "Survival and identity," in A.O. Rorty (ed.), *The Identities of Persons*, Berkeley: University of California Press, 17–40.

Loewald, H. (1988) *Sublimation: Inquiries into Theoretical Psychoanalysis*, New Haven: Yale University Press.

Lyotard, J.F. (1984) *The Postmodern Condition: A Report on Knowledge*, Minneapolis: University of Minnesota Press.

McCarthy, T. (1996), "Legitimacy and diversity: dialectical reflections on analytical distinctions," *Cardozo Law Review*, 17: 1083–125.

McDougall, J. (1980) *A Plea for a Measure of Abnormality*, New York: International Universities Press.

MacIntyre, A. (1967) *A Short History of Ethics*, London: Routledge & Kegan Paul.

—— (1981) *After Virtue*, Notre Dame: University of Notre Dame Press.

Mahler, M. (1968) *Infantile Psychosis*, Vol. 1 of *On Human Symbiosis and the Vicissitudes of Individuation*, New York: International Universities Press.

Mahler, M. et al. (1975) *The Psychological Birth of the Human Infant: Symbiosis and Individuation*, New York: Basic Books.

Makkreel, R. (1975) *Dilthey: Philosopher of the Human Studies*, Princeton: Princeton University Press.

—— (1990) *Imagination and Interpretation in Kant. The Hermeneutical Import of the* Critique of Judgment, Chicago: The University of Chicago Press.

Marcuse, H. (1960) *Reason and Revolution. Hegel and the Rise of Social Theory*, Boston: Beacon Press.

Margalit, A. and Halbertal, M. (1994) "Liberalism and the right to culture," *Social Research* 61 (3): 491–510.

Marx, K. and Engels, F. (1978) *The Communist Manifesto*, (1848), in R. Tucker (ed.), *The Marx–Engels Reader*, New York: Norton.

Maslow, A. (1968) *Toward a Psychology of Being*, New York: Van Nostrand Reinhold.

Mead, G.H. (1974) *Mind, Self and Society from the Standpoint of a Social Behaviorist*, (1934), Chicago: The University of Chicago Press.

Menke-Eggers, C. (1989) "Relativismus und Partikularisierung – Zu einigen Überlegungen bei R.Rorty," *Philosophische Rundschau*, 36 (1–2): 25–40.

Nagel, T. (1980) "Aristotle on *eudaimonia*," in A.O. Rorty (ed.), *Essays on Aristotle's Ethics*, Berkeley: University of California Press.

—— (1991) *Equality and Partiality*, New York and Oxford: Oxford University Press.

Nicholson, L. (ed.) (1990) *Feminism/Postmodernism*, New York: Routledge.

Nozick, R. (1981) *Philosophical Explanations*, Oxford: Clarendon Press.

—— (1989) *The Examined Life*, New York: Simon & Schuster.

Nussbaum, M.C. (1986) *The Fragility of Goodness*, Cambridge: Cambridge University Press.

—— (1992) "Human functioning and social justice: in defense of Aristotelian essentialism," *Political Theory*, 20: 202–46.

—— (1993), "Non-relative virtues: an Aristotelian approach," in M. Nussbaum and A. Sen (eds.), *The Quality of Life*, Oxford: Clarendon Press, 242–76.

—— (1995) "Aristotle on human nature and the foundations of ethics," in J.E.G. Altham and R. Harrison (eds.), *World, Mind, and Ethics: Essays on the Philosophy of Bernard Williams*, Cambridge: Cambridge University Press.

—— (1998) "The good as discipline, the good as freedom," in David A. Crocker and Toby Linden (eds.), *Ethics of Consumption: The Good Life, Justice, and Global Stewardship*, Lanham, MD: Rowman & Littlefield.

Pareyson, L. (1988) *Estetica*, Milan: Bompiani.

Parfit, D. (1984) *Reasons and Persons*, Oxford: Clarendon Press.

Parsons, T. (1951) *The Social System*, Glencoe: Free Press.

—— (1965) "General theory in sociology," (1959), in R.K. Merton, L. Broom and L.S. Cottrell (eds.), *Sociology Today. Problems and Prospects*, Vol. 1, New York: Harper & Row, 3–38.

—— (1966) *Societies. Evolutionary and Comparative Perspectives*, Englewood Cliffs: Prentice-Hall.

—— (1968) "The position of identity in the general theory of action," in C. Gordon and K. Gergen (eds.), *The Self in Social Interaction*, New York: Wiley.

—— (1971) *The System of Modern Societies*, Englewood Cliffs: Prentice-Hall.

Parsons, T., Bales, R. and Shils, E.A. (1953) *Working Papers in the Theory of Action*, New York: Free Press.

Parsons, T. and Shils, E.A. (with the assistance of J. Olds) (1962) "The Social System," (1951), in T. Parsons and E.A. Shils (eds.), *Toward a General Theory of Action*, New York: Harper & Row, 190–233.

Passerin-d'Entrèves, M. and Benhabib, S. (eds.) (1996) *Habermas and the Unfinished Project of Modernity*, Cambridge: Polity Press.

179

Rawls, John (1971) *A Theory of Justice*, Cambridge: Harvard University Press.

—— (1980) "Kantian constructivism in moral theory," *The Journal of Philosophy*, 88: 512–72.

—— (1993) *Political Liberalism*, New York: Columbia University Press.

—— (1995) "Reply to Habermas," *Journal of Philosophy* 92 (3): 132–80.

Raz, J. (1994) "Multiculturalism," *Dissent*, Winter 1994: 67–79.

Ricoeur, P. (1970) *Freud and Philosophy: An Essay on Interpretation*, New Haven: Yale University Press.

Rieff, P. (1973) *The Triumph of the Therapeutic*, Harmondsworth: Penguin.

—— (1975) *Fellow Teachers*, London: Faber & Faber.

Riesman, D. (1950) *The Lonely Crowd*, New Haven: Yale University Press.

—— (1963) *Individualism Reconsidered*, Glencoe: Free Press.

Rorty, R. (1989) *Contingency, Irony and Solidarity*, Cambridge: Cambridge University Press.

—— (1991) *Essays on Heidegger and Others. Philosophical Papers*, Vol. 2, Cambridge: Cambridge University Press.

Russell, B. (1905) "On Denoting," *Mind*, 14: 479–93.

Sacks, H. (1995) *Lectures on Conversation*, edited by G. Jefferson, Oxford: Blackwell.

Sartre, J.P. (1966) *Being and Nothingness*, (1943), New York: Washington Square Books.

—— (1972) "L'universel singulier," in *Situations IX – Mélanges*, Paris: Gallimard.

Scanlon, Thomas M. (1982) "Contractualism and utilitarianism," in A. Sen and B. Williams (eds.), *Utilitarianism and Beyond*, Cambridge: Cambridge University Press, 103–28.

Scheler, M. (1980) *Der Formalismus in der Ethik und die materiale Wertethik*, (1916), Berne: Francke.

Schiller, (1971) *Kallias oder über die Schönheit: Uber Anmut und Würde*, (1793), Stuttgart: Reclam.

Schleiermacher, F.D.E. (1977) *Hermeneutics: The Handwritten Manuscripts*, edited by H. Kimmerle, Missoula: Scholars Press.

Schluchter, W. (1981) *The Rise of Western Rationalism. Max Weber's Developmental History*, Berkeley: University of California Press.

Schnädelbach, H. (1986) "Was ist Neoaristotelismus?," in W. Kuhlmann (ed.), *Moralität und Sittlichkeit*, Frankfurt: Suhrkamp, 38–63.

Schneewind, J.B. (1990) "The misfortunes of the virtues," *Ethics*, 101.

Schoeman, F.D. (ed.) (1984) *Philosophical Dimensions of Privacy*, Cambridge: Cambridge University Press.

—— (1992) *Privacy and Social Freedom*, Cambridge: Cambridge University Press.

Searle, J. (1969) *Speech Acts*, Cambridge: Cambridge University Press.

—— (1972) "What is a speech act?," (1965), in P.P. Giglioli (ed.), *Language and Social Context*, Harmondsworth: Penguin.

—— (1980) "An interview," in J. Boyd and A. Ferrara (eds.), *Speech Act Theory: Ten Years Later*, special issue of *Versus*, 26/27: 17–27.

Seel, M. (1985) *Die Kunst der Entzweiung. Zum Begriff der ästhetischen Rationalität*, Frankfurt: Suhrkamp.

Selznick, P. (1992) *The Moral Commonwealth. Social Theory and the Promise of Community*, Berkeley: University of California Press.

Sennett, R. (1978) *The Fall of Public Man*, New York: Knopf.

—— (1990) *The Conscience of the Eye. The Design and Social Life of Cities*, New York: Knopf.

Shoemaker, S. (1963) *Self-Knowledge and Self-Identity*, Ithaca: Cornell University Press.

Simmel, G. (1890) *Über soziale Differenzierung. Soziologische und psychologische Untersuchungen*, Leipzig: Duncker & Humblot.

—— (1955) *Conflict and the Web of Group-Affiliations*, (1908), New York: Free Press.

—— (1967) "The metropolis and mental life", (1903), in *The Sociology of Georg Simmel*, translated, edited and with an introduction by K.H. Wolff, New York: Free Press, 409–24.

—— (1987) "Das individuelle Gesetz," (1913), in G. Simmel, *Das Individuelle Gesetz. Philosophische Exkurse*, Frankfurt: Suhrkamp.

Slater, P. (1976) *The Pursuit of Loneliness. American Culture at the Breaking Point*, Boston: Beacon Press.

Smelser, N.J. (1988) "Depth psychology and the social order," in J. Alexander (ed.), *The Micro–Macro Link*, Berkeley: University of California Press.

Smith, N.H. (1996) "Contingency and self-identity. Taylor's hermeneutics vs. Rorty's postmodernism," *Theory, Culture and Society*, 13 (2): 105–20.

Sullivan, H.S. (1953) *The Interpersonal Theory of Psychiatry*, in *The Collected Works of Harry Stack Sullivan*, Vol. 1, New York: Norton & Co.

—— (1964) *The Fusion of Psychiatry and Social Science*, New York: Norton & Co.

Taminiaux, J. (1991) *Heidegger and the Problem of Fundamental Ontology*, Albany: SUNY Press.

Tarski, A. (1944) "The semantic conception of truth," *Philosophy and Phenomenological Research*, 4: 341–75.

Taylor, C. (1975) *Hegel*, Cambridge: Cambridge University Press.

—— (1985) "What is human agency?," in *Philosophical Papers*, Vol. 1, *Human Agency and Language*, Cambridge: Cambridge University Press, 15–44.

—— (1986) "Die Motive einer Verfahrensethik," in W. Kuhlmann (ed.), *Moralität und Sittlichkeit*, Frankfurt: Suhrkamp.

—— (1989) *Sources of the Self. The Making of the Modern Identity*, Cambridge: Harvard University Press.

—— (1992) *The Ethics of Authenticity*, Cambridge: Harvard University Press.

—— (1993) "The politics of recognition," in A. Gutmann (ed.), *Multiculturalism and "The Politics of Recognition"*, Princeton: Princeton University Press.

Thiebaut, C. (1995) "Authenticity or autonomy," *Philosophy and Social Criticism*, 23 (3): 93–108.

Tillich, P. (1952) *The Courage to Be*, New Haven: Yale University Press.

—— (1962) *Die verlorene Dimension*, Hamburg: Furche.

Tocqueville, A. (1969) *Democracy in America*, (1840), Garden City: Doubleday.

Trilling, L. (1972) *Sincerity and Authenticity*, Cambridge: Harvard University Press.

Van Dijk, T.A. (1977) *Text and Context. Explorations in the Semantics and Pragmatics of Discourse*, London: Longman.

—— (1980) *Macrostructures. An Interdisciplinary Study of Global Structures in Discourse, Interaction and Cognition*, Hillsdale: Erlbaum.

—— (1984) "Semantic discourse analysis," in T.A. Van Dijk (ed.), *Handbook of Discourse Analysis*, 4 Vols., London: Academic Press.

Vattimo, G. (1991) "Ricostruzione della razionalità," in G. Vattimo (ed.), *Filosofia '91*, Bari: Laterza, 89–103.

Vollrath, E. (1977) *Die Rekonstruktion der politischen Urteilskraft*, Stuttgart: Klett-Cotta.

Von Wright, G.H. (1963) *The Varieties of Goodness*, London: Routledge & Kegan Paul.

Walzer, M. (1987) *Interpretation and Social Criticism*, Cambridge: Harvard University Press.

—— (1990) "Two kinds of universalism", in *Nation and Universe: The Tanner Lectures on Human Values*, Salt Lake City: University of Utah Press.

—— (1994) *Thick and Thin. Moral Argument at Home and Abroad*, Notre Dame: University of Notre Dame Press.

Warnke, G. (1987) *Gadamer. Hermeneutics, Tradition and Reason*, Cambridge: Polity Press.

Weber, M. (1958) *The Protestant Ethic and the Spirit of Capitalism*, (1904), New York: Scribner.

—— (1975a) "Religious rejections of the world and their directions," in H.H. Gerth and C. Wright-Mills (eds.), *From Max Weber: Essays in Sociology*, New York: Oxford University Press, 323–59.

—— (1975b) "Science as a vocation," in H.H. Gerth and C. Wright-Mills (eds.), *From Max Weber: Essays in Sociology*, New York: Oxford University Press, 129–56.

—— (1975c) "Politics as a vocation", in H.H. Gerth and C. Wright-Mills (eds.), *From Max Weber: Essays in Sociology*, New York: Oxford University Press, 77–128.

—— (1978) *Economy and Society*, (1922), edited by G. Roth and C. Wittich, Berkeley: University of California Press.

Wellmer, A. (1991) *The Persistence of Modernity. Essays on Aesthetics, Ethics, and Postmodernism*, Cambridge: MIT Press.

Whitebook, J. (1995) *Perversion and Utopia. A Study in Psychoanalysis and Critical Theory*, Boston: MIT Press.

Wiggins, D. (1980) *Sameness and Substance*, London: Blackwell.

Williams, B. (1973) *Problems of the Self*, Cambridge: Cambridge University Press.

Winnicott, D. (1953) "Transitional objects and transitional phenomena," in *Playing and Reality*, (1971), Harmondsworth: Penguin, 1–30.

—— (1958) "The capacity to be alone," in *The Maturational Process and the Facilitating Environment*, (1965), New York: International Universities Press.

—— (1960) "Ego distortion in terms of true and false self," in *The Maturational Process and the Facilitating Environment*, (1965), New York: International Universities Press.

—— (1965) *The Maturational Process and the Facilitating Environment*, New York: International Universities Press.

—— (1971) *Playing and Reality*, Harmondsworth: Penguin.

—— (1986) *Home is Where We Start From. Essays by a Psychoanalyst*, New York: Norton.

—— (1988) *Human Nature*, New York: Schocken Books.

Young, I.M. (1990) *Justice and the Politics of Difference*, Princeton: Princeton University Press.

INDEX